THE UNITED STATES PONY CLUB
MANUAL OF HORSEMANSHIP

Also by Susan E. Harris

Horsemanship in Pictures

Grooming to Win, Second Edition

Horse Gaits, Balance and Movement

The United States Pony Club Manual of Horsemanship:
Basics for Beginners/D Level

THE
UNITED STATES
PONY CLUB
MANUAL
OF
HORSEMANSHIP

INTERMEDIATE HORSEMANSHIP/C LEVEL

written and illustrated by

Susan E. Harris

Ruth Ring Harvie, USPC Editor

Wiley Publishing, Inc.

Howell Book House

Published by Wiley Publishing, Inc., New York, NY

For general information on our other products and services or to obtain technical support please contact our Customer Care Department within the U.S. at 800-762-2974, outside the U.S. at 317-572-3993 or fax 317-572-4002.

Wiley also publishes its books in a variety of electronic formats. Some content that appears in print may not be available in electronic books.

Library of Congress Cataloging-in-Publication Data

Harris, Susan E.
    The United States Pony Club manual of horsemanship: intermediate horsemanship/C level / written and illustrated by Susan E. Harris; Ruth Ring Harvie, USPC editor.
        p. cm.
    Includes index.
    ISBN 0-87605-977-9
    1. Horsemanship. 2. Ponies. 3. United States Pony Clubs.
I. Harvie, Ruth Ring. II. United States Pony Clubs. III. Title.
IV. Title: Manual of horsemanship. V. Title: USPC manual of horsemanship
SF309.H3692   1995
798.2'3—dc20   94-23569
                                                                    CIP

Manufactured in the United States of America
15 14 13 12

Contents

Foreword

For many years I have watched Pony Clubs provide grassroots instruction and activities essential to the development and nurturing of future participants in the international equestrian disciplines. Although some children aspire to represent their country in competition, others choose a path of teaching, training, or simply a lifetime of dedication to a sport in which they take continuing pleasure.

This manual speaks to a variety of goals and interests. The subject matter is designed to accommodate children's attraction to, fascination with, and affection for horses as it introduces them to ever-increasing depths of knowledge. The emphasis on responsible use and care of horses at all times and in all phases of horsemanship should instill in young people a sense of pride and accomplishment based on high, yet attainable standards.

Susan E. Harris writes with charm and style, which speak to different ages directly and honestly. Her background as a teacher, trainer, author, and clinician makes this book attractive and useful to all those who teach children and horses. Her continued interest in and respect for the basics of good horsemanship worldwide should keep professionals, amateurs, and volunteers of both categories fresh, inspired, and informed. More importantly, her style promises to make this manual the "best friend" of children who love horses.

Donald W. Thackeray

A Note from the United States Pony Clubs, Inc.

We suspect that the first requests from USPC members for a manual of their own were received in 1954, when the first U.S. clubs were founded. By 1979, when the Instruction Council rewrote the USPC Standards, it was determined that there was a need for one source of information members could consult as they progress through the rating levels. The British and New Zealand manuals have served our members well, but thanks to the foresight of the USPC Board of Governors, its officers, staff, and instruction committees in the late 1980s and early 1990s, we finally have a text that matches our standards, uses terms specific to North America, and is written at a reading level comfortable for the majority of our members.

Author and illustrator Susan E. Harris, an experienced and successful riding instructor, has received guidance from an advisory panel that represents years of teaching, coaching, and examining riding and horse management skills within the USPC. We wish to express our thanks to Consulting Editors Laurie Chapman-Bosco, H. Benjamin Duke III, and Dru Malavase, as well as to Editorial Assistants Jessica Jahiel and Anne Colahan.

Carol Urbanc, formerly of the USPC National Office, has been a source of technical support and personal comfort to the advisory panel.

Madelyn Larsen, of Howell Book House, has been the patient, professional reason we have a manual available at long last.

Melanie Heacock, while Vice President, Instruction, and now President of USPC, has provided support and wisdom beyond the call of duty.

USPC editor Ruth Ring Harvie, as Chairman of the Manual of Horsemanship Committee and Curriculum Standards Committees, and through terms on the National Testing, Educational Resources, and Instruction Council, has served tirelessly to correlate, coordinate, update, and incorporate input from these vital educational groups, and has acted as the primary liaison between USPC, Susan Harris, and the publisher.

Although we do not claim to cover all special interest areas, we have carefully listened to and seriously considered all suggestions. We are grateful to all the members of the committees who have directly influenced this manual, especially Diane Hunter, Billie Stewart, Marilyn Yike, and the D and C Standards Committees.

The late Col. Donald W. Thackeray, who wrote the Foreword, has long been a friend, adviser, and committee member of the USPC, despite his duties as United States Representative to the Fédération Equestre Internationale and his activities as an "I" level dressage judge. For his tutelage and interest, we are extremely appreciative.

Plainly, this manual represents several years of research, reference checking, philosophical discussions, consultations with experts, proposals, and counter-proposals, and dozens of exchanges of letters. We hope that young riders everywhere enjoy Susan Harris's exceptional work as much as we do.

A Note to Parents

Pony Club started in Great Britain in 1928 with 700 original members. By 1992 there were more than 125,000 members in 27 countries, making it the largest junior equestrian group in the world. Each club is run by a volunteer District Commissioner and other elected officers. At this writing, the United States Pony Clubs have nearly 11,000 members in more than 500 clubs.

This *USPC Manual of Horsemanship* is written especially for Pony Club members and for the volunteers who lead and teach them, but it will also be helpful to anyone who wants to learn or teach good horsemanship. In this manual and in the manuals for the D and B/A levels, the emphasis is on how children learn, rather than on subject matter for its own sake. Progress along a continuum of learning is stressed, not the mere acquisition of facts.

This manual provides an introduction to the curriculum of the USPC and will help children meet the current USPC Standards of Proficiency. However, the levels of proficiency required by the standards cannot be achieved by book work alone. Much practical hands-on learning is essential, as is good mounted instruction at all levels. As in any course of study, effective teaching and learning require outside reading and supplemental material. Material from the USPC's most recently published standards and reading lists, as well as individual teachers' resources, will be necessary to augment this manual.

Pony Club supports the ideal of a thoroughly happy, comfortable horseperson, riding across a natural country, with complete confidence and perfect balance on a horse or pony equally happy and confident and free from pain or bewilderment

USPC'S MISSION

The United States Pony Clubs, Inc., an educational organization for youth, provides a program that teaches riding, mounted sports, and the care of horses and ponies, thereby developing responsibility, sportsmanship, moral judgment, leadership, and self-confidence.

USPC'S GUIDING BELIEFS

- USPC is an educational organization.
- The local club is the core of the USPC.
- USPC provides an opportunity for shared fun and cooperative work with others.
- Fair and friendly competitions develop teamwork and sportsmanship.
- USPC is beneficial for both horse and rider.
- USPC is committed to safety.
- USPC requires parental involvement and support.

This book is not intended as a substitute for professional advice and guidance in the field of horseback riding. A young person should take part in the activities discussed in this book only under the supervision of a knowledgeable adult.

All USPC tests in this book are current as of 1995.

A Note to the Reader

This book is for riders who have learned the material covered in The United States Pony Club Manual of Horsemanship: Basics for Beginners/D Level, and for Pony Clubbers who have completed the USPC D Level ratings (D-1, D-2, and D-3). Even if you are not a Pony Club member, you need to know the D Level work that forms the basis for this C Level manual. This book is meant to be used along with a regular course of instruction in riding, horse knowledge, and horse management, taught according to USPC Standards. No book can take the place of a good instructor, and some activities can be quite unsafe for you and for your pony if you try to do them on your own without instruction. Your instructor will help you progress at your own rate, and will know when you and your pony are ready to move on safely to the next level.

It's very important to read the D Level manual before going on to this one. Everything in the C Level manual is based on what is taught at the D Level, and some subjects covered there are not included here. As a Pony Club member, you are responsible for knowing D Level material that is not repeated in this book, and you can't pass Pony Club C, B, or A Level ratings unless you do. Even if you are not a Pony Club member, you need to know the D Level work first in order to learn from this book. Pony Clubbers will also need to do outside reading (see the USPC Recommended Reading List for your level, and also follow your instructor's and District Commissioner's recommendations).

The USPC Standards for C-1, C-2, and C-3 levels are used to determine when a Pony Clubber is ready to move on to the next level. These are given in Appendix A.

THE USPC C LEVEL

The C Level is an intermediate level of horsemanship. It follows the basic work at D Level and is a foundation for the advanced work of the B and A levels. As a C Level Pony Clubber, you are learning to become an independent horseperson. You are expected to take more responsibility for the care and management of your pony, for study and practice, and for conditioning and preparing your pony and yourself for rallies and other activities. (As mentioned in the *USPC D Manual,* the word "pony" is used in Pony Club to mean any mount a young person rides, regardless of size. Pony Club mounts may be horses or ponies.)

The most important thing in all horsemanship is your relationship with your pony. *Photo: Susan Sexton*

The C rating gives Pony Clubbers a good basis in horsemanship for the lifelong enjoyment of horses and horse sports. This level teaches you what you must know in order to own and care for your own horse or pony, and to ride independently and correctly on the flat, over fences, and in the open. In addition to "working rallies" (regular mounted Pony Club meetings), you may enjoy taking part in Pony Club activities like mounted games, foxhunting, competitive trail riding, tetrathlon, vaulting, or competitive rallies. All of these require additional specialized instruction.

From the C Level, you may go on to higher Pony Club ratings such as B, H-A, or A Ratings, or specialize in disciplines such as dressage, show jumping, eventing, or showing (which require more specialized instruction and coaching), or you may simply enjoy riding and caring for your own horse and participating in your favorite riding activities at your own level. You also become able to help teach younger and less experienced Pony Clubbers, and to contribute to your own club and Pony Club's national organization now and in the future. Most Pony Clubbers are Cs of one level or another; they are the backbone of Pony Club.

The C Level ratings require more time, study, and effort, and more regular riding and practice than the D ratings. You may have to budget your time in order to attain C Level ratings, as you will need to ride five or six days a week and take responsibility for your pony's care and condition. You will also need to take lessons regularly and practice the exercises your instructor recommends for your own riding and your pony's schooling. It is very important to ride correctly at your level, with good position, balance, and use of the aids. If any one of your basics is weak, it will have to be brought up to standard before you can go on to a rating test or to more advanced work. You will also need to practice your horse management skills, and read and study each week.

Horse care and management are especially important at the C Level because you are expected to take more responsibility for your pony's care and condition, and you may be doing more strenuous riding than you did at D Level. You will also need to learn some special skills for taking care of your pony at competitions and special events. (See the *USPC Horse Management Handbook* for more information, especially about horse care at rallies.) Good horse care and management means doing everything correctly, to Pony Club Standards, *at home every day*, not just before a rally or special event. This ensures that your pony is healthy and well cared for, and that you have practiced your horse management skills enough to perform

them safely and correctly at home as well as at testing and competitions. To take good care of your pony only at rallies or competitions, while letting things slide at home, is poor horsemanship.
Good daily care, keeping up to Pony Club Standards, shows up in
the condition of your pony, equipment, and stable area.

You don't have to be an extremely talented rider or have an
expensive horse in order to pass C Level ratings. Whatever horse you
ride must be safe, serviceably sound, trained, and able to perform C
Level work. You are not expected to be able to ride or train a green
horse at the C Level, and it is quite unfair to expect a green horse to
be a C Level Pony Club mount. You will need plenty of practical,
day-to-day horse care and management experience, following the
Pony Club Standards. If you don't own or lease your own pony, you
must make arrangements to take this responsibility by helping a
horse owner who is willing to keep horses according to Pony Club
Standards.

CHAPTER 1

C-1 RIDING

At the D Level, you learned the basics of riding on the flat, over low jumps, and in the open. In the C Level, you will learn to be a better rider and to improve the way your pony goes. You will also learn how to prepare yourself and your pony for different kinds of riding activities.

GOALS FOR C LEVEL RIDING: THE FOUR BASICS

Four basic principles are the foundation of good horsemanship. These are:

- Security (safety) for the rider
- Effective use of the aids for good control
- Non-abuse of the pony
- Unity between pony and rider (pony and rider together in balance)

As you improve each of these basics, you become a better, safer, and more effective rider, and you will be able to get a better performance from your pony. However, if any of the basics are weak, there will be problems in your riding.

Here's how each of the four basics work:

Security (Safety) for the Rider "Security" means a secure and independent seat—so that you can ride at all gaits without losing your balance. A rider who is loose, bouncy, or out of balance has security problems. He may grip with his legs or hang onto the reins to stay on, which upsets a pony and causes trouble for both pony and rider. Developing an independent seat takes time and practice.

Effective Use of Aids (Good Control)   A good seat puts you in position to control your pony easily and effectively. Your legs and seat must be secure and in correct position in order to apply leg, seat, and weight aids properly. A rider with a bouncy, insecure seat or poor shoulder, arm, or hand position will not be able to give smooth, clear, or correct rein aids. His pony will have a hard time understanding what his rider wants him to do.

Non-Abuse of the Pony   "Non-abuse" means riding in such a way that you don't confuse or upset your pony, or interfere with his balance and movement. Non-abusive riding is balanced and smooth, and makes it easy for your pony to carry you and to do what you want him to do. You must give your aids clearly and correctly so that he can understand them.

"Accidental abuse" means hurting or confusing a pony by mistake. This can happen if you lose your balance and thump down on your pony's back, or if you grab the reins to save your balance and accidentally catch him in the mouth. Riders sometimes commit accidental abuse by kicking or pulling too hard, riding in poor balance, or using conflicting aids (for example, kicking to go forward while pulling to stop). This can happen if you try to do something that is too difficult for your pony or for your own level of riding.

Accidental abuse is not being cruel on purpose or losing your temper, but it can ruin a pony's training and attitude. A pony who suffers accidental abuse may think he is being punished for trying to do what his rider told him to do. If it happens a lot, the pony may come to hate being ridden. The more aware you are of how your pony feels and how you are riding, the less likely you are to make mistakes that hurt and confuse him.

Unity Between Pony and Rider   "Unity between pony and rider" means that you and your pony are "united," or together in balance, as if you and he are one. This is a wonderful feeling, in any gait or over jumps. It can only happen when the other three basics are working well: Your seat is secure; you use your aids effectively; and you ride non-abusively, in cooperation with your pony. When you and your pony are in the best possible balance and work smoothly together in harmony, riding becomes easy and beautiful.

C-1 RIDING ON THE FLAT

Riding on the flat helps improve your seat and aids, and your pony's balance, suppleness, and responsiveness. It helps you develop the control you need for riding in the open and for better jumping. You will also learn how to prepare yourself and your pony for a simple dressage test.

Warmup for Flat Work

A good warmup:

- Is essential for every ride, on the flat or over fences.
- Lasts at least twenty minutes.
- Supples, stretches, and warms up muscles and improves circulation, which helps prevent injuries.
- Develops rhythm, relaxation, and free forward movement, and prepares pony and rider physically and mentally to do their best.

When warming up:

- *Always* start with ten to fifteen minutes at the walk (especially important for old or stiff ponies, or stabled ponies).
- Practice rider warmup and suppling exercises (see *USPC D Manual*).
- Change directions frequently to supple both sides of the pony. Use ring figures such as circles, half circles, figure 8s, serpentines, and broken lines (see illustration on page 98).
- Trot and canter in both directions, including 20-meter circles on the correct diagonal and canter lead in each direction.
- Post the trot at first; don't sit the trot until the pony's back muscles are warmed up and his trot becomes supple and springy.
- Work progressively (from easy to more difficult). Start with large, simple turns and figures (20-meter circles); gradually include smaller circles and turns (15 and 10 meters).
- Frequent transitions improve a pony's attention, balance, and response to the aids.

Improving Your Seat

Here are some ways to sit more smoothly and comfortably with your pony's gaits.

Balance   To sit comfortably and smoothly with your pony's movement, you must be in balance. If you are out of balance forward or backward, or off to one side, your muscles tighten up to keep you from falling farther out of balance. This makes you stiffen up and bounce.

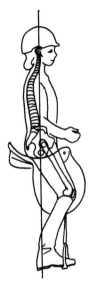

BALANCED RIDER:

- Vertical line through ear, shoulder, hip, and ankle
- Pelvis balanced on seat bones

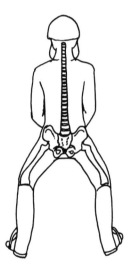

BALANCED RIDER:

- Head balanced
- Shoulders even
- Spine straight
- Weight evenly balanced on seat bones
- Stirrups even

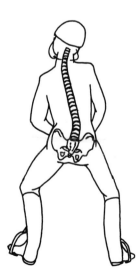

CROOKED RIDER:

- Tilted head
- Shoulders uneven
- Crooked back
- Collapsed hip
- Uneven weight on seat bones
- Uneven stirrups
- Elbow, knee, and toe sticking out

SLOUCHING RIDER:

- ◆ Looking down
- ◆ Round back
- ◆ Pelvis tilted backward
- ◆ Weight on buttocks
- ◆ Legs ahead of body
- ◆ Heels up

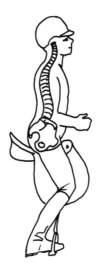

STIFF, HOLLOW RIDER:

- ◆ Head too high
- ◆ Neck cramped
- ◆ Hollow back
- ◆ Pelvis tilted forward
- ◆ Weight on crotch
- ◆ Knees pinching
- ◆ Leg too far back

When you are in balance,

- ◆ You sit evenly on both seat bones, without leaning to one side, dropping a shoulder, or collapsing one hip.
- ◆ Your pelvis is balanced. (If it tilts forward, it hollows your back and you ride too far forward on your crotch, which makes you stiff and can hurt your back. If your pelvis tilts backward, you ride on your buttocks and your back is round and slouched, which puts your legs forward and you out of balance behind your pony.)
- ◆ Your feet are directly under your body, not out in front or behind you.

- All your body parts stack up: head over shoulders, shoulders over upper body, upper body over seat bones, legs and feet under seat. (Imagine a line that passes straight down from your ear through your shoulder, center, hip, and ankle.)
- Your head is balanced. (It weighs 10-13 pounds; if it hangs down, sticks out in front or tilts, it puts your whole body out of balance.)

To check your balance, ride in a half-seat for several strides. If you have to lean way forward or pull your feet back to get into a half-seat, you are out of balance. If you can stay in a half-seat easily without holding on or gripping with your knees, you are in balance.

Breathing   Good breathing makes a big difference in your riding. When you get nervous, you hold your breath or breathe high up in your chest. This makes you stiff and tense; your pony feels it and gets tense, too. When you breathe deeply and naturally, you use your diaphragm, a big muscle that attaches below and behind your navel. This helps your seat relax, so you can go with your pony's movement better, without bouncing. Deep breathing makes your seat, legs, and hands feel relaxed and quiet, which helps your pony relax, move smoothly, and respond quietly to your aids.

The Following Seat   Having a "following seat" means that your body goes smoothly with your pony's movements. You must be supple and flexible instead of holding yourself stiffly in a "correct" position.

A following seat begins at the walk. Try having someone lead your pony for a few minutes so that you can safely close your eyes and concentrate on feeling how your pony moves your body. Let each seat bone move forward and backward, up and down, and around in a circle. Notice the way the movement ripples up your back. Does your head move slightly, or does it feel "stuck"? Let your hips and thighs, all the way down to your knees, move in rhythm with your pony's motion. Gripping with your knees makes you stiffen and stops the motion. Also, notice the swing of your pony's barrel as he walks. As his barrel swings out to the right, your left leg drops down and your knee bends a little, so your leg "follows the barrel." What other movements do you discover?

Next, open your eyes and ride at a walk. If you hold your breath, stiffen up, or grip with your legs, your pony's movement gets short and stiff or may even stop. When you breathe and relax, you move smoothly and freely with your pony, and he moves better, too. You may feel his strides get longer as you allow him to use his back and muscles freely.

At the trot and the canter, you can hold the front of the saddle with one hand while you handle the reins with the other hand. This helps you pull yourself deeper into the saddle, relax your seat and legs, and let the movement ripple through your whole body. If you start to tighten up or grip with your legs, you should take a breath, relax, and slow down your pony until you can let your body follow the movement again.

Finding Your Springs   Your knees, ankles, and hip joints are your "shock absorbers." To do their job, they must be relaxed and springy. Your legs should hang comfortably against the saddle and your pony's sides. Your knees and toes should not stick out, nor should they be forced in or pinched tightly against the saddle.

Tight, gripping knees and legs keep you from sitting smoothly with your pony. If you jam your heels down and forward, your ankles stiffen and you lose your balance. Tightening the muscles in your seat and thighs locks up your joints and makes your legs and seat stiff, making you bounce as your pony moves.

EXERCISE FOR FLEXIBLE JOINTS

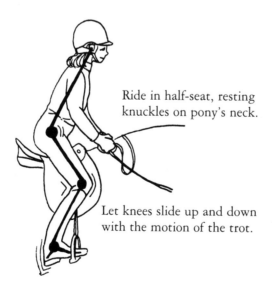

Ride in half-seat, resting knuckles on pony's neck.

Let knees slide up and down with the motion of the trot.

To find your springs, ride in a half-seat at a slow trot, pressing your knuckles down on your pony's neck. Let your knees relax and slide on the saddle as your pony lifts one of your knees and then the other with each step. As your knees relax, your ankles and hip joints also get soft and springy and take up the bounces. Try to keep them flexible in sitting trot and posting trot as well as in half-seat.

When you canter, the movement may feel more like a circle. Let the canter "roll" your flexible hips, knees, and ankles. Your knees must bend a little at each stride to keep your feet back under your seat. Cantering in a half-seat also helps you use your springs (hips, knees, and ankles).

Using the Aids

The aids are the means by which you communicate with your pony. Two kinds of aids exist: natural aids and artificial aids. (The basic aids and what they do are introduced in the *USPC D Manual.*)

The Natural Aids   The natural aids are your seat, legs, hands, and voice—all natural parts of you. You use them (the voice aid excepted) to apply pressure, which your pony feels through his sense of touch. A well-trained pony has been taught to respond to rein and leg pressure and to changes in your balance, which he feels through your seat bones. You must give the correct aids at the right time and with the right amount of pressure so that he can understand and respond to them. You must also ease up on the pressure at the right time, to thank him for doing what you asked, and to avoid annoying and confusing him.

The Artificial Aids   The artificial aids are crops, whips, and spurs. They are used to help the natural aids (especially the leg aids) in training, and when a pony is lazy or does not pay attention. They should be used to teach a pony to respond better to the natural aids, not to punish him. Crops, whips, and spurs are a big responsibility; you must never lose your temper or use them unfairly. You should not use artificial aids (especially spurs and dressage whips) until your instructor recommends that you do so and shows you how to use them correctly.

Crop (or Bat)   A short stick with a loop or flat "popper" on the end. It is carried pointing down.

USING A CROP

  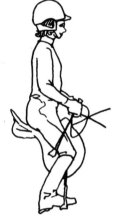

1. Bridge reins in one hand.

2. Tap behind leg.

3. Return hand to reins.

To use a crop, or bat, always put both reins in one hand first, and then reach back and tap the pony on his side, close behind your leg. Then return your hand to the reins without pulling on them.

Never use a crop behind your leg without first taking your hand off the rein. Otherwise you will jerk your pony in the mouth when you tap him, and you will also give him conflicting aids, which is very unfair to the pony.

Beginners sometimes use a crop by turning their wrist and tapping the pony on the shoulder. This method doesn't work very well and may cause a jerk on the pony's mouth.

Dressage Whip   A whip about 3 feet long that you can use without taking your hand off the reins. You carry it pointing down and backward across your thigh. To use a dressage whip, you turn your wrist and tap the whip against your thigh so that the tip of the whip taps your pony on his barrel, behind your leg. Be careful not to jerk on your pony's mouth when you use a dressage whip. You must use it with a light tap, never a hard blow, because it stings more than a crop. Some ponies are nervous about a rider carrying a dressage whip, so don't use one unless your instructor recommends that you do and shows you how to use it properly.

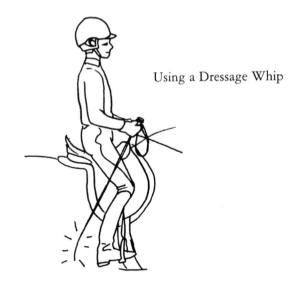

Using a Dressage Whip

When riding in a ring, you usually carry a crop or whip on the inside, to keep the pony from cutting corners. When you change directions, you change your crop or whip to the new inside hand. (Sometimes a crop may be carried in the outside hand for training purposes.)

Wrist loops on crops and whips are dangerous. For example, if you need to drop the crop but have your hand through a wrist loop, you may not be able to drop it in time. The crop could catch in the reins during a fall and cause an injury. If your crop has a wrist loop, cut it off!

Spurs   Don't use spurs until your instructor recommends that you use them. This will not be until you have enough control of your legs to use spurs properly, and until your legs are steady enough to keep from accidentally digging the pony with the spurs. To use spurs sooner would be unfair and unkind to your pony.

Spurs must be blunt and not too long. The Prince of Wales type, about 1/2 inch long, is the best kind to start with. It is worn high on a boot, with the sides of the spur level (not pointing up or down), and the curved end of the spur pointing down. If your boots have spur rests, the spurs should be just above them. If not, the spur should run along the upper "welt," or stitching. You buckle the spur straps on the outside, and you should cut off the long ends of the straps or tuck them neatly underneath the spurs.

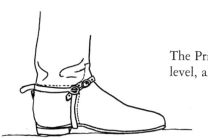

The Prince of Wales spur is worn level, along the seam of the boot.

You use spurs to remind a pony to pay attention to your leg aids. Always give a correct leg aid first, with a brief squeeze of your calf muscle. If your pony doesn't respond, turn your toe out and give a brief nudge inward and upward with your spur; then instantly rotate your foot and leg back into the proper position. Never kick with spurs or nag your pony with them. Use them with just a strong enough touch to make your pony pay attention to a correct leg aid.

Loose Reins, Long Reins, and Riding on Light Contact

There are three basic ways to use the reins: riding with loose reins, riding with long reins, and riding on light contact. (There is also a fourth way, riding "on the bit," which comes at a more advanced stage.) Each is a step in learning to ride, and gives you a certain kind of control and communication with your pony.

Loose-Rein Riding When you ride on loose reins, there is a loop in your reins between your hands and the bit, except when you give a rein aid. This allows the pony to move his head freely and stretch his neck out as far as he wants. Loose reins are used to let a pony relax and stretch; to cool out, in western riding; and to do "no-hands" exercises.

In loose-rein riding, your weight aids prepare your pony just before your hands tell him what to do. Sitting up deep and tall tells him to fix his balance or prepare to slow down or stop; swivelling your body prepares him to turn. Your hands "check and release"; that is, they take the slack out of the reins, apply a little pressure, and then immediately ease up again. Even when riding with loose reins, you and your pony must stay alert and pay attention to each other. If your reins are too long, your pony may get careless and you will not be able to give good rein aids.

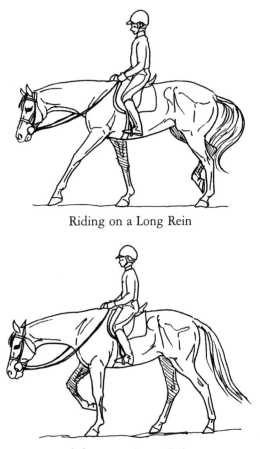

Riding on a Long Rein

Riding on a Loose Rein

Riding on a Long Rein (Light Rein)   Riding on a long rein (also called a light rein) is similar to loose-rein riding, but the reins are slightly shorter and have less slack. This method allows the pony freedom to relax and stretch, but gives you more control and communication with him.

When you ride on a long rein, your reins must be just long enough to sag a little when your hands and the pony's head are in a normal position. Squeezing your hands should apply gentle pressure to the bit. You should be able to control the pony with small movements of your hands. If the reins are too long, you may pull back and move your hands too much, which results in rough, crude rein aids.

At the walk and the canter, your pony must be able to move his head and neck freely without feeling little jerks that come from stiff hands and arms. At the trot, his head doesn't move as much, but your hands must be relaxed and quiet so that they don't bounce and jerk his mouth or go up and down when you post.

Riding with Light Contact   "Light contact" means you have a light, steady feel of your pony's mouth through the reins all the time. The reins are lightly stretched and are straight from your hand to the bit, not loose or sagging. With light contact, you give rein aids by squeezing and relaxing your fingers to change the pressure on the bit. This method, in which the rein aids are almost invisible, gives you finer control and also helps your pony pay closer attention to your rein aids.

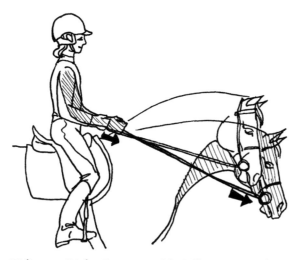

Riding on Light Contact, with Following Hands

You can begin to ride with light contact only when you have a correct seat and good balance and can ride smoothly without bouncing or catching the reins for balance. If you try to ride with contact before your position and seat are good enough, you can't help but make mistakes. With each mistake you make, you pull on your pony's mouth, which upsets him and can ruin his training. Your instructor will tell you when you are ready to start riding with contact.

As your pony walks, his head and neck stretch out and come back with every stride. Your hands must follow his natural head motion without bumping, pulling, or losing contact. This is called "following hands," or "passive contact." If your hands don't let him stretch out enough, or, worse, if you bump his mouth, he cannot walk properly; then he may shorten his strides, stiffen up, or toss his head.

To begin riding with contact, you adjust your reins so that there is only about half an inch of slack in the reins when your hands and your pony's head are in a normal position. Your shoulders must be relaxed; your elbows should hang next to your sides. Use your legs to ask your pony to move out in a big-striding walk. As his neck stretches out, you will feel his mouth reach out and gently pull your hands forward. As his head comes back, let your elbows come back to your sides. The contact (the touch or feel of the reins) should stay the same—light and steady—as the pony's head moves forward and back.

If you forget to use your legs, your pony may walk slowly. He won't stretch out his neck and you may lose contact; the reins will go slack. If your shoulders, arms, elbows, or hands tense up, they freeze in one place. Then your pony will feel a jerk each time he tries to stretch his head out. This is called "intermittent contact" and is a serious fault because it teaches your pony not to reach out or trust your hands. If your hands go too far forward or are too loose and floppy, your pony cannot feel your contact at all.

When you can follow your pony's mouth with soft, steady contact, ask him to stop by stopping your elbows and squeezing your fingers on the reins *without pulling back*. As he feels the pressure and responds, relax your fingers, but don't move your hands forward or

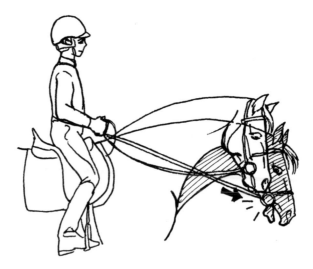

Wrong: Intermittent contact. Reins go slack and tight as pony bumps into rider's rigid hands.

let the reins go loose. Just reduce the pressure and go back to the light, steady contact. To turn, squeeze the fingers of one hand. You may find that your pony pays attention to much smaller, lighter rein aids than you thought he could feel.

At the trot, the pony's head does not move forward and back as in the walk, so your hands stay in one place. However, you must be careful not to let them move up and down as you post or bounce when you sit the trot. You must adjust your reins to the right length, and use your legs to ask your pony to take long strides so that he will stretch out his neck and "put his mouth in your hands."

At the canter, a pony's head and neck move forward and back almost as they do in the walk, but his back rocks more. You must sit the canter smoothly, with relaxed shoulders and arms, so that your hands can follow your pony's mouth with soft, gentle contact.

Practice riding on contact for a part of every ride, but let your pony relax on loose reins from time to time.

Free Forward Movement

A pony must move forward when you ask him to. In "free forward movement," he is willing to move forward easily from a light leg aid, and he uses his body well when he moves. A pony that lacks free forward movement might act lazy, stubborn, or reluctant to move; or he may move with short, "sticky" strides.

Free forward movement doesn't mean going fast. It means that the pony takes long, even strides, using his hindquarters, back, and muscles freely with each stride. It also means that he wants to go forward and to do what you ask but is calm and relaxed about it. A pony that goes fast with short strides and stiff muscles, lacks free forward movement and is difficult to ride.

To move forward freely, a pony must be sound and comfortable, must be ridden well, and must understand and trust his rider. The pony must also pay attention to and obey his rider's leg aids. If the pony is sore, confused, or unhappy, he will be reluctant to move freely. A rider riding out of balance, tight reins, rough hands, too severe a bit, or confusing signals can make a pony afraid to go forward.

Improving Your Pony's Response to Light Leg Aids Some ponies don't want to work any harder than they have to and will ignore leg aids if they can get away with it. The more you nag, kick, and thump, the harder it is to get them to go forward. These ponies must be taught to respond promptly to a correct, light leg aid. Here's one way to do it:

Free Forward Movement

Sticky, Reluctant Movement

1. Test your pony by asking him to trot from a walk. Notice how strong a leg aid you must use to get him to trot, and how long it takes him to respond to your leg aid.
2. Ask your pony to trot again, giving just two short, light leg aids. If he responds properly by trotting *within three seconds*, reward him with a pat and praise him. If he doesn't trot, immediately tap him once with a crop behind your leg, just hard enough to make him trot. When he does trot, pat and praise him immediately, and let him keep trotting.
3. Test him again; ask him to trot from two short, light leg aids. If he responds correctly in three seconds or less, pat and praise him. If he is sluggish, tap him immediately. Repeat this exercise until he trots easily from a light leg aid without your having to use the crop.

Be careful not to pull on the reins when using the crop or when making your pony trot. Don't wave the crop or threaten him with it. Your pony should pay attention to your leg aids, not to the crop. Remember to pat and praise him immediately when he responds properly.

Teaching Your Pony to Move Forward and Out from the Inside Leg Aid When you squeeze with both legs, your pony goes straight forward. Now he must learn to move forward and out when you squeeze one leg. This helps him respond better to leg aids for turning, bending, and going forward. You can also use this method to tell him not to cut corners and to stay out on the track.

Start by teaching him to move forward and out from your inside leg, as he moves from a halt to a walk. Here's how:

1. Halt on the "inside track" (about 10 feet inside the regular track), facing straight ahead.
2. Give one or more short squeezes with your *inside* leg in its normal position, right behind the girth. (Don't move your leg back; this may confuse your pony.) Keep your outside leg, seat, and hands quiet and relaxed.
3. Your pony should start to walk by stepping forward and out toward the rail on the first step. If he moves forward and out, even a little, pat his neck and praise him right away, and let him keep walking forward.
4. Instead of moving forward and out, your pony might make a mistake. If he walks straight ahead without moving out (the most common mistake), stop him gently and repeat the leg aid. You may have to use stronger leg aids or your reins to guide him out for the first step. (Always use your leg first, however.) If he goes sideways but doesn't go forward, make sure you are not pulling on the reins. Use a stronger leg aid and give a "cluck," to teach him that "forward" is just as important as "out." If he pushes in against your leg aid, keep giving short taps with your leg aids, and help with your reins until he goes forward and out. Then pat and praise him, and let him keep walking.

Practice this simple forward-and-out step several times, until your pony moves out easily from one leg aid. Then change directions and try it with the other leg. You will find that one side is easier for your pony. The other side will need more practice before he moves forward and out as easily.

FORWARD-AND-OUT EXERCISE

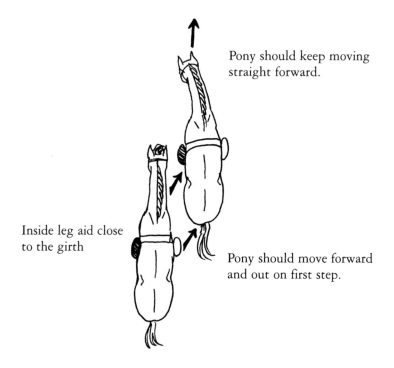

Pony should keep moving straight forward.

Inside leg aid close to the girth

Pony should move forward and out on first step.

Teaching the Pony to Move His Hind Legs Sideways from a Leg Aid   Your pony should learn to step sideways with his hind legs when you ask him to. This makes it easy to move his hindquarters over when you need to make a tight turn, open or close a gate while you are riding, or get out of someone's way.

To teach a pony this signal, first try practicing while you are on the ground. You can do this while you are grooming your pony, if he will stand quietly while tied. (If he won't stand quietly while tied, ask your instructor to help you.)

1. Start on the pony's left side. Place your fist on his side, right where your leg would be if you were riding. Then move your fist back about 4 inches. Say "Over" as you give a short nudge and release, like a leg aid. If your pony steps sideways with his hind legs, away from your hand pressure, stop pressing, pat him, and praise him right away. If he doesn't step sideways, keep repeating the short nudge and release, using just enough pressure to make him pay attention. Pressing too hard makes some ponies push back instead of stepping sideways.

2. When your pony has learned to take one step sideways, ask him to take another step. Always stop and pause between steps, and praise him. Ask for only one step at a time. He should not take several quick steps.

3. Next, repeat the exercise on the right side. You may find that it is easier for your pony on one side and harder on the other. Keep practicing and rewarding him when he gets it right, until he steps over in either direction.

TEACHING PONY TO STEP SIDEWAYS FROM PRESSURE

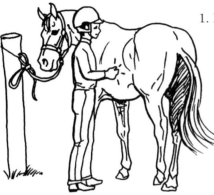

1. From the ground, from hand pressure

2. When mounted, from leg pressure

After you have succeeded in making your pony perform this exercise while you are on the ground, you can teach him to do so while you are mounted. At first, it may help to halt him facing a fence or wall. This keeps him from moving forward by mistake, without your having to pull on the reins.

Put your leg in exactly the same place (about 4 inches behind the girth) that you put your fist when you were on the ground and teaching him to step sideways. Sit up tall (don't lean forward) and stretch your leg back from your hip joint, instead of bending your knee and pulling your heel up. Give a short nudge with your leg to ask him to step sideways. When he takes a step sideways, pat and praise him. If he doesn't respond, use short, repeated leg aids until he steps over. If your pony doesn't seem to understand, or if you have trouble, ask your instructor for help.

When a pony is learning to step sideways, it is important that he not back up. This makes him awkward at stepping sideways and can start a bad habit that is hard to cure. If he tries to back up, your reins may be too short, or you may be leaning forward. Sit up very tall (even tip backwards a little) and relax your reins to tell him not to back up. Walk him forward, then try again. If he tries to back up again, get help from your instructor before you continue.

Better Transitions

A "transition" is a change from one gait to another or from a gait to a halt. Going from a halt or a slower gait to a faster one is an "upward transition." A "downward transition" means going from a faster gait to a slower one or a halt.

Transitions give a pony practice in adjusting his balance, or "rebalancing" himself, and responding to your aids. They help him move better in all his gaits. However, only smooth, well-ridden transitions help a pony. Rough and sudden transitions are awkward and hard on both pony and rider.

Here are some ways to improve your pony's transitions and the way you ride them:

- Prepare for every transition. A pony needs several strides to get ready for a transition. If you are riding in a ring with dressage letters, start preparing for a transition at least one letter before the spot where you want to make a transition.
- Wake your pony up with a leg squeeze before you ask him to change gaits. This gets him ready to respond to your aids— especially your leg and seat aids.

◆ When you sit up deep and tall, with your feet under your seat, and take a deep breath, you rebalance yourself. This helps your pony adjust his balance and get ready for a transition. Several quick rebalancings in a row work better than one. Rebalancings are also called "half-halts."

◆ Use several short aids, squeezing and relaxing in rhythm with your pony's gait, instead of one long, hard one.

◆ Taking a deep breath makes your body more relaxed and supple, and helps you ride transitions without stiffening up or bouncing.

Riding Accurate Ring Figures

Riding ring figures is good practice for you and your pony if you ride them carefully and correctly. Riding them teaches you to plan ahead, to look where you are going, and to ride accurately. (This pays off later on jump courses.) Practicing ring figures can also make your pony more supple and obedient.

To ride good ring figures, you must know their correct size and shape. You must decide how big your figure will be and exactly where it starts and finishes. It helps to set up markers for the quarter point, the half-way point, and the three-quarter point of a circle or other figure. Another good way to learn is to walk through ring figures on foot.

Ponies do not make perfect ring figures by themselves, no matter how well-trained they are; their minds are usually on something else. If your pony wants to go back to the barn or other ponies, he may "bulge out" on the side of the turn or figure that is close to where he wants to go. On the far side, he may cut the corner or "fall in." A pony may try to slow down or break down to a slower gait when going away from the barn, the ring gate, or other ponies; or he may hurry too fast when coming back. You must think ahead every step in order to keep him moving steadily and going exactly where you want him to go.

When you ride ring figures, your eyes are especially important. On a circle, you should look about one-quarter of the circle ahead. When changing directions, look ahead to the marker where you will return to the track. When riding a serpentine or a figure 8, make your change of direction at the center line of the ring. Make your circles or loops the same size, and keep them round. If you look down or forget to look where you are going, your pony may cut in and make a loop smaller, or he may bulge out.

Dressage Arena   The best place to work on ring figures is in a dressage arena. This gives you a standard-size ring in which you can learn where your figures should start and finish and how big they should be. Riding in a dressage arena also gets you used to the dressage letters, which are used in all dressage tests and Pony Club tests.

If you don't have access to a dressage arena, you can set up buckets or jump poles to mark off a level area 20 meters by 40 meters (66 feet by 132 feet). These are the measurements of a standard small arena. A large arena is 20 meters by 60 meters (66 feet by 198 feet) and has four additional letters. You can paint letters on buckets or squares of plywood and set them up as shown in the illustration.

Preparing for a Simple Dressage Test   You may ride a dressage test for a rally or competition, as part of a Pony Club rating test, or simply as a challenge to test your riding and your pony's training. Your first dressage test should be a simple one. You should move on to more difficult tests only when you are doing the easier ones well. A test that is too difficult for your level of experience or your pony's training is hard for both you and your pony, and can hurt your pony's training. Dressage tests are available from Pony Club, along with rules for dressage competitions. Ask your instructor to help you

DRESSAGE ARENA

Make your own dressage letters:

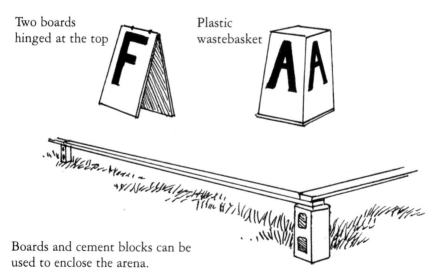

Two boards
hinged at the top

Plastic
wastebasket

Boards and cement blocks can be
used to enclose the arena.

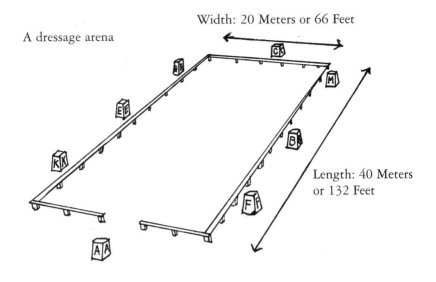

A dressage arena

Width: 20 Meters or 66 Feet

Length: 40 Meters or 132 Feet

choose the right test and prepare for it. Riding requirements for Pony Club Dressage Competitions or open dressage shows may be more advanced than those for a Pony Club rating test, so you may need special preparation and coaching for these.

You will need to learn your test and be familiar with every movement. In some competitions, a "caller" may read the test out loud to remind you, but this is not permitted in all competitions. You should learn your test anyway for practice, and you *must* memorize the test if you ride in a combined training event. The best way to do this is to walk through the test on foot several times, thinking about where you ride your ring figures, turn, or prepare for transitions. You can lay out a dressage ring indoors with paper letters and walk through the test, or copy the dressage arena illustration and "ride" the test with a pencil, drawing the movements and ring figures as you go.

You may ride a test a couple of times for practice, but don't ride the test over and over. Ponies learn dressage tests and patterns faster than people do. If your pony learns a test too well, he will anticipate: He may start to slow down for a transition before you ask him to, or cut into the center because he knows a circle is coming up. Anticipating will cost you points on your test score, because it shows you are not completely in control.

When practicing for a dressage test, warm up your pony carefully. Work on the movements and parts of the test, such as 20-meter circles at the trot and canter, changing the rein on the diagonal, making good corners, and performing transitions. This kind of practice helps you and your pony improve on specific parts of the test but does not teach your pony to anticipate. Always finish with something your pony does well so that you can praise him and quit on a good note. Don't make him bored and sour by drilling him on the same things too many times. Take time to relax and go on a trail ride now and then.

There are many other things to learn about riding a dressage test, especially in competition. For more information, see the *USPC Rules for Dressage Competitions.*

C-1 RIDING OVER FENCES

At the C-1 Level, you will jump some new kinds of fences and ride over more challenging courses. You will need to develop a more secure and independent seat over jumps and also work on your timing, so that you go smoothly with your pony as he jumps. An important goal is to learn to ride a course, keeping your pony at a good, steady pace.

Warmup for Jumping

A good warmup is even more important for jumping than for riding on the flat, because jumping is harder on your pony's legs and muscles. You must always warm him up at a walk, trot, and canter, in both directions, for at least twenty minutes before jumping. Practicing circles, changes of rein, and transitions will help him pay attention and make him easier to ride during your jumping work.

Check Your Basics

Before starting C-1 jumping, you must review D-3 jumping work. Your instructor must be sure your basics (jumping position, balance, eyes, release, and control) and your confidence are solid. Trying to do more difficult jumping with weak basics is unsafe and can give you and your pony bad experiences.

Improving Balance and Timing

"Timing" is your ability to feel when your pony starts to jump and to go with him, instead of getting into jumping position too early or too late. Timing has a lot to do with balance. If you are in balance with your pony, then going with him as he jumps is much easier. If you are out of balance, even a little, you may jump ahead of him or get left behind.

Here are some exercises to help your balance and timing:

POSTING WITH AND BEHIND THE MOTION

If you post correctly, "with" your pony's motion, then jumping with him will be easy, too. Riders who post behind the motion ride behind the motion when they jump, and often get left behind. If you post ahead of the motion, you tend to jump ahead of your pony, which is incorrect and dangerous.

To post with the motion, you must get your balance together with your pony's balance. When you both are in perfect balance, he does all the work of making you post; you do not have to lift yourself up. Posting this way is easier for you and your pony, and teaches you to let your pony close your angles (at your hips, knees, and ankles) as he jumps.

To post with the motion, trot in half-seat. Open or close your hip angle until you find the point where you can easily keep your balance without gripping with your knees. Now, count "One, two" with your pony's trot. Touch your seat bones down on "One," and let your pony push you back up again on "Two." When you feel your pony "posting you," you are with the motion.

Posting "behind the motion" means you are behind your pony's balance. This makes you work harder, and it is harder on the pony's back. If you open your hip angle and post almost straight up and down for a few strides, you will be posting behind the motion. Sometimes a rider may post behind the motion on purpose to control a strong horse or drive him forward. However, riding behind the motion in jumping interferes with the pony's jumping movements, is hard on his back, and can make you pull on his mouth or get "left behind."

Posting "ahead of the motion" means your balance is too far forward, ahead of your pony's balance. This happens when you close your hip angle too much, lean too far forward, or stand up forward. Jumping ahead of the motion is quite unsafe and can easily cause a fall.

Practice riding with the motion in posting trot and in half-seat, and do just enough posting behind the motion and ahead of the motion to know what each feels like. You can also post over a ground pole, then over a "trotting grid" (a series of ground poles spaced for trotting). Try riding a cross-rail in a posting trot, allowing your pony to "post you" over the low jump. This helps you relax and wait for your pony to jump, and improves your balance.

1. Posting with the motion

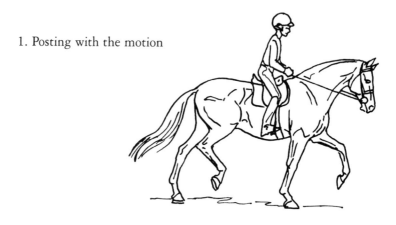

2. Posting behind the motion

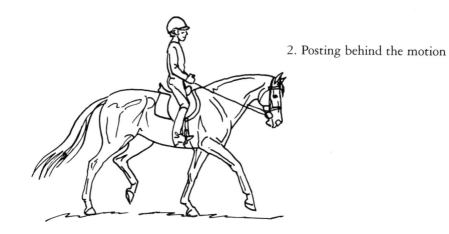

3. Wrong: Posting ahead of the
   motion is incorrect and unsafe.

CLOSING YOUR ANGLES AS YOU JUMP

When you jump, the thrust of your pony's takeoff must close your angles, making you bend at the hips, knees, and ankles. Your angles are "open" when they are straighter (when you sit or stand up straight). They "close" when your body folds at your hips, your knees bend, and your heels sink down. To jump well, you must fold (or close your angles), not stand up.

Your pony's jump determines how much your angles close. If he makes a big, powerful jump, he closes your angles tightly. If he only hops a little, your angles close just a little. You cannot guess just how big a jump he will make, so you must stay in balance and wait for him to close your angles.

You must be relaxed to wait and let your pony close your angles. Tight, tense muscles keep you from feeling when your pony pushes off and stop your angles from closing. Tight, tense muscles also make you bounce and lose your balance. Deep breathing helps keep your joints and muscles relaxed and springy. Try breathing out (as if you were blowing out a birthday candle) just as your pony takes off. Keeping your eyes on your "target" also helps you stay relaxed and wait for the jump.

Gymnastic jumping exercises (such as bounces, jumping grids, and one-strides) help you learn to let your pony close your angles and make you fold.

AN EXERCISE TO IMPROVE TIMING

When your pony jumps, you must let your body fold into jumping position just as he takes off. If you try to guess when he will jump

The thrust of the pony's jump closes the rider's angles.

and you stand up forward, you may be too late or too early. You must learn to relax, wait for him, and feel your pony's timing.

Here is an exercise to help your timing:

Start at a walk, sitting in normal position, with loose reins, and ask your pony to trot. On the *first step* of trot, fold into jumping position and stay there, without posting, holding the mane or neckstrap, or pulling on the reins.

When you do this exercise perfectly, you fold into jumping position just as your pony pushes off into the trot, and you are "with" him, just as you should be when you jump. If you are behind the motion or a little late, you may sit in the saddle for a second or two before you get up, or you might post or fall back onto the saddle. Over a jump, you would be "left behind." If you are ahead of the motion, or if you move too soon, you may stand up before your pony begins to trot. Over a jump, you would be "ahead" of your pony.

Repeat this exercise on loose reins until you are "with" your pony every time. Next, tie a knot in the end of your reins and try the exercise with "no hands." To test yourself, ride an approach to a low cross-rail in a sitting trot. If you automatically fold into jumping position just as your pony jumps, you are jumping with good timing.

Hands and Reins: Jumping with a "Bridge"

You have already practiced jumping with a basic release, a long release, and a short release. Now you can learn to use a "bridge" when you jump. A bridge gives you some support on your pony's neck and helps you keep your hands in the right position as he jumps.

To make a bridge, your right hand holds the end of the left rein, with about 6 inches of rein between your hands. You press this piece of rein (the bridge) down over the top of your pony's neck, with your hands pressed down against the sides of his neck.

It's important to have your reins at the right length when using a bridge. If the reins are too long, you will have no contact and no control. If they are too short, you will pull on your pony's mouth and keep him from stretching his head and neck when he jumps. You can use a long or short release with a bridge. Keep the bridge pressed down against the top of your pony's neck throughout the jump, until he has landed.

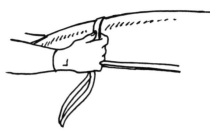

1. Bridging the reins

2. Press the bridge down over the pony's neck when jumping.

Simple Gymnastic Jumping

Gymnastic jumping comprises jumping exercises that develop the pony's and the rider's jumping style (the way you and your pony use your bodies over jumps). The exercises are usually a series of carefully spaced jumps, or ground poles and jumps. The spacing of the poles and jumps makes a pony adjust his strides and balance, and take off and land at certain places. When used correctly, gymnastics can help a pony jump better and make it easier for a rider to jump well. The jumps, however, *must* be used carefully and must be set at the right distances and heights for your pony. The wrong kind of gymnastics can be difficult or even dangerous for both pony and rider, even if the jumps are not very high. Always have your instructor set up and check all gymnastics for you and your pony.

The distances given for gymnastic jumping exercises are average distances for various sizes of horses and ponies. Some ponies have a longer or shorter stride than average. The distances must be adjusted so that your pony can handle them comfortably. To do this, you need an experienced helper on the ground (preferably your instructor). Set up the gymnastic, using ground poles in place of jumps, and ride through it. Your helper should watch to see whether your pony's feet land in the middle of the spaces. If he scrambles, misses poles, "reaches" (stretches his legs out), or shortens his strides, your helper should adjust the distances until the pony can do the gymnastic easily with normal strides. Only then should you add the actual jumps.

Most gymnastics should be approached in a posting or sitting trot (cantering into gymnastics is for advanced jumpers only, as it is easier to make a serious mistake). The pony must be alert but relaxed, with a steady rhythm, not rushing. Fold into jumping position and release at the first jump or ground pole, and keep your release until your pony has finished the last jump. A basic release, crest release, or bridge are best for beginning work over gymnastics.

Following are some basic gymnastic jumping exercises.

TROTTING POLES TO A CROSS-RAIL

Trotting poles (also called a "trotting grid") teach the pony to approach a jump with a steady, even stride and to watch where he puts his feet. When placed the right distance from a cross-rail, they make him take off at the right spot. They also encourage him to stretch his neck, round his back, and jump in good form. Trotting poles can be used to help steady a pony that tends to rush.

This exercise is good for the rider's balance; helps relax knees, ankles, and hip joints; and gets the heels down. It can help both pony and rider develop confidence over low jumps.

Following are the average distances between trotting poles and on takeoff.

Between trotting poles:

- Large horses: 4 feet 6 inches to 4 feet 9 inches
- Small horses, large ponies: 3 feet 9 inches to 4 feet 3 inches
- Smaller ponies (under 13.2): 3 feet 3 inches to 3 feet 6 inches

The distance from the last ground pole to the cross-rail should be approximately twice the distance between trotting poles.

Takeoff distance (from the last trotting pole to the jump):

- Large horses: 9 feet to 9 feet 6 inches
- Small horses, large ponies: 8 feet 6 inches to 9 feet
- Smaller ponies: 7 to 8 feet

DOUBLE WITH ONE SHORT CANTER STRIDE

A "double" is an exercise with two jumps close together. A double with a short canter stride encourages a pony to rebalance himself after the first jump and take off at the right place. It can help a quick pony to relax and jump quietly, and jump the second fence carefully.

It helps to set a grid of three or four trotting poles before the first cross-rail, to keep the pony steady. The second jump, a cross-rail or low vertical, is placed one short canter stride away. (See distances on the following page.)

This exercise gives a rider practice in waiting for the pony to jump, in rebalancing on landing, and in riding a canter stride before a jump. Release at the first ground pole, and keep your release until your pony has landed over the last jump. Remember to keep your eyes on your target, sink into your heels, and let your pony close your angles as he takes off.

Average distances for a double with one short canter stride (approached in trot):

- Large horses: 17 to 18 feet
- Small horses, large ponies: 16 to 17 feet
- Smaller ponies (under 13.2 hands): 14 to 15 feet

Double with One Short Canter Stride

CANTER GRID (GROUND POLES ONLY)

A "canter grid" is a series of ground poles spaced to help the pony canter with even, steady strides. It makes him canter with rounder strides and more energy, and pay attention to where he puts his feet. Riding a canter grid helps you keep your balance and go easily with your pony's motion. It's a good way to practice sinking your heels down, letting the pony close your angles, developing your rhythm, and using your timing.

To set a canter grid, you will need four or five ground poles spaced for your pony's canter stride. The ground poles should have "feet" or should be fixed in place so that they won't roll under your pony's feet if he should hit one. You must space them so that his feet land in the middle of the space between the poles. Then he won't have to "reach"; take short, choppy strides; or trip.

When riding a canter grid, keep your seat bones close to the saddle, but close your hip angle a little and keep all your angles flexible. Don't stand up or take an exaggerated jumping position; just let your pony rock you as he canters over the poles.

Average spacing for canter grid (ground poles):

- Large horses: 11 to 12 feet
- Small horses, large ponies: 10 to 11 feet
- Smaller ponies (under 13.2 hands): 9 to 10 feet

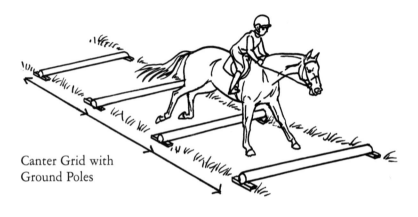

Canter Grid with
Ground Poles

SINGLE BOUNCE (NO-STRIDE)

A bounce, or a "no-stride," is two small jumps set so close together that the pony lands and takes off again without taking a stride in between. A bounce teaches a pony to jump with good balance and energy, to push off with his hocks, and to fold his front legs properly. Riding over bounces teaches a rider keep his balance and, especially, not to stand up and get ahead of the motion. It makes your angles close, open, and then close again quickly.

Setting trotting poles before the first jump helps you approach in a steady, lively trot and take off at the right place. You must make sure your pony has enough energy to jump two jumps. If he has barely enough energy to jump the first one, he may slow down or even stop in the middle. Keep your eyes on your target; sink your heels down; and let the pony close your angles as he jumps, lands, and jumps again.

Average distances for a single bounce (approached in trot):

- Large horses: trotting poles spaced 4 feet 6 inches to 4 feet 9 inches
  takeoff distance: 9 feet to 9 feet 6 inches
  bounce: 9 feet 6 inches to 11 feet
- Small horses, large ponies: trotting poles spaced 4 feet to 4 feet 3 inches
  takeoff distance: 8 feet 6 inches to 9 feet
  bounce: 9 feet
- Smaller ponies (under 13.2 hands): trotting poles spaced 3 feet 3 inches to 3 feet 9 inches
  takeoff distance: 8 feet to 8 feet 6 inches
  bounce: 7 to 8 feet

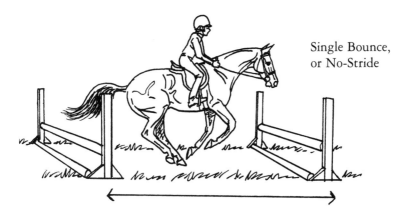

Single Bounce, or No-Stride

STEERING DURING GYMNASTIC JUMPING

When you ride a gymnastic jumping exercise, release either at the first pole or as your pony takes off at the first jump, and keep your release until he has landed over the last jump. However, if a pony tries to swerve or duck out, you must steer while he jumps in order to keep him straight.

If your pony wants to swerve to the right, take your left hand off his neck and hold it out to the side in an opening rein aid. Your other hand should be on his neck or holding the mane. You can "thumb a ride"—briefly rotate your hand so that your thumb points out in the direction of the opening rein. Never pull backward; you would catch him in the mouth and might make him stop. Carry your crop on the side he likes to swerve toward. You can also use this steering method to prevent a pony from swerving or running out at a single jump.

Steering in a gymnastic:
Rotate hand out to the side.

Jumping New Kinds of Fences

Before you jump higher fences, you and your pony need experience jumping different types of fences at a height at which you both are comfortable. This makes jumping more interesting and fun, and teaches your pony to go freely and confidently over any kind of jump you meet.

Different Types of Show-Jumping Fences   Show-jumping fences (also called "stadium jumping obstacles") are made of standards with rails or planks that can be knocked down. These fences also include walls, gates, panels, brush boxes, flower boxes, or other "fillers" (jump materials that fill in the space and make a jump look more substantial). Show jumps are often brightly painted. Jumps for hunter classes are more natural looking, such as brush, walls, coops, and natural rails.

The two basic types of jumps are:

Verticals (also called uprights or straight fences): Fences that are built "straight up." These include vertical rails, planks, gates, panels, and walls.

Spreads: Fences that have width as well as height. They use two or more "elements" (sets of standards with rails and other materials).

There are several kinds of spreads:

TYPES OF JUMPS

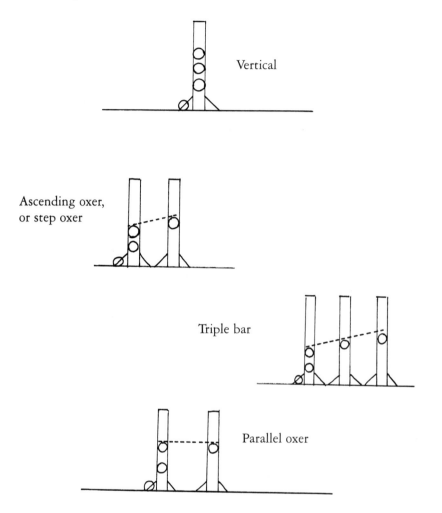

- *Ascending spreads (also called "staircase fences")*: Spread jumps that slant up and away from the takeoff side, like steps. They are the easiest kind of spread fence to jump because they give a pony more time to fold up his legs. An "ascending oxer" (also called a "step oxer") is a spread with two elements, with the back element higher than the front. A "triple bar" is an ascending spread with three elements.
- *Parallels*: Spreads with front and back elements the same height. A "square oxer" is a parallel that is as wide as it is high. Parallels are harder to jump than ascending spreads, and square oxers are the most difficult type of parallel to jump.

Safety Considerations   Oxers, triple bars, and parallels are made to be jumped in one direction *only*. Jumping them the wrong way creates a false ground line, which is dangerous. For safety, the last element of any spread (the one closest to the landing side) must be no more than a single pole. Planks, gates, and panels should have metal handles that allow them to balance safely on flat cups. These should be supported by flat cups only. Rounded cups will not allow a gate or panel to fall if it is hit hard. Gates or "ladders" (panels with spaces in them) must have a safe distance between the bars so that a pony cannot catch his hoof in them. You can use straw bales or barrels for fillers, but they must be fixed so that they cannot roll.

(For more about safe jumps, see the *USPC D Manual*, pages 73-74.)

How to Jump a New Fence

Ponies are naturally suspicious of new fences, especially white or brightly colored fences. At home, your pony can look at a new jump before he jumps it. In competition, however, you cannot practice over the fences or show your pony a fence before jumping it. You must teach him to trust you so that he will jump a new fence when you ask him to, without looking it over first.

To teach your pony to jump new fences, your goal is to get him to jump each new fence the first time you ask him, without a refusal or runout. Start with a single painted pole, cross-rail, or very low fence. Ride an opening circle to the right that aims you at the center of the jump; then change direction and ride a circle to the left so that you ride a figure 8 in front of the jump. Each time your pony goes toward the jump, notice his attitude. Does he pay attention to the jump and go forward with confidence, or does he tense up, shorten his stride, weave and wobble, or hold back? Each time he sees the jump ahead, use your legs to ask him to move forward freely. When you are sure he is willing to go forward, give a firm leg aid, cluck to him, and ride straight on over the middle of the jump. Don't ask him to jump until you are quite sure that he will go forward freely. Be ready in case he jumps extra high over the new fence. After the jump, pat him and praise him, and let him walk.

If the pony should refuse or run out, you must stay calm but in control. Bring him back to the center of the jump and let him have a good look at it. Then use your legs firmly, perhaps adding a tap of your crop behind your leg to remind him to go forward. Keep your eyes firmly on your target, over the middle of the jump. It may be necessary to lower the jump or to let him follow another pony over it to give him confidence.

Remember that your goal is to give your pony confidence and a good experience on his first try over new and different but easy fences. If you ask him to jump fences that are too big and scary (especially a jump that cannot be lowered) before he is ready, you may cause a bad experience for both of you.

Striding and Jumping in Stride

When a pony canters, he should cover about the same amount of ground at each stride. The average length of strides at the canter are the following:

Large horse: 12 to 13 feet

Small or short-striding horse, large pony: 11 feet

Small to medium ponies (under 13.2 hands): 9 to 10 feet

A normal jump is the same length as a normal canter stride. For instance, if your pony canters with an 11-foot stride, his jump is about 11 feet long. Jumping "in stride" means that he canters with even strides and that his jump is the same length as his strides. This makes jumping smooth, steady, and easy to ride. Jumping shorter than a normal canter stride (called "popping") is rough and harder to ride. A jump that is longer than a normal canter stride is big and powerful but can catch a rider by surprise.

To find the length of your pony's normal cantering stride, rake the dirt smooth, canter over it, and measure the distance from one set of hoofprints to the next.

At this stage, you should try to ride with a steady pace, even strides, and free forward movement. Later on, you will learn how to shorten and lengthen your pony's strides to help him take off at the right spot.

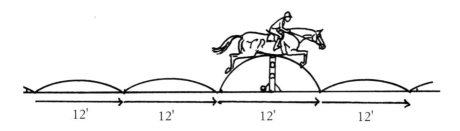

12'   12'   12'   12'

Jumping in Stride

Developing a Good Pace for Stadium Jumping

It is easier to ride a good course if you ride at a steady, even pace. This helps your pony jump in stride and helps you to go with him smoothly.

A good pace starts with free forward movement. A pony cannot move at a good pace or jump well if he is "sticky," reluctant to move, or not paying attention. He must be willing to move forward with energy when your legs ask him to, and you must use your leg aids correctly to keep him going forward. He must also be calm and relaxed enough to pay attention to you and to the jumps. A pony that is tense, rushing, or fighting your control is not ready or safe to jump, especially over a course.

Your pony must be in good balance to canter and jump well. This means an ordinary canter that feels safe, steady, and comfortable (not leaning or scrambling) for turns and jumping. You must also be in balance with your pony, riding with the motion, not ahead or behind the motion. Never let a pony take you to a jump in poor balance. During your opening circle, check his balance and your own. If it doesn't feel right, circle again while you rebalance yourself and use your aids to get a better canter. (In competition, you cannot take an extra circle, so you must get the right balance on your first circle.)

Your pace should be the kind of canter from which your pony jumps best. Once you have found his best jumping canter, try to keep that pace all the way around the course. If your pony begins to go slower, use your legs at each stride to keep him going forward. If he starts to go faster, sit up a little more and squeeze your hands at each stride to steady him.

An exercise that helps you develop a good jumping pace is to ride a course of ground poles at a canter, concentrating on making straight lines and good turns, and keeping the canter steady and well-balanced. When your pace is good and steady over the ground poles, you can build them up into jumps.

C-1 RIDING IN THE OPEN

At C-1 Level, you will learn to ride in the open at faster gaits, to handle different kinds of terrain, and to jump a variety of cross-country fences. You must be comfortable with D-3 riding in the open, and have confidence in yourself and your pony. You *must* ride a pony that you can control safely, especially for group riding and cross-country jumping. Being overmounted (riding a pony that is too much for you) is no fun at any time, but in the open it is simply dangerous.

Control in a Group in the Open

Control is never more important than when you are riding outside with other riders. Most ponies act more lively when ridden outside, especially if the weather is cool or windy. Also, their herd instinct is stronger when outside in a group, especially when trotting and cantering. Herd instinct makes ponies want to stay close to other ponies, take off if another pony spooks or runs, and never be left behind the herd. Ponies often get excited when two or more ponies are moving fast.

When herd instinct takes over, a pony may stop paying attention to his rider, which is not safe. Your job is to keep him listening to you, even when you are doing exciting things. Here are some tips for better control, especially when you are trotting or cantering in a group in the open:

- Use equipment that helps you keep control. Some ponies may need a stronger bit or a martingale for cross-country riding, especially in a group.
- Review the pulley rein for emergency control. (See *USPC D Manual*, page 125.)
- Keep a safe distance from other ponies (at least one pony length, more at a trot or canter). You should be back far enough to see the hind feet of the pony ahead of you over your pony's ears.
- Don't try to keep your pony so far behind the group that he gets upset. If he is too far back and gets excited, trot and catch up, or ask the group to wait for you. Never leave a pony behind when his rider is trying to mount, close a gate, or fix his tack. This can make the pony upset and hard to control.
- To keep your pony paying attention, ride him on contact and every now and then ask him to slow down just a little.
- Stay in line. Don't pass without permission.
- Never go fast toward home.

Trotting and Cantering in a Group   Before you trot on, ask others in the group if they are ready to trot. Keep at least one pony length (two lengths is better) between ponies. Don't pass others unless you ask first and there is plenty of room. If you must pass, give the other pony plenty of room and keep your pony's head turned slightly toward the pony you are passing. The person being passed should keep his pony's head turned toward the passing pony, and his heels turned away, to prevent kicking.

When you canter in a group, it should be on good footing, going slightly uphill and *away* from home. The safest way to canter outside is to follow a good leader (preferably your instructor). Everyone *must* stay in line without passing or crowding the pony ahead. The leader should ask whether everyone wants to canter. No one should canter unless everyone is comfortable cantering in a group. Each rider opens up a little extra space—at least two pony lengths. When all are ready, the leader sets the pace at a brisk trot, and you may canter as long as you can stay in line and keep your spacing. If your pony tries to pass or crowd the others, you must bring him back to a trot immediately. If anyone becomes uncomfortable cantering or if any pony gets excited or hard to control, the whole group must come back to a walk.

Emergency Control   Someday you may have to control a pony that is frightened, excited, or disobedient. It's important to stay as calm as you can and to think, not panic. Taking deep breaths and sitting up deep and tall help you stay strong and calm while you get control.

Some ponies get "strong" at a canter: They pull and are hard to stop. Sit up deep and tall and use a pulley rein upward several times, as sharply as you must to get his attention. Even if a pony is hard to stop, you can usually steer him. You can turn in a large circle and gradually make the circle smaller until he comes back under control. (Don't, however, turn sharply downhill or on slippery ground.)

Some ponies might buck when they get excited at a canter or after a jump. To buck, a pony must round his back and put his head down. If you sit up and lean back and use a pulley rein to lift his head, this corrects him for bucking and makes it much harder for him to buck or run.

When a pony kicks at another pony, he usually puts his ears back first and then swings his rump toward his victim. *Instantly* turn his head toward his victim and his heels away, and correct him sharply with your voice, reins, and crop. When choosing a Pony Club mount, remember that a pony that kicks is dangerous to other ponies and to people, and should not be ridden in company.

CROSS-COUNTRY CONTROL

Circling to slow pony down

Using a pulley rein

Riding over Different Kinds of Terrain

Riding Up and Down Hills   When riding uphill, stay in half-seat to be in balance with your pony and to let him stretch his neck and back as he climbs. Keep him moving steadily; don't let him rush. On a long hill, he may need to stop and rest if he gets out of breath.

When riding downhill, you must stay in balance with your pony. On gentle slopes, it usually works best to stay in a half-seat, without leaning too far forward. On a steeper slope, sit up deep and tall, keeping your legs under your seat. Don't lean back or let your legs get out ahead of you, or else your pony will have difficulty using his hind legs to keep his balance. Keep your eyes up to help yourself steer and to keep your balance. And make your pony go slowly enough to be safe.

When riding down a steep slope, it is very important to keep your pony straight. If he goes downhill at an angle, he could slip sideways and fall. If he goes straight, he can sit down on his hindquarters to keep his balance.

Riding over Ditches   At first, you should ride over only easy ditches: shallow, with sloping banks and good footing. (Riding over deep ditches or those with steep banks requires more experience.) There are two ways of riding a ditch: walking through it or jumping it.

If a ditch is wide and shallow with sloping banks, you may walk through it. Ride in a half-seat, keeping your eyes up and staying in balance with your pony. Keep your pony straight and under control as you ride down the bank. At the bottom, sink your heels down and hold the mane or the neckstrap in case he jumps. Stay in half-seat as he climbs up the far bank.

If a ditch is fairly narrow and has good footing on both sides, you can jump it. Approach in a steady trot or canter, keeping your seat in the saddle and your eyes on a target beyond the ditch. Use your legs firmly to keep your pony going forward, and remember to close into jumping position and release as he jumps. If you look down, lean forward too soon, or drop your contact, you may surprise your pony and cause him to stop. If your pony is reluctant to cross a ditch, it may help to follow another pony at a safe distance.

Crossing Streams   When crossing a stream, you must first be sure about the safety of the spot where you want to cross. Look for a shallow place with gently sloping banks, good footing, and clear water so that you can see the bottom. Don't cross where it is steep, slippery (especially fast water with large, slippery rocks), or boggy. If you can't tell how deep the water is or what the bottom is like, it is unsafe to cross. There could be wire, rocks, or even quicksand under the surface.

To ride across a stream, stay in balance with your pony, keep your eyes up, and use your legs firmly. Keep your pony moving steadily forward. You can let him drink if he wants to, but don't let him paw or splash. Some ponies like to lie down in water; they usually lower their heads and paw first. If your pony should try this, pull his head up and use your legs and crop firmly to get him going forward.

Some ponies do not like to cross water, perhaps because they cannot tell how deep the water is by looking at the surface. Keep your pony straight, and sit up deep and tall while you use your legs firmly, over and over. Be firm, but be patient. It is not a good idea to get off and try to lead your pony across, as he might jump and knock you down. It may help to follow another pony across the stream at a safe distance.

Jumping Low Banks A low bank is a simple step up or down. To jump onto a bank, a pony needs to be in good balance with extra energy (impulsion), and must get his hind legs underneath him and "jump off his hocks." Use your legs to keep him going forward but not too fast, in a bouncy trot or canter. (Riding too fast at a bank can make a pony stumble.) As he jumps up, stay well forward and hold the mane or neckstrap until he has landed. If you slip backward or sit up too soon, you could make him drop his hind legs and slip.

To jump down off a bank, you must stay in balance with your pony as his back tips down and then comes back to level. Approach the bank in a fast walk or slow but lively trot, keeping your seat

Jumping a simple step up

Jumping down a step

close to the saddle. Keep your eyes on your target. Don't look down, which could make you lose your balance. Use your legs to keep your pony moving straight and forward; and let your body fold into jumping position; then "open" just as you do when landing over an ordinary jump. Your legs should be right under your seat, with your heels down and your ankles and knees absorbing the shock. Keep your hands firmly on his neck, using either bridged reins or a neck-strap, so that you won't pull his mouth by mistake.

Banks look easy and natural to ponies, and most ponies jump them well. But you must be "positive" (sure and strong) and go straight, steady, and not too fast.

Riding in Flat, Open Areas   Flat, open areas are places where you may want to trot or canter. Before you do, be sure of your footing. High grass or weeds could hide holes, ditches, wire, or even farm machinery, so don't canter blindly across a field.

Watch out for holes made by groundhogs, prairie dogs, and other animals. The main hole may have dirt piled at the entrance, but there may be other "blind" holes nearby that are very hard to see. If you spot a hole, point it out to other riders behind you and call "Ware hole!"

When you want to trot or canter in an open area with others, first make sure that everyone is ready to move on and is in control. If someone takes off without warning or passes other riders, the ponies may get excited and become very hard to control. If your pony should begin to get strong (pull or go too fast), then you should sit up, use a pulley rein, and circle him to get control again. If one pony gets strong, all the others must come back to a walk until he is under control.

Riding in the Woods   When riding in the woods, watch out for low branches, large tree roots, and trees close to the trail. When you ride under a branch, duck your head and let the branch slide over your helmet. Never try to hold a branch out of the way for a rider behind you. When you let go, it will swing back and could whip across either his or his pony's face.

Watch out when riding on a narrow trail with trees close by, as a pony does not notice how far your knees stick out. If you turn his head slightly toward the tree and use your leg on his side, you can bend his body a little and keep him from bumping your knee on the tree.

Cross-Country Jumping

"Cross-country jumping" means jumping fences in the open. This may include jumping natural fences while hacking out cross-country, jumping foxhunting panels (such as coops, walls, and post and rails), jumping fences on an outside hunter course, or the cross-country phase of combined training events.

The basics for jumping in the open are the same as for jumping in the ring. The main differences are that the fences are usually solid (cannot be knocked down), and you must pay attention to terrain and the natural conditions around a jump, which can change the way a jump "rides." Also, because many ponies are more lively when jumping outside, you must ride with good control in order to be safe.

Dos and Don'ts for Safe Cross-Country Jumping

- Do warm your pony up thoroughly and check your tack first. Be sure that your stirrups are at the correct jumping length.
- Don't *ever* jump alone! There must always be another responsible person with you in case of accident.
- Do check the approach, takeoff, and landing of each jump first. Watch out for hazards such as holes, bad footing, or wire.
- Don't jump a pony that you can't control safely in the open, especially in a group.
- Do ride with a positive attitude—strong and sure. Jump only fences that you feel positive about jumping.
- Don't get ahead of your pony, stand up forward, look down, or "drop" your pony (suddenly loosen the reins) when jumping cross-country. These actions are dangerous and can throw him off balance and make him refuse.
- Do keep your pony straight and in good balance, moving freely forward to his jumps. You should jump most cross-country jumps in a steady, well-balanced canter.
- Don't let your pony gallop fast, carelessly, or out of control at his fences.
- Do seek the advice of an expert and learn to ride cross-country fences correctly.

Techniques for Jumping Cross-Country Obstacles

Control, Impulsion, and Free Forward Movement   Just as in ring jumping, your pony must go forward freely when your legs ask him to. If he is lazy, sticky, or reluctant to move forward, he can get into trouble jumping solid cross-country fences. When he does go forward, you must be able to control him safely. In free forward movement, your pony goes forward willingly when you ask him to and uses his hind legs strongly without going fast or running away.

Before you begin jumping in the open, check your pony's responsiveness to your aids by asking him to "go forward" and "come back," first in a trot and then in a canter. When you squeeze your legs, he should move forward more strongly. If he seems sluggish or slow to respond to your legs, remind him with a tap of your crop behind your leg. Ask him to "come back" by sitting up taller, sinking deeper into the saddle, and squeezing your hands on the reins. If he does not respond by slowing down, use a pulley rein to bring him to a halt.

Steering: Holding a Specific Line Over a Fence   When you jump a fence in the open, your pony must jump straight and exactly where you aim him. There could be an important reason for him to jump where you tell him; for instance, you might have to avoid a hole or bad footing on one side of the jump.

To ride a specific line over a fence, you must pick a target in line with the place you plan to jump. Keep your eyes on your target before, during, and after the jump. Use your hands to steer your pony straight if you need to (see page 34), and use your legs to push him over if you feel him starting to drift sideways.

At first, you should jump all fences squarely. Later, you can ride a simple vertical fence at a slight angle. You must ride this kind of approach as a straight line before, during, and after the jump (not a last-minute turn); and you must be careful not to let your pony run out. Practice jumping straight, and at a slight angle from the left and from the right.

Footing and Terrain   "Terrain" is the shape of the ground you ride over: flat, uphill or downhill, steep or gently rolling. "Footing" is the condition of the ground underfoot: firm, hard, deep, muddy, or slippery. Both can affect the way a pony moves and jumps, and can make a particular jump easier or harder.

Galloping and jumping uphill is hard work. On an uphill slope a pony may get tired and "strung out": stretched out, leaning on his forehand, with his hind legs trailing behind him. To jump well, he must be in balance, with his hind legs underneath him, not leaning on his forehand. You should ride him uphill in a lively, bouncy trot or canter, not in a sprawling, stretched-out gallop.

Downhill slopes tend to make a pony go faster and lean on his forehand. If his balance is too far forward, he may scramble faster and faster, just as a child running downhill must run faster to keep from falling down. This can make him stumble or slip, especially if he turns quickly or has to jump before he catches his balance. You should ride downhill slopes at a slow to medium speed, in a bouncy, well-balanced trot or canter, with the pony's hind legs well under his body. When riding downhill, always slow down and check your balance before you turn.

The best footing for cross-country riding and jumping is firm but springy turf. Deep or soft footing is tiring; it makes a pony work hard with every step and makes the jumps seem bigger. Slippery footing feels insecure; a pony will shorten his stride and may be afraid to jump on slippery footing. Very hard footing makes a pony's feet sting when they hit the ground, so he may shorten his strides and be reluctant to jump. Hard ground with short grass can be both hard and very slippery, especially when wet. Rough ground with stones, bumps, and uneven footing can cause injuries from twisting a fetlock joint, and should be taken slowly and carefully.

Types of Cross-Country Obstacles and How to Ride Them

Simple Verticals (Post and Rails, Gate, Panel, Etc.) Simple verticals are usually quite straightforward and can be ridden just as you would ride them in the ring. Be sure that your pony is moving forward freely (not too fast) and is in good balance, and stay in rhythm. Keep your eyes up and wait until your pony closes your angles as he takes off.

TYPES OF CROSS-COUNTRY FENCES

Verticals

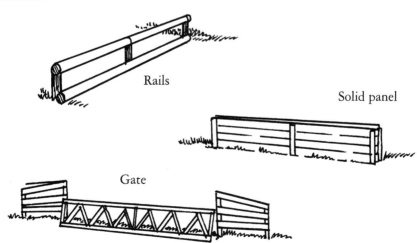

Rails

Solid panel

Gate

Spread Fences

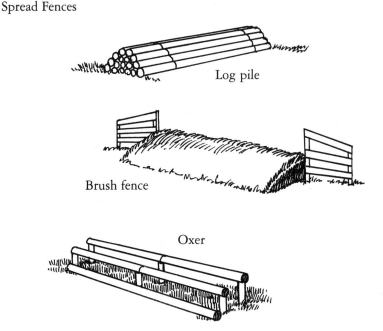

Log pile

Brush fence

Oxer

Spread Fences   Cross-country spread fences for C-1s should be simple, easy to see, and not too wide. They should be ascending spreads, not parallels or square oxers. Some examples include a log pile, a brush pile (or "aiken"), a wide stone wall, and an oxer made of poles.

Approach a spread fence at a steady canter with free forward movement, but not too fast. If your pony takes off too far back, the spread becomes wider, and he could hit the back side of the jump. Help him wait for the best takeoff spot by riding a steady approach in good balance. Stay in jumping position until he has landed, and use a long release that allows him to stretch his neck as far as he needs to. Sitting back too soon or restricting your pony's use of his neck or back can make him jump short or drop his hind legs into the fence.

CHAPTER 2

C-2 RIDING

C-2 RIDING ON THE FLAT

At the C-2 Level, you should be riding with free forward movement and a light, steady feel of your pony's mouth, and making progress toward riding with an independent seat and coordinated use of the aids. This requires a good foundation: a correct and secure seat, riding in balance, and using the aids correctly. Riding without stirrups in all gaits will help your seat become more secure and independent. You will also learn techniques for improving your hands and contact; how to coordinate your aids for better transitions and halts; how to bend and straighten your pony; and how to ride the hand gallop.

Improving Your Seat: Riding without Stirrups at All Gaits

Riding without stirrups is good for developing strong legs, suppleness, security, and an independent seat, but you must do it correctly. Incorrect work without stirrups can cause bad habits (such as pinching with your knees or riding with your legs out in front of you). Your instructor should make sure you are doing it correctly.

When you ride without stirrups, remember to move the buckle away from the stirrup bars before crossing your stirrup leathers over in front of the saddle, and fold the leathers flat so that there is no lump under your leg.

Sitting Trot without Stirrups

Why: To develop a deep, supple seat and go smoothly with the trot.

Tips for Sitting the Trot:

- Your pelvis must be balanced, not tipped forward or backward, and your back must be tall, straight, and relaxed.
- Sit in balance (head, shoulders, and upper body over seat bones; legs and feet under seat), and straight (weight balanced evenly on both seat bones).
- Legs should hang relaxed, but your heels must not come up and dig into your pony's sides.
- Ride by balance, not by grip (which tightens your seat and makes you bounce).
- Breathe deeply and allow the movement of the trot to lift one hip, then the other.

Sitting Trot without Stirrups

Cantering without Stirrups

Why: To develop a deep, supple seat; to follow the movement of the canter smoothly without bouncing.

Tips for Sitting the Canter:

- Sit deep and tall, as in sitting the trot. Ride by balance, not by grip. Your legs should be relaxed, but don't let your heels come up and dig into the pony's sides.
- Sit up straight. Do not lean forward or you will bounce. Keep your balance in the center, without leaning to either side.
- The canter motion is more rolling, like a big circle. Let it open and close your hip joints, and "roll" your seat with each stride.
- Deep breathing or humming along with the canter helps you relax and go with the rhythm.

Posting without Stirrups

Why: For muscle control and balance; develops strong legs and independent seat. Especially important for security in jumping.

Posting Trot without Stirrups

Tips for Posting without Stirrups:

- Posting without stirrups is easy if your balance and position are correct. However, even small errors in balance or position make it very difficult.
- Keep the same position as when riding with stirrups: legs under body, knees bent, calves in contact with your pony's sides, toes higher than heels.
- Close your hip angle until you find the body angle at which your pony "posts you." The thrust of the trot lifts your seat up and forward; don't lift yourself up or post too high.
- As you post, roll forward onto the inner part of your thighs, then back onto your seat bones.
- Keep your legs steady on your pony's sides, with knees bent and toes up. If your toes drop down, or you grip with your knees, or your legs get loose and floppy, you will lose your balance.

Half-Seat without Stirrups

Why: This exercise is more difficult than sitting or posting without stirrups. It develops strong legs and good balance, and can help you get ready to jump without stirrups.

Tips for Riding in Half-Seat without Stirrups:

- Ride as when posting without stirrups (toes up and legs under you, legs in contact with your pony's sides). Close your hip joints by tilting slightly forward until you are in balance with your pony.
- Don't lean too far forward, or your legs will slip backward and you will lose your balance.
- This exercise takes more strength than posting without stirrups, because you do not let your pony lift you up and down. Try alternating posting without stirrups and half-seat for several beats. As your legs get stronger, you will be able to stay in half-seat longer.
- If you start to lose your balance or if your legs get too tired to stay in position, come back to a sitting trot or a walk and give your muscles a short rest.
- When posting or riding in half-seat without stirrups, you *must not* use the reins for balance. It may help to use a neckstrap.

Improving Your Hands and Contact

Riding correctly on contact gives you smoother and more precise control of your pony.

Good Hands   Good hands give aids by changing the pressure on the bit, not by pulling. To have good hands, you must be able to squeeze, resist (hold against a pull), and relax without pulling.

- "Squeezing" means briefly squeezing your fist (like squeezing water out of a sponge). This causes a brief, stronger pressure on the bit.
- "Relaxing" means relaxing your hands back to a soft fist, not letting the reins slip away or get longer.
- "Resisting" (or "holding") means that you squeeze your hands, stop following with your arms, sit deep and tall, and wait. Your hands (and arms, shoulders, and body) do not pull backward, but they do not let go. As your pony feels the pressure he causes by pushing against your hands, he "gives" by relaxing his mouth and slowing or stopping. You then relax your hands, without leaning forward or moving your arms forward.

Learning Not to Pull   One of the worst (and most common) habits a rider can have is pulling on the pony's mouth. You may pull without realizing that you are doing it, or if you are having trouble controlling a pony. Pulling is often the result of incorrect shoulder, arm, or hand position, or of catching your balance on the reins. It can also happen if you are overmounted, or trying to do things that are too difficult for your level.

Pulling hurts and annoys a pony instead of giving him clear and correct signals. He will soon learn to defend himself by opening his mouth, tossing his head, pulling against his rider, or developing a "hard mouth." If you pull on your pony, whether on purpose to control him or by accident, you will spoil his mouth and his responsiveness to your aids, and he will become difficult to ride with correct contact.

Rider resists pull from helper.

To help you learn how to resist (or hold) instead of pulling, your instructor or a helper can take the reins and pull against you. Keep your shoulders wide and arms hanging close to your sides. As your helper pulls, sit deep and tall, and take the pull down your shoulders and back so that you sink deeper into your saddle. Keep your elbows still and your fingers closed, and *wait without pulling.* You should resist exactly as much as your helper pulls—no more, no less. When your helper stops pulling, your hands, arms, and seat should stay just as they were; they should not fly backward. As you practice, you will realize when you are resisting correctly or pulling (or leaning back).

Shoulders, Arms, and Hands You can't have good hands without good shoulders and arms and a good seat. If your seat is incorrect or stiff, you get bounced around, which makes your hands jerky. If your shoulders, arms, elbows, or wrists are stiff or in the wrong position, you will pull on your pony by accident.

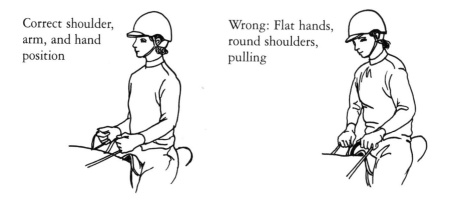

Correct shoulder, arm, and hand position

Wrong: Flat hands, round shoulders, pulling

Your shoulders should feel wide and relaxed and hang in a natural position. Hunched shoulders are caused by tension, especially in the upper chest.

Here is an exercise to help your shoulders:

1. Touch your fingers to the tips of your shoulders.
2. Unfold your hands and arms slowly, stretching them straight out to the sides, palms up.
3. Turn your hands over, palms down.
4. Let your arms fall gently to your sides.

This exercise widens your shoulders and helps them drop into a natural position. It also helps to take a deep breath and lift your shoulders up toward your ears, then let them relax and drop down again.

Upper arms that are stuck out ahead of your body make your hands stiff and jerky. When you halt, slow down, or resist a pull, let the muscles in the back of your upper arms do the work. This gives you more power without pulling.

Relaxed elbows are an important key to good contact. Your elbows must bend enough to let your arms hang under your shoulders, with your hands at the right height for your pony's head position. Elbows act as shock absorbers, keeping bounces from going all the way to your pony's mouth.

SHOULDER EXERCISE

1. Start with fingers touching shoulders.
2. Open arms out, palms up.

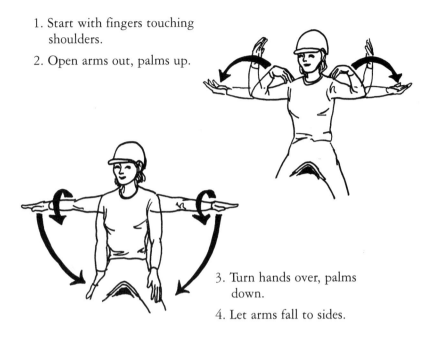

3. Turn hands over, palms down.
4. Let arms fall to sides.

Your forearms should be turned so that the edges of your wrists are on top. If your forearms turn so that the flat sides are up, then your hands are in an incorrect knuckles-up position, which is hard on your pony's mouth. This also hunches your shoulders and makes your elbows stick out.

The correct way to carry your wrists is straight but relaxed, as you do when you shake hands with someone. Your hands should be held in a natural, soft fist, with knuckles vertical or very slightly tipped inward (no more than 30 degrees inside the vertical). Incorrect hand positions or open fingers make you tense your hands and arms, producing a stiff, uncomfortable touch on your pony's mouth. They also let your reins slip, which interferes with control.

A common cause of pulling is "flat" hands (knuckles on top). In this position, you drop the weight of your arms and hands onto the reins and pull every time you use a rein aid. You also hunch your shoulders and stick out your elbows.

Straight Line from Elbow to Bit When you ride, there should be a straight line from your elbow through your wrist, hand, and rein to the bit (seen from the side). Then your hands are in position to give rein aids properly without pulling up or down on the bit, and the bit can work as it is designed to do. When your pony changes his head position, your hands must adjust their position (up or down) to keep the straight line from elbow to bit.

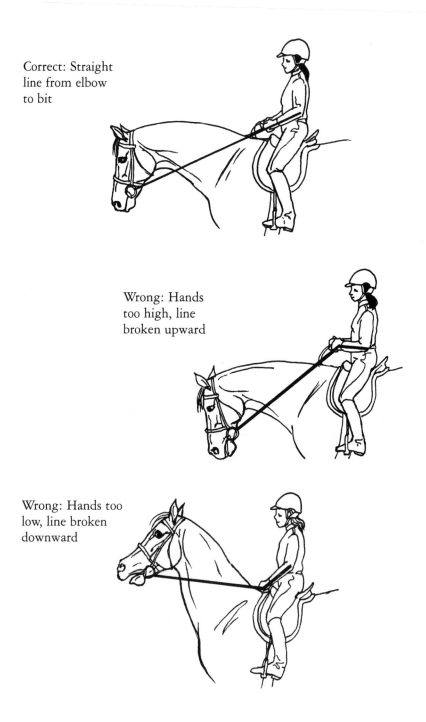

Correct: Straight line from elbow to bit

Wrong: Hands too high, line broken upward

Wrong: Hands too low, line broken downward

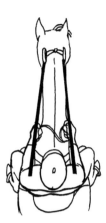

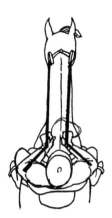

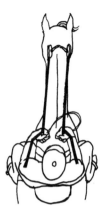

Correct: Straight line from elbow to bit, with straight wrists

Wrong: Broken line from elbow to bit; wrists broken inward

Wrong: Broken line from elbow to bit, wrists bent

There should also be a straight line from your elbows to the bit, when seen from above. This means your wrists are straight, not bent in or out, and your hands are several inches apart, not locked together or spread too wide apart. Riding with hands too close together or with bent wrists breaks the straight line inward. The result is that your wrists, arms, and hands stiffen, which makes the contact with your pony's mouth harsh and uncomfortable.

Improving Your Use of the Aids

The aids can be used in three ways: as driving aids, restraining aids, or guiding aids. There are several degrees of aids, from the lightest to the strongest. A good rider always starts with the lightest aids and increases them only as much as necessary to make his pony pay attention, then returns to a lighter aid.

The Driving Aids The driving aids are those that send the pony forward and ask for more energy. These are legs, seat, and voice (natural aids), and whips, crops, and spurs (artificial aids).

- *Legs* are the main driving aid. You use them in their normal position, just behind the girth, by squeezing (a short increase of pressure with the calf muscles, like a brief hug), nudging, or sometimes tapping.
- The *seat* makes your leg aids more powerful when you sit deep and tall. Briefly stretching your spine along with your leg aids can help make a reluctant pony move forward.

- The *voice aid* for forward movement may be a word or a short, sharp "cluck" used along with your leg and stick. You should not use voice aids too often, or your pony may stop paying attention.
- *Spurs* may be used to reinforce the leg aids with a gentle touch or a brief nudge.
- *Whips or crops* are the most powerful artificial aids to reinforce the driving aids. To apply a crop, you take the reins in one hand while you reach back with the other hand and tap the pony's side close to your leg. You can use a dressage whip to tap the pony's side without taking your hand off the reins. Never pull on the pony's mouth when using a whip or a crop.

The Restraining Aids   The restraining aids are those that ask your pony to stop or slow down, or prevent him from going forward. They include seat, hands, and sometimes voice (natural aids).

- *The seat* is the most important restraining aid. Sitting deep and tall, rebalancing yourself, and briefly stretching your spine helps your pony adjust his balance to stop, slow down, or collect himself.
- *Hands* should squeeze, not pull. They may squeeze briefly, or resist (or hold) by applying steady pressure. The strongest rein effect is a pulley rein (bracing one hand against the pony's neck and lifting sharply up and back with the other), which is used only for emergency control.
- *Voice*—for example, a quiet, soothing "Whoa"—can sometimes help out the other restraining aids. This should not be overdone.

The Guiding Aids   The guiding aids are those that ask your pony to turn, bend his body, or move sideways. You may also use them to prevent him from turning or moving sideways. They include seat, legs, and hands.

- *The seat* is the most important aid for turning and bending your pony. When you "swivel," or turn deep in your center, your pony feels the motion through your seat bones. Sometimes, during a turn, you shift a little more weight onto the inside seat bone. *Never*, however, lean sideways; this upsets your balance and your pony's balance.

- *Legs* help guide your pony in two ways: *One leg at the girth* asks him to bend or turn in that direction, and to move forward and out. *One leg used 3 to 4 inches behind the girth* asks him to move his hind legs sideways, away from the leg aid. You can also use these leg aids to prevent a pony from turning, moving sideways, or cutting in on a turn.
- *Hands* are used with one of the four basic rein aids (direct rein; opening rein; indirect rein; neck, or bearing, rein), to guide the pony through a turn or ask him to bend or move sideways.

Coordinating the Aids

"Coordinating the aids" means using the aids together. This makes your aids clear and easy to understand and gives you smooth, precise control. The opposite is "clashing the aids," or using them so that one aid conflicts with another (for example, using a leg aid to go forward while your hands hold the pony back). Clashing aids confuse and upset a pony, and teach him bad habits such as pulling, balking, and rearing.

To coordinate your aids, you must be able to feel how much pressure you are applying with your hands, legs, and seat, and be able to add or reduce pressure with each. Above all, you must know clearly what your aids are asking your pony to do.

Coordinating the Aids in Upward Transitions Making an "upward transition" means moving forward from a halt or increasing the pace. There are two ways to coordinate the aids for upward transitions:

- For beginner riders (and green ponies), the hands must release (relax pressure on the bit) before the legs ask for forward movement. This opens the door for forward movement and avoids a clash of aids.
- For more advanced riders and better-trained ponies, the rider may close his legs and sit up deep and tall an instant before relaxing the pressure of his hands. This prepares the pony and allows him to gather his energy before he moves forward.

Coordinating the Aids in Downward Transitions Making a "downward transition" means coming back to a halt or decreasing the pace to a slower gait. There are two ways to coordinate the aids for downward transitions:

- For beginner riders (and green ponies), the rider should sit up deep and tall, relax leg pressure, and then squeeze his hands to ask his pony to stop or slow down. His legs remain softly resting on his pony's sides but are passive during the downward transition.
- For more advanced riders and ponies, the rider sits deep and tall, briefly stretches his spine, and closes his legs softly as he squeezes and resists with his hands. This helps the pony bring his hindquarters under himself and stay alert and balanced in the downward transition. The legs must be used tactfully, just enough to keep the pony in balance, and not so strongly as to clash the aids.

Coordinating the Aids in Turns   The most important aid in turning is the swiveling of the rider's seat. (Looking in the direction of the turn turns your eyes and head, which also helps.) This makes it easy and natural to coordinate the other aids: the inside leg squeezes close to the girth, while the outside leg slides back a little to control the hindquarters. The inside hand squeezes softly to lead the pony through the turn, and the outside hand presses toward (but never across) the neck, with a supporting rein.

Coordinating the Use of Leg, Cluck, and Stick   "Leg-cluck-stick" is a sequence of aids that can be used to make a pony respond better to the driving aids. It can be helpful in jumping as well as for producing better responsiveness in flat work.

Give your pony a brief leg aid to go forward (squeeze briefly with both legs). If he does not move forward immediately, give a single short, sharp cluck. If he still does not move forward (within one second), bridge your reins and tap him firmly with a crop, close behind your leg. Test him by squeezing your legs again. If he does not respond right away, repeat the leg-cluck-stick until he does. You must apply leg-cluck-stick within three seconds, or he will not understand.

Once your pony has learned to respond better to your leg aids, you should use your leg instead of clucking to him, except in rare cases where your leg aid is not enough and you do not have time to use your crop (for instance, if he begins to lose impulsion right before a jump). If you cluck too often, a pony will learn to ignore you, and the noise can interfere with other horses' and riders' concentration. Clucking is not permitted in dressage tests and is penalized.

Rhythm and Gaits

To move well, a pony must move with proper rhythm in every gait. A pony that changes his speed and rhythm is very hard to ride. Such changes may be due to nervousness, lack of training, his not paying attention, or poor riding. Finding your pony's best working rhythm is not difficult and will improve his movement and your riding.

"Rhythm" means the beats or pattern of a gait. For instance, the walk has a four-beat rhythm; the trot, two; and the canter, three. Each gait should have a clear, steady rhythm. If a pony loses his rhythm, his gaits become a mixed-up shuffle, and he may break from one gait into another.

"Tempo" means the speed of the rhythm: quick, slow, or medium, like playing a tune quickly or slowly. For example, a pony could walk with a four-beat rhythm in a quick tempo, slow tempo, or medium tempo. The tempo should be steady; it should not change from slow to fast to slow again.

The more aware you are of rhythm and tempo, the easier it is to help your pony move well. A metronome, which is a device used by musicians to keep a steady beat, can be set to match your pony's tempo. Every aid you use, whether a driving, restraining, or guiding aid, should be applied with a squeeze and release in rhythm with your pony's gait. Pay special attention to rhythm and tempo when you leave the rail or ride through a turn, circle, or ring figure, or when you ride toward or away from the stable. If you can keep your pony in a steady rhythm in spite of distractions, you help to keep his attention on his work and discourage shying.

Making Square Halts

You and your pony should learn to make square, well-balanced halts, and to stand still at the halt for several seconds. This takes a good working attitude, with a calm, obedient pony that pays attention to your aids.

A good halt is always ridden from "back to front." This means that you ask your pony to step under himself with both hind legs in order to balance himself as he halts. You do this by sitting deep and tall, rebalancing yourself, and stretching your spine briefly while softly closing your legs on your pony's sides. A split second later, your hands gently squeeze and resist, asking your pony to halt. You may need to repeat this sequence (seat, leg, hands, relax) several times in rhythm with your pony's gait before he learns to balance himself and halt.

Correct: A good halt comes from behind.

Wrong: A poor halt is "all in the hands."

A bad halt is "all in the hands." When a rider pulls or hangs on his pony's mouth, the pony first stiffens his mouth and neck, then hollows his back, braces his legs, and stops out of balance with his hind legs sprawled out behind him. He may throw his head up, open his mouth, lean on the bit, or halt crookedly. This kind of halt is even harder on a pony if his rider tries to halt quickly from a fast gait.

At this stage, you should make your halts gradually, through the walk. This means that your pony takes a few steps to slow down and walks a step or two before he halts. Only quite advanced ponies (and riders) are able to make smooth halts directly from the trot or the canter.

To get your pony to stand quietly at the halt, you must relax but stay in contact with him through your seat, legs, and hands.

Breathing out and allowing your seat to relax helps him relax and stand still. If your pony doesn't like to stand, ask him to halt for only a second; then move forward. You can work up to asking him to stand for two seconds, then three seconds and longer. Remember to stay straight and even, or he may move sideways.

A perfect halt is well balanced, straight, and "square"; the pony halts with front legs and hind legs lined up, and his head, neck, and back straight. Straightness is most important. Ride a straight line before and during your halt, with your eyes on a target ahead. You must be perfectly straight, with your weight balanced evenly on both seat bones, and your rein contact even, or the halt will be crooked.

Developing a straight, square halt takes time and training. You must be aware of what your pony's hind legs are doing. A pony stops with one hind leg, then the other. The last hind leg to stop is usually left behind and must take a half-step to square up. It helps to have a helper tell you which hind leg is left behind.

Improving Your Pony's Suppleness

"Suppleness" means a pony's ability to shift his balance forward and backward quickly and smoothly, and to turn easily. A supple pony is handy, flexible, easy to turn, and comfortable to ride. The opposite of suppleness is "stiffness." A stiff pony has trouble bending and balancing in turns and may move crookedly, which makes him awkward to ride and harder to control. A pony may be stiff because he is green, poorly trained or ridden, or unsound.

Frequent transitions help to improve a pony's balance and suppleness. You must ride them smoothly, from back to front (using your seat and legs to prepare your pony, then your hands).

All ponies have one side that is naturally more supple and one side that is stiffer, just as people are right- or left-handed. Good riding and training help a pony to become more even—stronger on his weaker side and more supple on his stiff side. A pony that is not ridden and trained well may become one-sided. He will have trouble carrying a rider on one diagonal at the trot or on one lead at the canter, and may be hard to turn.

Straightness and Bending

A supple, well-trained pony moves straight on straight lines, not crookedly or carrying his head or hindquarters off to one side. On curves or circles, he bends evenly, looking in the direction in which he is going. His back legs follow in the tracks of his front legs on curves and on straight lines. This keeps his spine properly lined up.

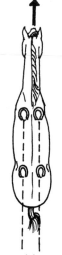

| Correct: Pony moves straight. | Hind legs are tracking front legs. | Wrong: Pony moves crookedly. | Hind legs do not track front legs. |

When a pony bends on a circle or a turn, his inside hind leg reaches farther forward under his body, so he doesn't slip or scramble. This helps him lift his back so that he can carry his rider through the turn with better balance. The pony looks in the direction of the turn, and his hind feet follow in the tracks of his front feet. He turns without leaning in, falling out with his shoulders, or skidding sideways with his hindquarters. A pony normally should bend toward the inside of a turn or circle. Bending to the outside is usually a mistake (except in a few special movements).

The aids for bending are the same as the aids for making a proper turn. The most important aid is the turning, or swivelling, of your seat while you look in the direction in which you want your pony to bend. Use an active inside leg aid close to the girth; the outside leg slides back a little to keep the pony's hind legs following the tracks of the front legs. The inside hand is active, softly squeezing to ask your pony to look in the direction of the turn. The outside hand uses a supporting rein, which keeps the pony from bending his neck too much or falling out.

You should just be able to see the pony's inside eyelashes; if you can see the whole side of his face, he is bending his neck too much. He must bend at the poll just behind his ears. Bending too far back in his neck is called "rubber-necking" and makes him hard to steer.

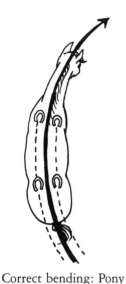  

Correct bending: Pony is evenly bent on track of circle. Hind feet follow in tracks of front feet.

Wrong: No bending

Wrong: Bent to the outside

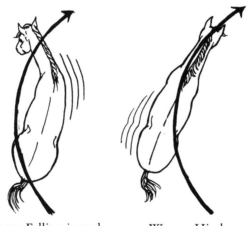

Wrong: Falling in and "rubber-necking"

Wrong: Hindquarters swinging out

It's important to practice bending in both directions, with a little extra practice on the pony's stiffer side. When you change directions, you must change the bend. To do this, ride straight for a stride or two, then change your bending aids to the other side.

To improve your pony's bending, practice ring figures such as circles, half-circles, figure 8s, serpentines, and changes of direction.

Don't make circles too small, especially at first. It's better to bend correctly on a larger circle than to have a hard time on a tight circle.

Riding the Hand Gallop

A hand gallop is a controlled gallop, faster than a canter but not as fast as an all-out run. The speed is about 15 to 18 miles per hour, or 400 to 425 meters per minute. When a pony goes from a canter to a gallop, his strides get longer and lower, and you hear four beats instead of three. During a hand gallop, your pony should be "in hand," or under control.

Riding a Hand Gallop

For a hand gallop, your stirrups must be short enough to allow you to ride in a well-balanced half-seat, but not so short as to put you too far out of the saddle. Bridge your reins and set your hands down alongside your pony's neck. Ride in a half-seat with your heels down, legs in contact with your pony's sides, seat close to the saddle, and shoulders just over your knees. Your contact with the pony's mouth may become stronger but should not be harsh or pulling.

A hand gallop should begin from a canter (not from a standing start). Shorten your reins and squeeze your legs in rhythm with your pony's strides; then shift into a half-seat as he lengthens his strides. He should take longer strides, not faster short ones. When you are ready to pull up, you should sit up and open your hip angle so that you are sitting upright, with your seat deep in the saddle. Use your seat, legs, and hands to bring your pony down to a canter and then to a walk. If he pulls or doesn't want to slow down, you may use a pulley rein, but no harder than necessary. Another way to control a strong pony is to turn him in a large circle and gradually make the circle smaller until he slows down.

Hand galloping should only be practiced on good footing, with plenty of room to make safe turns. It can help to wake up a lazy pony and make him want to go forward, but don't overdo it with a "hot" or nervous pony.

C-2 RIDING OVER FENCES

By now, you should be jumping confidently with good basics over a variety of fences up to 2'9" high, and you should be able to ride a course of fences at a steady pace. In C-2 jumping, you will become more secure over fences, with and without stirrups; and you will learn to jump with more control. You will also begin jumping combinations, and learn how to walk a stadium jumping course and develop a riding plan.

Jumping and Stirrup Length

In different kinds of riding, you use different stirrup lengths in order to ride safely and in good balance. You must adjust your stirrups correctly for the kind of riding you are doing; this is especially true for jumping.

To check stirrup length, take both feet out of the stirrups and let your legs hang down. Notice where the stirrup irons hang in relation to your ankle bones: below the point of ankle bone, at the ankle, or above the ankle.

There are four stirrup lengths for different kinds of riding:

1. *Long stirrups (dressage length)*: Bottom of the ankle bone. Only for dressage, never for jumping.
2. *Medium stirrups (general-purpose length)*: Center of the ankle bone. For riding on the flat, hacking, and cavaletti only.
3. *Short stirrups (jumping length)*: Top of the ankle bone. For ordinary jumping and cross-country riding.
4. *Very short stirrups (high jumping/galloping length)*: Above the ankle bone. For jumping big fences, galloping, and cross-country jumping.

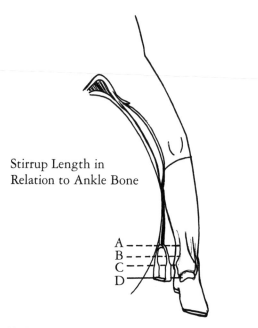

Stirrup Length in
Relation to Ankle Bone

A. Above ankle bone: Galloping or high jumping length

B. Top of ankle bone: Jumping length

C. Center of ankle bone: All-purpose, flat-work length

D. Bottom of ankle bone: Dressage length

You must use the right stirrup length for the job you are doing. It does not make sense to ride dressage with galloping-length stirrups or to jump with dressage-length stirrups. Jumping with stirrups that are too long makes your lower leg loose and unsteady. This is unsafe and spoils your balance.

Jumping without Stirrups

Working without stirrups over ground poles and low fences strengthens your legs, improves your balance, and makes you more secure over fences. Before you jump without stirrups, you must be able to ride without stirrups at a posting trot for several minutes, and to ride in a half-seat without stirrups for short periods at trot and canter. You should cross your stirrups over correctly, and, for safety, you should use a neckstrap when you first begin jumping without stirrups.

To jump without stirrups, you must keep your legs in the same position you use when posting without stirrups: toes up, legs in contact with your pony's sides, knees springy and not gripping. As in posting, you must let your pony fold you into a jumping position.

Start with a single ground pole. Approach at a posting trot without stirrups, letting your pony post you over the pole. You can also practice sitting the trot and folding into jumping position over the pole. When you feel secure trotting over a ground pole without stirrups, you can practice cantering over it. This is good practice in learning to wait and let your pony fold you into jumping position.

You can work up to jumping cross-rails without stirrups. However, don't try to jump big fences without stirrups. And do be sure you are jumping in balance and using a good release at every fence.

More about Releases

By now you should be using all the releases (long crest release, short release, and jumping with a bridge) well. Your timing should be good, and you should almost never be caught ahead of or behind your pony when he jumps. When you can do this, you are ready to learn the most advanced release—"jumping out of hand," or the "automatic release." This gives you the most control, but you must do it correctly or you can hurt your pony's mouth and spoil his jumping.

Automatic Release or
Jumping out of Hand

Jumping Out of Hand (Automatic Release)   "Jumping out of hand" is jumping on contact. You ride into the jump on contact, with your hands off the pony's neck and a straight line from your elbows to the bit. As your pony takes off, your hands do nothing—they simply maintain contact. As your pony stretches his head and neck forward, he pulls your hands forward, and your contact stays the same throughout the jump. As you land, your contact should have the same light, steady feel as before and during the jump. Your hands and arms should always be in a straight line from your elbow to the bit.

To jump like this, you must have a very secure seat and be able to ride with light, steady contact and relaxed, gentle hands and arms. If anything goes wrong (you get behind the motion, your legs slip forward, or your arms tense up), you will pull your pony in the mouth. If you aren't able to jump this well every time, it is better to use a crest release, a short release, or a bridge while you improve your jumping. Even experts jump out of hand only when everything is going right.

When you are learning to jump out of hand, you should avoid making the following mistakes. Don't shove your hands forward, hoping to guess how your pony will move his head. This can make you lose contact abruptly, dropping your pony and upsetting him. Don't drop your hands too low. This pulls down against the sensitive bars of your pony's mouth and restricts the use of his head and neck. Don't let your hands hover above the crest of his neck; keep your hands, wrists, and forearms in a straight line from your elbow to the bit. Don't open up your fingers and let the reins slip through, except in an emergency (in case you get left behind, to avoid jerking on your pony's mouth). This leaves you with long reins and no control on landing. Don't tense up your hands, wrists, and arms or lock your elbows; when your pony stretches his neck, he will run into your stiff hands and get a jerk in the mouth.

More Gymnastic Jumping Exercises

Continuing work in gymnastic jumping will help your balance, security, and timing over fences. It can also improve your pony's jumping. Always measure distances carefully, and have your instructor check to be sure they are right for your pony. Jumps used in gymnastics should be low to medium height, not maximum height.

Never leave extra empty cups on standards. These can injure you or your pony in case of a jumping mistake or fall. Extra cups, standards, or rails should be stored in a safe place, out of the way.

Most gymnastics should be approached in a steady but lively trot. Using a crest release or jumping with a bridge gives your pony more freedom to use his head and neck. Don't hold your pony back or "rate" him through a gymnastic, as this restricts the way he uses himself and defeats the purpose of the exercise. The closely spaced poles and jumps will teach him to slow down, keep his balance, and pay attention. If he tries to go too fast, bring him in more slowly and stop on a straight line after the last fence. Your job is to keep your pony going forward and straight with enough energy; he must find the right rhythm, takeoff distances, and way of using his body over the jumps.

Progressive Gymnastics A "progressive gymnastic" is one that begins with a ground pole or trotting grid and leads to bigger jumps. It is a combination of exercises you already know. The elements (parts) of a gymnastic must be put together so that they make sense to your pony; they must not surprise him, scare him, or make him jump with an uneven rhythm. Your instructor must help you set up gymnastics that are safe and useful for your pony.

Riding a straight line through a gymnastic. *Photo: Ruth Harvie*

Here are two examples of progressive gymnastics, with average distances:

- Trot poles, bounce, one-stride
- Trot poles, one-stride, two-stride, spread

PROGRESSIVE GYMNASTICS

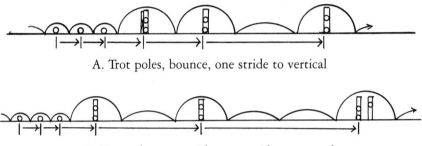

A. Trot poles, bounce, one stride to vertical

B. Trot poles, one stride, two strides to spread

Multiple Bounces (No-Stride Grid)   "Multiple bounces" are a series of three or four bounces or no-stride jumps. These improve rhythm and timing, and teach your pony to take off and land correctly, stay in balance, and push off with his hocks. They must be set at the right distance for your pony and should be fairly low: cross-rails to about 2 feet high.

Average distances for multiple bounces are:

- Large horses: 10 feet to 12 feet
- Small or short-striding horses, large ponies: 9 feet
- Small to medium ponies (up to 13.2 hands): 7 to 8 feet

Multiple bounces or a no-stride grid should be approached in a lively trot. It may help to use trot poles leading into it. (See distances on page 30.)

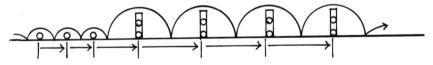

Multiple Bounces (No-Stride Grid)

A no-stride grid may be built in a chute by placing it along the rail of the ring and enclosing it with extra rails. This keeps the pony straight and prevents runouts. If your pony is quiet and steady over a no-stride grid, you can practice jumping no-hands. This exercise teaches you to jump with good balance and independent hands, stay in rhythm with your pony, and let him fold you into jumping position.

Tie a knot in your reins first, then ride into the grid with the reins in one hand. At the first pole, drop the reins and keep your hands over your pony's neck as you ride through the grid. If you lose your balance, hold the mane or neckstrap. Pick the reins up after the last jump. As you get better at jumping no-hands, you can ride through the grid with both arms straight out from your shoulders.

Riding Better Approaches

Good approaches (and good jumps) are a combination of several important factors: balance, line, impulsion, pace, and distance.

Pony and rider in good balance on approach

Poor balance: Pony on the forehand; rider standing up ahead of the motion

Balance (Horse and Rider)   To jump well, your pony must be in good balance. For ordinary jumping, this means a normal, well-balanced trot or canter. If he is not paying attention, leaning on his forehand, moving crookedly, or fighting you with his head up, he is hard to ride and cannot jump well. Never let your pony go to a jump in poor balance.

You must be in balance with your pony—not ahead of or behind his motion. Check your balance and your pony's balance during your opening circle. If he is out of balance, sit up and rebalance yourself, use your legs, and squeeze your hands in rhythm with his strides. If you are out of balance, sit up, drive your heels down, and open or close your hip angle until you are "with" him.

Line   A "line" begins where you finish your opening circle or turn and start your approach. Your eyes, looking at a target over the middle of the jump, pick out the line and keep you on it before, during, and after the jump. The line goes on after the jump to the next fence, or to where you begin to turn.

It's important to ride a good line to every jump and each line of jumps. This means that you must make good turns. If you turn too early or too late, your line may start in the wrong place and bring you in crookedly. This can cause a runout.

A good exercise for riding better lines is to jump a single fence or two fences in line, keeping your eye on your target all the way. After the last fence, halt on the line. If your pony has drifted sideways, move him over with your leg until he is perfectly straight and in line with your target; then pat him and move on.

Impulsion   "Impulsion" is energy. It comes from the pony's desire to go forward. Without impulsion, you cannot have free forward movement or good jumping. Impulsion is *not* speed or wild, runaway energy. If impulsion isn't under control, it is of no use and can even be dangerous.

Check your pony's impulsion by squeezing your legs briefly as you trot or canter. He should respond by increasing his stride right away. If he feels lazy or sticky, you may need to use the leg-cluck-stick lesson (see page 60) to remind him to go forward when you ask him to.

Pace   "Pace" means the pony's speed, rhythm, and length of stride. You must find the pace at which your pony jumps best. This is usually a medium canter, not too fast or too slow. (When riding in special conditions such as muddy ground or when making sharp turns, you may have to modify your usual jumping pace.)

A good jumping round is ridden at an even pace, with a steady canter rhythm. Changing the pace a lot (going fast, then slow, then fast again) is hard on your pony and makes your riding rougher.

Distance The spot where a pony takes off at each jump is called the "distance." He must take off at a safe spot at each jump. If he jumps too close (too short or deep) or too far back (too long), you will have difficulty staying with him, and he may hit the jump.

An experienced jumping pony will usually take off at a good distance by himself if you bring him in to the jump with good balance, line, impulsion, and pace, and stay in balance with him. An inexperienced pony needs help from an experienced rider who can "see a distance." A green pony and an inexperienced rider are a bad combination, especially when jumping at the canter, because neither one is able to help the other.

Twelve-Foot Stride and Twelve-Foot Jump

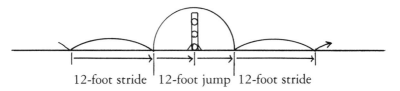

12-foot stride 12-foot jump 12-foot stride

Striding and Takeoff Distances

You have already learned about jumping in stride and how to measure the length of your pony's stride at the canter. Now you need to learn about correct takeoff distances and how to see a distance, or know where your pony will take off at a jump.

Correct Takeoff Distances As you jump bigger and more demanding fences, it's more important for your pony to take off at the right place. If your pony takes off correctly, he can jump safely and is easier to ride. If he gets too close to his jumps or takes off too far back, he may hit the jump with his front or hind legs.

The correct takeoff distance depends on the size and type of jump and the length of your pony's stride. If a horse's canter stride is 12 feet (the average canter stride for horses, used by most course designers for competitions), his jump should also be 12 feet. Half of the jump is takeoff; the other half is landing. This means that the *normal takeoff distance* is about 6 feet from the jump, and he lands about 6 feet beyond it.

TAKEOFF DISTANCES

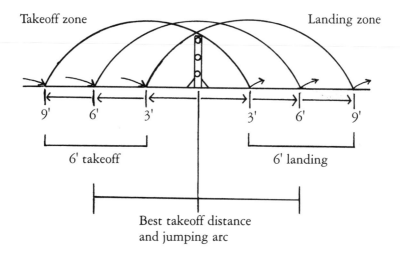

6' takeoff

6' landing

Best takeoff distance
and jumping arc

- *The closest safe takeoff distance* is the same as the height of the jump. For instance, for a 3-foot vertical jump, the closest safe takeoff distance is 3 feet from the jump. If a horse takes off at 3 feet and jumps with a normal 12-foot jump, he lands farther away—about 9 feet.
- *The closest safe landing distance* is also the same as the height of the jump (for example, 3 feet for a 3-foot jump). This means that a horse could take off as far back as 9 feet from the jump and still land safely, although his jump would be early.
- *The longest safe takeoff distance* is 9 feet from the jump. This would make the horse land close, 3 feet away.
- *The safe takeoff zone* is the space between the longest safe take-off distance (9 feet from the jump) and the closest safe takeoff distance (3 feet). In this case, the safe takeoff zone is 6 feet wide. A horse can make a safe, normal jump from anywhere in this takeoff zone and land safely, but the perfect takeoff spot is in the middle: 6 feet from the jump.

Note: These examples are based on a horse with a 12-foot stride. For a small horse or pony that canters with a shorter stride, the lengths of the jump, takeoff, and landing distances will be shorter.

When you and your pony are jumping a spread, the closest safe takeoff distance is the height of the first element. The closest safe landing distance is the height of the last element. The best place to take off is usually closer to the base of the fence than for a vertical.

If you take off too far back, it makes a spread wider, and your pony could hit the back rail.

When jumping small- to medium-size fences, it's more important to get to the fairly large safe takeoff zone in good balance and with enough impulsion (energy) than to take off from the perfect take-off spot. As the jumps get bigger, the safe takeoff zone becomes smaller. Jumping big fences requires a much more accurate takeoff, as well as good balance and impulsion.

Placing Poles for Correct Takeoff Distances A "placing pole" is a ground pole that helps a pony jump from the correct takeoff distance. You trot or canter over the placing pole, which helps him place his feet in the correct takeoff spot. This teaches him the habit of taking off right, and helps you learn what a correct takeoff feels like. A placing pole must be set at just the right distance for your pony, and it must be fixed so that it cannot roll under your pony's feet. Your instructor should check the distance to be sure it is right for your pony.

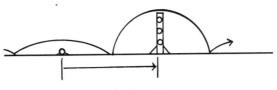

Placing Pole

Average distances for placing poles are the following:

- Large horses: 9 feet
- Small or short-striding horses, large ponies: 8 feet
- Small to medium ponies (up to 13.2 hands): 7 to 8 feet

Learning to See a Distance

"Seeing a distance" means being able to tell where your pony will take off (short, long, or just right) several strides before a jump. This seems to come easily and naturally to some people but is harder for others. Before you can learn to see a distance, you must be able to ride to a jump with good balance, free forward movement, and a steady pace. And your jumping basics (legs, timing, eyes, jumping position, and release) must be habits.

EXERCISE FOR SEEING A DISTANCE

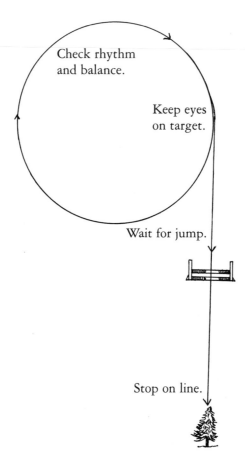

Seeing a distance could just as well be called "feeling a distance," because your "feel" for balance, rhythm, and impulsion is just as important as your eyes. You feel the kind of stride you have, and your eye gets a "flash picture" of the distance to the jump. You think "If we keep going like this, we will take off just right (or long, or short)."

Here is an exercise to help you learn to see distances:

1. Set up two standards with a single ground pole halfway down the long side of the ring. Ride a preparatory circle at the canter, with good balance and steady rhythm.
2. As you canter through the turn and line up with the pole, keep your eyes up on your target, and keep your pace and rhythm steady.

3. If you see a distance (long, short, or just right), relax and keep the same rhythm and balance. If you don't see it, keep going steadily on over the pole.
4. After each jump, ask yourself if the takeoff was short, long, or just right. (A ground person can watch and tell you.) If you knew ahead of time, you saw a distance.

You can't make yourself see a distance by looking hard. This makes you tense up, and you lose your rhythm and feel. It is better to keep riding in good rhythm and balance and to wait; you may see the distance on the next stride or the next. If you don't see it, your pony will see it for you. At first, you may see a distance on some jumps and not on others. With practice, it will become easier and more natural. You cannot rate your pony (shorten or lengthen his stride) to make it come out right until you can see a distance three or four strides away.

Combinations

"Combinations" are jumps set one or two strides apart (usually 39 feet or less). They may be doubles (two jumps) or triples (three jumps). When jumping a combination, the pony must jump the first jump and then take one or two strides of just the right length in order to jump the second. Combinations may include verticals, spreads, or both. The kind of fences and the distances between them make a difference in how easy or difficult a combination is to ride.

The first combinations you jump should be simple two-stride doubles, with two vertical fences no more than 2'6" high. Using spreads in a combination changes the distances; you will learn more about this later.

Here are the average distances for a two-stride double:

- Large horses: 35 to 36 feet
- Small or short-striding horses, large ponies: 33 to 34 feet
- Small to medium ponies (up to 13.2 hands): 30 to 32 feet

Practice over gymnastics helps you prepare to jump combinations. The difference is that combinations are approached in a canter, and you do not have trot poles or placing poles to make your pony take off at the right distance. You must ride the first fence of a combination on a straight line, with good balance, pace, and impulsion. Keep your pony going forward in rhythm over the first and second fences.

TWO-STRIDE DOUBLE

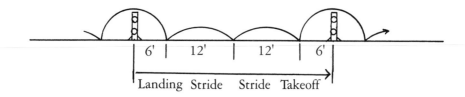

6' | 12' | 12' | 6'

Landing Stride   Stride   Takeoff

Walking a Course and Developing a Riding Plan

Before you ride a stadium jumping course, you should walk the course and plan the best way to ride it.

Start at the in-gate and plan your opening circle; it should finish with the line to your first fence. Always ride strongly to your first fence, especially if it is going away from the gate or other ponies.

Learning a course is easier if you remember the lines of fences rather than each fence by number. Pick a target to aim for to keep you on line over the first fence and through each line.

Plan each turn. Notice where your pony might want to cut in on a turn or where he might go wide. Usually, you should make your turns as wide as possible in order to give yourself room for the best approach to the next line of fences. Think about where your pony might be slow or sticky and need more leg (going away from the gate), and where might he get strong and need to be steadied (going toward the gate).

Which fences might look strange or spooky to him? These may need careful riding and extra leg to prevent a refusal. Finally, plan to finish with a closing circle after the last jump.

If you walk your course carefully and think through your riding plan several times, you will remember your course better, and you can ride smart, thinking your way around as you ride.

C-2 RIDING IN THE OPEN

Safety Measures for Different Types of Footing

The kind of footing you ride on is very important—for your safety, your pony's safety, and your pony's soundness. The best footing is slightly springy and not too deep or slippery.

A pony can injure himself, slip, or fall on slippery footing, especially if you go fast or make sharp turns. Very hard footing causes extra concussion (shock) on his feet and legs, which can make him sore. Avoid hard or fast work and, especially, jumping on very hard footing.

Mud, Bog, and Water   Muddy footing is slippery, so ride slowly and avoid making quick turns. A pony's feet sink into deep mud. As he pulls them out, he can easily pull off a shoe, pull a tendon, or twist an ankle, especially if he's going fast. A pony is more likely to over-reach when galloping or jumping in muddy conditions. Over-reaching occurs when the toe of a hind foot "grabs" the back of the front leg or heel, resulting in injury. Bell boots are used to protect the heels and prevent over-reaching.

Bog is very deep, soft mud. It can be dangerous because you cannot tell how deep it is or how far your pony might sink. In some places, there could even be quicksand or very deep mud that could trap your pony. Ponies fear being stuck in a bog and may lunge violently if they get into deep mud and feel themselves sinking. For your pony's safety and your own, don't ride into deep, boggy places! (If you should get into a bog by accident, hold the mane and give your pony a long rein so that he can use his head and neck to balance as he works to get out.)

When riding in water, a pony cannot see how deep the water is, so he must trust you to ride him only where it is safe. Pay attention to the banks and the bottom. Watch out for slippery rocks, boggy places, hidden holes, and hazards such as wire or trash under the water. Moving in water is hard, so go slowly. On a trail ride, it's a good idea to let your pony drink whenever you come to a stream.

Snow and Ice   Riding in snow is fun, but you must be aware of the footing. Light, powdery snow is easy and fun to ride in, but be careful that you don't run into ice underneath the snow. In deep, heavy snow, a pony has difficulty moving and can strain muscles (try running in it yourself). Snow with a frozen crust may break under a pony's weight and let him sink; and the sharp crust can cut his legs. Wet snow can pack up in a pony's feet, making him walk on slippery snowballs, especially if he is shod. Shoeing with special "anti-snowball" pads may help, or you can coat the bottoms of his hooves with mineral oil. Ice is very dangerous and should be avoided at all costs; a pony can easily slip and fall on it. Hard-packed snow can be as slippery as ice. If your usual winter riding area has icy patches (often in low places), apply a melting agent or block off the dangerous spots so that nobody will ride into those areas by accident.

Sand, Rocky Ground   Firm, sandy footing is usually good to ride on because it is a nonslip surface. However, moving in deep sand is hard on a pony's muscles and tendons, and can make him sore, especially if he is not used to working in it. Go slowly, take frequent rest breaks, and don't overdo it.

Rocky ground is hard on a pony's feet and legs. Rocks can make a pony stumble or slip, so go slowly. Riding too fast on rough ground can make him lame. If you ride often over hard, rocky ground, your pony should be shod so that he doesn't wear his feet down and get sore. He can get stone bruises or pick up rocks in his feet. After riding on rocky ground, check his feet to make sure he has not picked up stones in them.

Hard Ground, Deep Grass   When the ground is baked hard in summer, or frozen hard in winter, it can become almost as hard as concrete. If the ground is rough and uneven, with holes and hard lumps caused by hoofprints, it is very difficult to ride on, and a pony can easily twist an ankle or stumble. Hard ground jars his feet and leg joints at every step. Don't jump when the ground is hard; most of your riding should be done at slow gaits. Smooth hard ground with short grass can be very slippery, especially when wet.

Deep grass can hide hazards such as holes, ditches, or even farm machinery. Don't canter blindly through deep grass; slow down and watch out ahead.

Pavement and Road Surfaces   Pavement is very hard on a pony's feet and legs, and can be dangerously slippery, especially if your pony is shod. Avoid riding on pavement if possible; if you must ride on pavement, keep to a walk.

Gravel, crushed rock, and hard-packed dirt roads are hard on a pony's feet and legs. Unshod ponies may wear their feet down and get sore if they are ridden on gravel or rocky roads, and hard dirt is jarring if you ride on it very much or very fast. Soft dirt or sandy roads are better surfaces. Try to avoid riding on roads as much as possible.

Control Exercises for Riding in the Open

The following exercises will help you control your pony more easily when riding outside in a group. They are also good preparation for foxhunting, group trail riding, or just enjoying your pony with friends. However, you *must* do these exercises safely. Your instructor or another experienced rider should be in charge, and you must make sure that no pony becomes excited. Whenever you are passing or being passed by another pony, keep a safe distance (at least one pony length) and turn your pony's head toward the other pony. A pony that kicks is too dangerous to people and other ponies to be ridden in a group.

For these group-control exercises, you will need at least three riders. Do the exercises at a walk and slow trot first, then at a slow trot and faster trot. No one should canter until all ponies are doing the exercises quietly and obediently at the trot.

GROUP-CONTROL EXERCISE

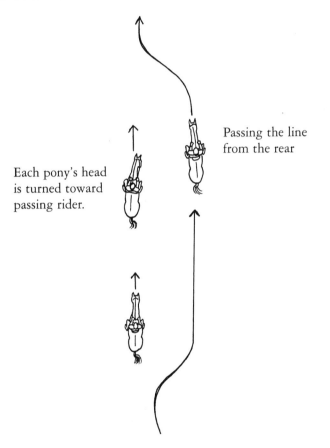

Passing the line from the rear

Each pony's head is turned toward passing rider.

PASSING AND BEING PASSED

Ride in line at a walk, two pony lengths apart. The last rider moves out to the side (at least one pony length) and trots to the front of the line. Each rider keeps his pony's head turned toward the passing pony. Repeat until everyone has had a turn; then do the exercise again, passing on the other side.

SPEED CONTROL AND SPACING EXERCISE

Ride in a line, keeping *exactly* one pony length apart. Walk, then trot, keeping the spacing. On command from the leader, spread out the spacing to two pony lengths, then three lengths, then back to one length. You must adjust the speed of your pony's gait to keep the exact spacing you want.

STOPPING AND STANDING

The leader moves out to the side (at least one pony length) and halts. His pony must stand still (with his head turned toward the others) while the whole line passes him at a walk; then he joins the end of the line. Repeat until everyone has had a turn. If all ponies are quiet and well-behaved, repeat the exercise at a trot and then at a canter.

GROUP CONTROL EXERCISE

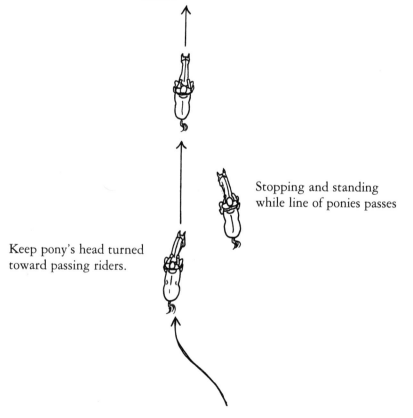

Stopping and standing while line of ponies passes

Keep pony's head turned toward passing riders.

LEAVING THE GROUP AND RETURNING UNDER CONTROL

The leader leaves the group by making a large circle (20 meters or larger). He should trot the first half of the circle (leaving the group) and walk the second half of the circle (returning to the group). The group keeps walking on, so the leader finishes his circle by returning to the end of the line. Each person circles away from the line in turn, returning to the end of the line. When all ponies are quiet and obedient, you can do this exercise cantering away from the line and walking back.

GROUP-CONTROL EXERCISE

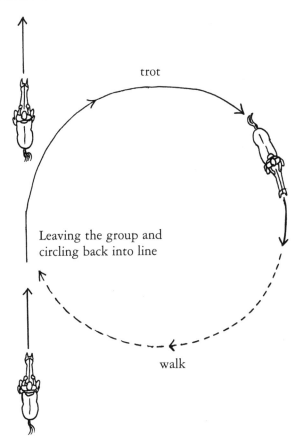

trot

Leaving the group and circling back into line

walk

Learning to Ride at the Gallop

Learning to gallop can be great fun, but you must do it safely. You need a safe place to gallop (a large, fairly level field with good footing, preferably enclosed), and a pony that is easy to control outside at the canter and gallop. Your instructor will tell you when you are ready to begin galloping outside, and should watch and help you.

You have already learned to hand-gallop in a large arena. Galloping outside is much the same, but it is more important to stay well-balanced and to control your pony's speed, because some ponies may get strong and pull when they gallop in the open. It's important to keep a pony in good balance when he gallops, especially over rolling terrain. If he runs along leaning on his forehand, he is out of balance and will become hard to stop; this can also lead to bucking.

Before you start, shorten your stirrups to cross-country length (stirrups at the top of your ankle bones). Warm up your pony, and then "check your brakes" by halting from the trot and canter. Use a circle or a pulley rein to bring him back if necessary. Start out in a canter, going *away* from the stable or gate. Shorten your reins and make a bridge with your hands resting on each side of his neck as you shift into a half-seat. Your contact may be a bit stronger than usual, and the reins must be short enough to control your pony and help you keep him in good balance. To move him out, squeeze briefly with your legs at each stride. This asks him to take longer strides, not quicker ones. At first, gallop only for a short distance (50 yards or so); then come back to a canter and then to a walk. When you have good control, you can gallop for longer distances.

Developing a Feel for Pace   When you gallop, keep a fairly steady pace. This is easier on your pony than racing fast and then being pulled up sharply, and makes it easier to stay in control. You must find the pace at which your pony can gallop freely and easily, with good balance, and is easy to control. This will be the pace from which you jump most cross-country fences. Slow down if you encounter a slight uphill or downhill slope (at this stage, you shouldn't be galloping on anything but the *slightest* of slopes!)

A good starting cross-country galloping pace for C-2 riders is about 400 meters per minute, or one mile every four minutes (approximately 15 miles per hour). (This pace is for horses; the

Good control at the gallop, with rider and pony in good balance. *Photo: Susan Sexton*

pace for medium or small ponies is slower.) You can measure off a galloping track 800 meters (874 yards, or 2,622 feet) or 1/2-mile long by walking over the track with a measuring wheel. Or someone can drive over it and measure it with the odometer (.5 miles). If you ride this track in two minutes, you are galloping at the standard pace of 400 meters per minute.

Importance of Conditioning, Signs of Tiring   When you gallop your pony, you *must* be aware of his condition and notice when he starts to get tired. Galloping is hard work for a pony's heart, lungs, muscles, and tendons. Many ponies get so excited when they gallop that they will keep on going even after they are so tired that they are in danger. You must be responsible for knowing when your pony has had enough, and you must never allow him to be overworked. (See Chapter 7 for more information about conditioning and fitness.)

When you gallop, pay attention to your pony's breathing. Galloping makes any pony breathe hard, but if he seems to be having trouble breathing or if the sound of his breathing changes, he needs to rest. If he begins to slow down or feels sluggish, he is getting tired and should stop. A tired pony will begin to lean on his forehand and will gallop heavily. If you are having trouble keeping him in good balance, he needs a rest. A tired pony is not safe, so it is important to recognize when he has had enough.

Riding Different Types of Cross-Country Fences
(Novice to Training Level)

At this level, you may encounter cross-country fences that require more specialized riding and training techniques: water fences, open ditches, uphill and downhill fences, in-and-outs, and jumping from light into shadow or from shadow into light. Learning to jump them safely and confidently requires help from your instructor, good judgment, and a step-by-step approach to training. Never "over-face" yourself or your pony by trying to jump a fence that is too difficult for either of you; this is dangerous and can give you both a bad experience. If you keep each training step simple and easy, and master each step before going on to the next, you and your pony will build confidence in each other while learning to jump different types of fences.

Water Fences: Jumping into and out of Water　It is hard for a pony to jump into or out of water because he cannot see how deep it is and because the drag of the water on his legs makes it more difficult to move and to jump. Because jumping out of water requires extra effort, a small jump may feel bigger to you. When jumping into water, you will have to learn to keep your balance as your pony's balance changes. Start with the easiest water-jumping exercises and work up to the more difficult ones. If you "overface" your pony (ask him to jump something too hard for him), you can make him afraid of jumps involving water.

Start by finding a suitable stream crossing. It must be nearly level, with shallow water and firm footing on the banks and bottom—no steep banks, boggy footing, or slippery rocks. Cross the stream at a walk several times in both directions; then trot across until your pony is used to the splash.

Next, place a pole or small log on the ground about 30 feet from the edge of the water. Trot through the water and on over the ground pole. Stay in balance, with your seat close to the saddle, and use your legs firmly, as the drag of the water will slow your pony down.

Now, approach from the other side—trot over the ground pole and then on across the water. Keep your seat close to the saddle, sit up, and use your legs firmly to keep your pony going and in balance.

Next, replace the ground pole with a low cross-rail. When your pony trots freely and easily through the water and over the cross-rail in both directions, move the cross-rail one stride closer to the water (about 22 feet from the edge). When he does this well, move the cross-rail one stride from the edge (9 to 10 feet), and practice at a trot. Then set the cross-rail at the edge of the water, and trot through the water and out over the cross-rail. (It helps if you set up this exercise so that you are heading toward home.)

Finally, jump the cross-rail into the water. Approach in a steady sitting trot with good contact and impulsion, and keep your eyes up. If you go too fast, look down, or drop your pony, he may be surprised and refuse. When you jump into water, your pony is suddenly slowed down by the drag of the water. You must keep your seat close to the saddle and only close your hip angle a little bit, and sit up immediately as he lands.

Learning to Jump Uphill and Downhill Jumping uphill and downhill takes good balance. As in learning to jump water, you must start with easy exercises and gradually work up to more difficult ones. For schooling uphill and downhill, you need good footing and a *gentle* slope, with level ground at the top and bottom.

Start by riding a square (about 80 feet on each side) with one line uphill, one line on the level at the top of the hill, one line downhill, and one line on the level at the bottom. Going uphill, your pony must work harder and may want to slow down. Ride in half-seat to stay in balance with him, and use your legs firmly to keep him moving. Going downhill, he may tend to go faster and lean on his forehand. Sit up deep and tall in good balance, and use your hands, legs, and especially your balance to keep him slow, steady, and in balance. It's important to keep him straight, with his hind legs in line with his front legs.

UPHILL AND DOWNHILL JUMPING EXERCISE

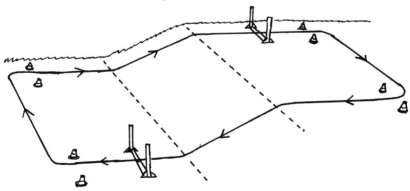

Safe turns are important when riding uphill and downhill. When you turn from level to uphill, use your legs firmly to keep the pony going forward. Turning from uphill to level is easier. When turning from level to downhill, you must have your pony well-balanced and in control so that he doesn't go faster downhill after the turn. The turn from downhill to level is the most difficult. You must slow the pony down and check his balance *before* you turn. If you turn while your pony is going too fast or out of balance downhill, he could slip or even fall.

When you ride the uphill and downhill square well at a walk, begin trotting on the level and uphill lines, but come back to a walk for the downhill line. Then begin trotting *slowly* on the downhill line. When your balance and control are good enough, trot the whole square. Cantering downhill is the most difficult and requires really good balance and control to do this safely.

Next, place a ground pole on level ground about 22 feet after the uphill line and another about 22 feet after the downhill line. Ride the uphill line straight on over the pole; then turn about 30 feet afterward. Do the same on the downhill line. This exercise teaches you to balance your pony for uphill and downhill jumps but gives you room to get ready. Just as you did when learning to jump water fences, you gradually move the ground pole closer to the edge of the hill, then onto the hill itself. When you are riding over ground poles easily, uphill and downhill, they can be built into small cross-rails.

When you are jumping uphill, the jump may feel bigger because of the uphill slope. Keep your heels down and stay well forward so that you don't come down onto your pony's back. Jumping downhill fences requires good balance, especially on landing and after the jump. Keep your eyes up, sit close to your saddle, and don't lean too far forward or drop the contact. When you jump downhill, keep your seat touching the saddle and sit up and back immediately on landing.

Jumping from Light to Shadow and Shadow to Light
Jumping from light into shadow (for instance, at the edge of the woods) makes a jump more difficult. A pony's eyes adjust slowly from light to darkness, so he cannot see what is on the other side. In order to jump, he must trust you. For this kind of fence, you must ride a strong, positive approach with a steady pace, but not too fast.

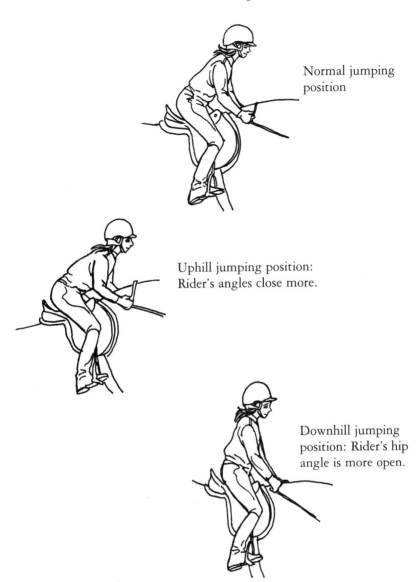

Normal jumping position

Uphill jumping position: Rider's angles close more.

Downhill jumping position: Rider's hip angle is more open.

(The faster you go, the greater the element of surprise and the more likely your pony is to refuse.) Sit deep in your saddle, use your legs firmly, keep your eyes up, and keep contact with his mouth.

Jumping from a shady area into light is more inviting, so it is easier. Your pony's eyes, however, need time to adjust to the brighter light.

JUMPING FROM LIGHT INTO SHADOW

Open Ditches   You have already jumped small natural ditches. Now you may jump ditches that have steeper sides, are "revetted" (the sides are braced with wood), or have water at the bottom.

When jumping a ditch or water, your pony must understand that he should jump over the whole thing, not step into it or go through it. You must be clear about what you mean to do. If you are undecided, weak, or hesitant, he will be confused and may stop or make a mistake.

JUMPING AN OPEN DITCH

When approaching a ditch or water, ride at a strong canter without going too fast. Use your legs to keep him moving freely forward, but use your seat and hands to keep his balance back so that he can jump. Sit up and keep your eyes on your target, beyond the jump. If you lean too far forward, look down, drop your contact, or let your pony gallop too fast leaning on his forehand, he might gallop right into the ditch or water, or refuse at the last minute. Riding a strong, balanced canter and using your legs (and perhaps a cluck) to ask him to take off will give you a good jump.

Simple Two-Stride In-and-Outs An "in-and-out" is two fences one or two strides apart. You may find an in-and-out when crossing a lane or jumping into and out of a pen. A cross-country in-and-out is jumped much like a double combination in the ring. Ride a straight line, and keep your eyes on your target during your approach and through the combination. Ride at a strong, steady (but not too fast) canter, and stay with your pony's rhythm as he jumps, lands, takes two strides, and jumps again.

When you jump an in-and-out with two or more panels, or sections, you *must* keep your pony straight and jump the second panel in line with the first. If he swerves or "crosses panels," he may run out or take off at the wrong spot. When foxhunting or jumping with others, if you let your pony swerve or cross panels, you could cut off another rider and cause an accident.

Riding a straight line
through an in-and-out

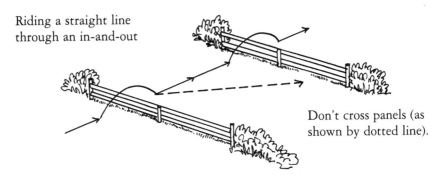

Don't cross panels (as
shown by dotted line).

CHAPTER 3

C-3 RIDING: THE GATEWAY TO ADVANCED RIDING

C-3 riding is really the beginning of advanced horsemanship. It lays the foundation for the more advanced B and A levels. You will need strong basic skills; correct riding at a more advanced level; and serious, organized work in order to ride safely and well enough to pass the C-3 Standard.

Some riders would rather enjoy many different activities at the C-2 level than work as hard as they must to pass the C-3 Standard. For them, it might be better to be a really good C-2 rider than a not-so-good C-3.

Before you take on the challenge of C-3 Level, you and your instructor should review your riding up to this point: your strong and weak points, goals, and what you and your pony need to work on. Do you have the interest, confidence, and willingness to work hard to take on the challenge of the C-3 Level? Does your instructor think you are ready?

C-3 RIDING ON THE FLAT

Flat work (dressage) is training. It makes a pony obedient, better balanced, and easier to ride on the flat, over fences, and in the open. Some riders think flat work is something to put up with in order to get to the "fun" things such as galloping and jumping. The better a rider, however, the more importance he puts on flat work. Even jumper trainers say, "A jumper is made on the flat." It's impossible to succeed in any riding activity without good flat work.

The purpose of flat work is to improve your pony's suppleness, responsiveness to the aids, and way of moving, as well as your own riding. It's important to ride correctly, with good form, when schooling. Everything you have learned has a purpose: to make it easier for your pony to feel, understand, and carry you well—not just to look nice or to please a judge. Never ride in a sloppy or incorrect position because you are "only schooling." The better you train, the better you will ride, and vice versa.

About Mounting

As you become a more advanced rider, good mounting habits become even more important. Sloppy, inconsiderate mounting is unsafe. As you become a better rider, you may ride green or sensitive horses that might react badly if you mount poorly.

A good rider mounts smoothly, carefully, and in control. Adjust the reins for good control, but never pull on them while mounting. Spring up lightly, without hauling yourself up or pulling on the cantle, which pulls sideways on the pony's back and can damage the saddle tree. When you swing your leg over, catch yourself on your knees and stay up for a moment; then settle gently into the saddle. Finally, make sure your reins and stirrups are properly adjusted and that you are sitting correctly *before* allowing your pony to move off.

While it is usual to mount on the left (near) side, there may be times when you need to mount on the right (off) side. This takes some practice. A well-trained pony should stand quietly while you mount and dismount from either side.

Warming Up

You already know how important it is to warm up your pony properly for every ride. A warmup should be progressive, working from simple exercises to more difficult work. Pay special attention to your pony's rhythm, relaxation, and free forward movement.

During warmup and work on the flat, it's important to change directions and exercises often, to keep the pony interested and attentive. A pony (or rider) gets bored doing the same thing over and over, or going around the ring. Changing directions works his muscles evenly on both sides; frequent transitions improve his balance and responsiveness.

To fine-tune your pony's responses, try riding a random pattern, putting circles, figure 8s, serpentines, changes of direction, etc., together in any order. When your pony wants to turn left, smoothly ask for a circle to the right instead. If he wants to speed up, make a downward transition to a slower gait, or halt. When he wants to slow down or stop, ask for an upward transition. When done smoothly and tactfully with light aids, riding random patterns makes a pony alert and responsive, ready to do whatever you ask promptly.

Riding Accurate Ring Figures

Good riding and training require precision; a ring figure is only as good as the rider makes it. When riding a turn or schooling figure, you must be aware of the size and shape of the figure and exactly where your pony should go. Straight lines must be straight, circles must be round, and curves must be even. In figure 8s or serpentines, circles or loops must be of equal size. Study the ring figures in the diagram on page 98, and walk through them on foot to learn the size and shape of each figure, and the points where they start and finish.

Ponies often want to go toward the gate, other horses, the center of the ring, or the stable. This can cause sloppy figures if you don't pay close attention. Watch out for "falling out" (drifting sideways, making a turn too wide), and "falling in" (leaning in and cutting a turn too short).

Inside and Outside Aids   Correct seat, leg, and rein aids help your pony turn, track, and bend correctly. You must use both inside and outside aids to keep him on the track you have chosen. The inside aids are the seat bone, leg, and rein on the inside of a bend or turn. The outside aids are those on the outside. Swivelling your seat and upper body in the direction of the turn asks the pony to turn and bend. Your inside leg (close to the girth) keeps him moving forward, asks him to bend, and prevents falling in. The inside rein asks him to look in the direction of the turn. The outside rein and outside leg behind the girth set a limit on how far out he may go and how much he bends, and keep him on the track you have chosen.

During a turn, you must keep a steady contact on the outside rein without pulling on it. If your outside rein loosens, your arm straightens out, or your elbow sticks out, the outside rein becomes ineffective, and your pony will fall out. Pulling him around with the inside rein results in a crude, unbalanced turn and throws you both off balance.

Even rhythm and tempo are important in schooling. It is harder work for a pony to keep moving correctly through a turn than on a straightaway, so he may try to shorten his strides or slow down when

RING FIGURES

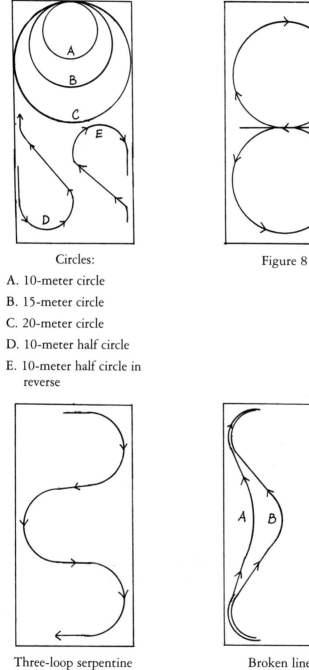

Circles:

A. 10-meter circle

B. 15-meter circle

C. 20-meter circle

D. 10-meter half circle

E. 10-meter half circle in reverse

Figure 8

Three-loop serpentine

Broken lines:

A. Shallow broken line

B. Broken line to center line

he turns or leaves the rail. Use your aids in rhythm with his gait to keep him working steadily all the way through each ring figure.

Improving Contact and Response to the Bit

During most work on the flat, you should be riding on light contact. (Give your pony a break on long reins now and then to keep him relaxed and cooperative.) Up to now, you have been riding on passive contact except when asking for a halt or downward transition. Now you will begin to ask your pony to respond to your aids with his mouth, body, and overall balance.

Where Contact Begins: Making the "Leg Connection"   True contact really begins with your legs. Each leg aid tells the pony to use the muscles of his hindquarters to push harder and take a longer step with that hind leg. Reaching forward with the hind legs is called "engagement"; this is where his power comes from in all gaits. As he reaches farther with his hind legs, his back comes up, rounds, and stretches. This stretches out his neck and head, and if your reins are the right length, you feel your pony's mouth reach out and "take contact" with your hands, lightly stretching the reins. This whole process is called "making the connection"—from your legs, through his hind legs, back, neck, and mouth, into your hands.

When a pony is "connected," he responds to all the aids (seat, legs, and hands). Your aids affect his whole body, especially the way he uses his hind legs. This lets you influence his balance and way of moving; it gives you a new level of control and communication.

Making the Leg Connection

Problems That Spoil the Connection   The "connection" from legs to mouth and hands is a sensitive thing. It can be spoiled by rider mistakes such as the following:

- *No legs*: If you fail to use your legs correctly, your pony has no reason to stretch out and make the connection. He takes short, lazy steps instead of engaging his hind legs and moving freely forward.
- *Poor seat*: If your seat is stiff, bouncy, or out of balance, it hurts your pony's back. He will not want to stretch his back; instead, he may stiffen, hollow his back, and raise his head. This makes it impossible for him to engage his hind legs.
- *Uncomfortable bit or hands*: If the bit or your hands hurt the pony's mouth, he will be afraid to reach out and make contact. He may carry his head too high or too low, open his mouth, or tuck his head to avoid contact with the bit. Severe or ill-fitting bits; stiff, bouncy, or pulling hands; or too-short reins can spoil the connection.
- *No hands*: If your hands are too weak and limp, or your reins are too long, the pony cannot "find the bit" no matter how much he stretches out.

Accepting the Bit (Accepting Contact)   When a pony is relaxed, happy, and comfortable when working on contact, we say he "accepts the bit." This is important for a good mouth, so he understands what you want and is easy to ride. A pony can accept the bit only with good riding and training. Signs of accepting the bit are:

- The pony carries his head in a normal position, with a slightly arched neck. His head is not carried stiffly, too high or too low, or tipped sideways.
- He keeps a light, steady contact without leaning, pulling, tossing his head, or dropping the contact.
- His mouth is closed, but he chews the bit gently, which makes his mouth wet and moist.
- The muscles of his jaws, poll, and neck are relaxed, not stiff, tense, or braced.
- He responds to rein and hand signals by "giving to the bit" (relaxing his jaw, softly chewing the bit, and flexing slightly), not by resisting, stiffening, or fighting the bit.

ACCEPTING THE BIT:

- Poll is the highest point of the neck.
- Pony reaches forward to the bit with light, steady contact.
- Relaxed jaw
- Closed mouth
- Pony chews the bit softly.

Accepting the Other Aids A pony cannot work on contact properly or have a good connection between legs and the hands unless he accepts all the other aids, too. Accepting the legs means responding to leg aids by using his hind legs more powerfully (engaging his hind legs). He doesn't ignore leg aids or resist by acting sticky, refusing to go forward, or switching his tail when he feels a leg aid. Accepting the rider's seat means that his back is relaxed and springy, not stiff, tight, or tense. He is willing to round and stretch his back and carry the rider's weight on it, instead of sinking his back down or tensing it up against his rider.

In order to accept the aids, a pony must be comfortable and must trust his rider. If you apply your aids incorrectly or confuse your pony, he may resist, act up, or respond incorrectly. However, a pony that deliberately ignores the aids or tries to bully his rider may have to be disciplined. Make sure that he understands what you are asking him and that he is not resisting because of pain. If your pony resists your aids, ask your instructor to help you find the cause of the problem and to suggest what to do about it.

Resistance to the Bit Resistance to the bit is a distress signal. Some common resistances are head tossing, pulling, leaning on the bit, carrying the head too high ("above the bit"), tucking the chin in too far ("overbending"), opening the mouth, or refusing to take any contact with the bit (getting "behind the bit").

RESISTING THE BIT

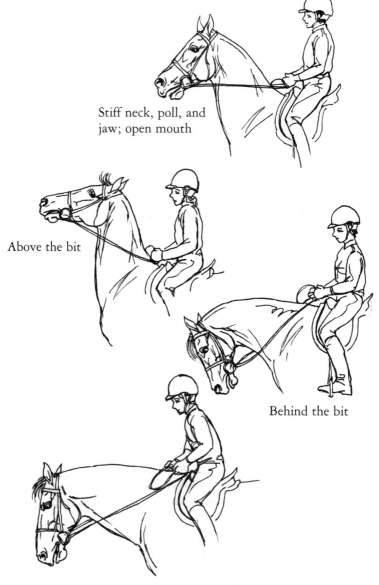

Stiff neck, poll, and jaw; open mouth

Above the bit

Behind the bit

Leaning on the bit

A pony may resist the bit because he is upset, confused, in pain, or unable to respond correctly. *The most common reason for resisting the bit is pain.* This could be due to an incorrectly adjusted bit, too severe a bit, a sore mouth, a bad tooth, or the rider's rough hands. It can also come from pain in the pony's back from an ill-fitting saddle or a rider who is out of balance. The first thing to do is check the pony's mouth and the fit of the bit, and any other places in which he may feel physical pain. You may have to change or adjust the bit, have the pony's teeth checked, or call your veterinarian.

Two other important things to check are the rider's hands and seat, which are often the cause of the pain. If you catch your balance on the reins, have stiff or bouncy hands, pull, use reins that are too short, or "clash the aids," you may make a pony resist your hands. You must go back to slower and easier riding activities while you work on improving your seat and developing independent hands.

Hands and Arms   To help your pony accept the bit, you *must* have a good hand and arm position, with a straight line from your elbow to the bit. When your hands are too low, they make the bit press severely downward, against the sensitive bars of the pony's mouth. This causes a pinching effect on his lower jaw, hurts his mouth, and makes him resist. The opposite problem, hands too high, can make him carry his head too high. Hunched shoulders, stiff arms and elbows, bent wrists, and "busy" hands create a stiff, uncomfortable contact that leads to resistance.

Stiffness and tension in the rider can cause tension and resistance in a pony. If you are nervous, angry, or tense, your muscles tighten up, and your pony feels it. This upsets him and can make him resist your aids, which may make you even more tense. Breathing deeply helps unlock your tense muscles. If you start to get upset with your pony, *stop, dismount,* and *take time to settle down* before you try to work with him again. Ask your instructor for help; otherwise this situation can become unsafe.

More About Rein Aids

You should review the basic rein aids that you learned at the C-1 Level. Now you will use these aids in a more advanced way.

A rein aid is a change of pressure, never a pull. For rein aids to work correctly, you must have a light, steady contact with your pony's mouth. You must coordinate rein aids with seat and leg aids, which keep your pony going forward and in contact with your

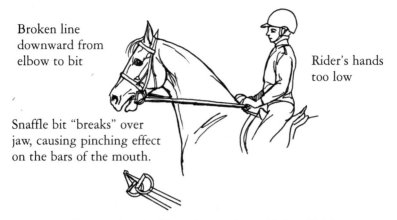

Broken line
downward from
elbow to bit

Rider's hands
too low

Snaffle bit "breaks" over
jaw, causing pinching effect
on the bars of the mouth.

Pony resists the bit and may throw his head higher.

hands. You can use each aid with varying degrees of pressure, from very light to very strong, depending on what your pony needs at the moment.

Here are the four basic rein aids and how they are applied:

1. *Opening or Leading Rein*: Applies pressure sideways but not backward, "leading" a pony through a turn without slowing down. It works best when supported by the other rein. It can be used to turn while jumping because it does not pull backward.

    To apply this rein aid, briefly rotate your hand so that your fingernails are on top and your thumb points in the direction of the turn. This brief twist of your hand changes the pressure on the bit sideways and outward.

2. *Direct Rein*: Applies pressure straight back, affecting the hind leg on the same side. If applied with both hands, it asks a pony to slow or stop. If used with one hand, it asks him to bend and turn in that direction.

    Always apply a direct rein by holding or resisting the pony's forward movement, *never by pulling backward*. Squeeze your fingers briefly into a stronger fist, then relax back to a soft fist. If you need a more powerful rein aid, hold (but never pull) with your elbows and back muscles as you squeeze your hands. Always relax your fingers as soon as your pony begins to give to your hand.

3. *Neck Rein or Bearing Rein*: Usually used as an outside supporting rein, along with an opening or leading rein. It can be used when the reins are held in one hand.

Opening or leading rein

Left opening or leading rein (left hand rotates to left).

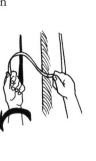

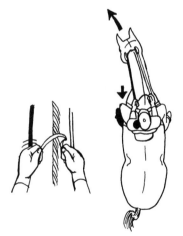

- Left leg at girth, right leg supports behind girth.
- More weight on left seat bone.
- Right supporting rein.

To apply a neck rein, keep your thumb up and move your hand toward but not across the center of the neck. Press the rein against the side of the pony's neck. Don't turn your hand flat, with knuckles up, as this makes you pull instead of pressing correctly.

If you use a neck rein incorrectly (pull too hard and move the hand too far across the neck), it pulls backward on the side of the bit as well as across the neck. This makes a pony tip his head sideways, open his mouth, and resist the bit.

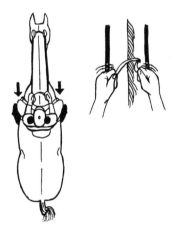

Both direct reins (both hands squeeze backward).

- Both legs support at girth.
- Weight on both seat bones.
- Stop or slow down.

Left direct rein (left hand squeezes backward).

- Left leg at girth, right leg supports behind girth.
- More weight on left seat bone. Right supporting rein.
- Bend and turn left.

4. *Indirect Rein*: Applies pressure inward and upward on one side of the bit. It asks a pony to position his neck and head in the direction of the rein, and to move his shoulders slightly sideways. The indirect rein is used to position the head and neck, to encourage bending, and to discourage cutting corners or leaning inward on a turn. It must *always* be used with a coordinated leg aid.

To apply an indirect rein aid, briefly rotate your hand so that your fingernails are on top and your thumb rotates outward. This brings your lower fingers (little finger and ring finger) and the rein in and up for a moment. Don't hold the rein in this rotated position; just give it a brief turn, then return to a normal position. Don't bend your wrist (this makes you pull) or pull backward. An indirect rein aid should act in a diagonal direction, toward the rider's opposite hip.

An indirect rein can be used by only one hand at a time. Using two indirect reins at once would be conflicting aids and would confuse the pony.

There is another kind of indirect rein aid (the indirect rein behind the withers), which you will learn at a more advanced level.

Half-Halts and Balance

To understand half-halts, you must know how your pony moves and changes his balance. His hind legs push him forward at each stride; the longer the strides, the more "pushing power" he has. Sometimes a pony moves like a wheelbarrow, with too much weight on his front legs; this is called "moving on the forehand." This is awkward and makes it harder for him to turn, slow down, or handle his balance. To improve his balance, he must tuck his hindquarters under and change from "pushing power" to more "carrying power." This helps him bring his balance back and makes it easier for him to stop, turn, and move with good balance.

A half-halt is a brief, almost invisible signal that tells a pony to use his hindquarters to balance himself, pay attention, and get ready to do something. (It is *not* a stop or a pull!) Because a half-halt asks a pony to improve his balance, it is often called a "rebalancing." You can use half-halts to prepare your pony to halt smoothly and in balance, to make accurate transitions, to give you more energy and attention, and to improve his balance in any gait. Good half-halts are a key to advanced riding.

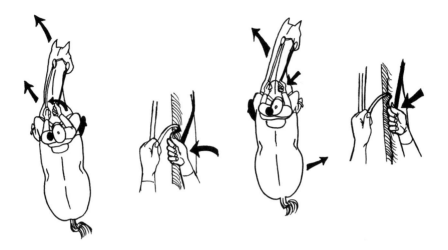

Right neck rein or bearing rein (right hand rotates and presses rein against neck).

- Right leg at girth, left leg supports behind girth.
- More weight on left seat bone.
- Bends neck to right, moves diagonally to left.

Right indirect rein (right hand rotates and presses toward rider's left hip).

- Left leg behind girth, right leg supports at girth.
- More weight on left seat bone.
- Bends to right, forehand moves left, hindquarters move to right.

Half-halts begin with sitting deep and tall. You must be in balance, with your legs under you and weight properly balanced on your seat bones. You use all the aids in a half-halt, but your seat is the most important.

To give a half-halt, your spine stretches briefly. Your seat bones go deeper into the saddle, your back gets longer and taller, and your stomach muscles feel stronger for a moment. (Taking a deep breath helps, too.) Your legs stretch down around your pony's sides, and your fingers close briefly on the reins—they don't pull. All this happens in a split second, like a heartbeat; then you relax. If you try to hold a half-halt too long or push too hard with your muscles, you tense up, which prevents your pony from responding correctly. Remember, a half-halt is a quick rebalancing; you can't hold a half-halt.

Hind legs move with pushing power.

On the forehand

Hind legs move with carrying power.

Because half-halts are so brief, you can give several in a row in rhythm with your pony's gait. Each half-halt asks him to use his hindquarters and rebalance for one stride. When a pony responds to a half-halt, you may feel him "wake up" and pick up his balance a bit. It takes several half-halts to make a smooth, well-balanced transition, to correct a balance problem, or to halt.

Half-halt or rebalance before and after each corner, before every transition, and any time you feel your pony is leaning too much on his forehand. When your pony responds to half-halts in the walk, begin using them in other gaits. In the posting trot, half-halt each time you sit. At the sitting trot, half-halt every stride (on every other beat). In the canter, half-halt at the moment when your seat goes down in the saddle.

HALF-HALT

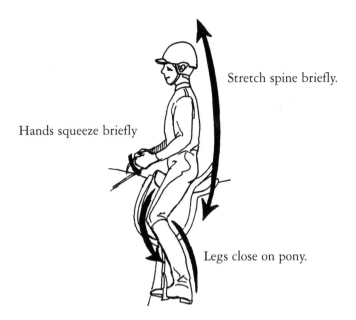

Stretch spine briefly.

Hands squeeze briefly

Legs close on pony.

Making Accurate Transitions

As your balance and control and your pony's response improve, you can make more precise transitions. In a dressage test, transitions must be accurate (as your body reaches the correct letter), but they must also be smooth and quiet, with invisible aids. Sudden, rough transitions; strong, crude aids; or resistance from your pony just won't do. You must prepare for each transition far enough ahead so that your pony can execute it smoothly at the right place.

Plan to make a transition at a certain letter (for example, from walk to trot at E.) Several strides before the letter, prepare your pony with several half-halts in rhythm with the walk. He should feel as if he wants to trot, so you must hold him back a little to keep him from trotting too soon. Just as you reach the letter, give a quiet leg aid and allow him to trot. If he responds a little early or late, notice how far before or after the letter he trotted. On the next walk-to-trot transition, you may have to prepare earlier or wait a little longer, until you get it just right. You may need a slightly stronger or lighter leg aid to make a smooth transition.

For downward transitions, use several half-halts in rhythm with the gait to prepare to walk at the letter. In a good downward transition, your pony feels as if he "sits down" but keeps moving forward freely. To help your pony, you must feel if he is too much on the forehand or balanced just right. Notice how long it takes for a downward transition, and start your preparation far enough before the letter. Use your legs to keep enough energy, or he may drop to a slower gait too soon. If he leans, falls on his forehand, or slows to a crawl, he needs more half-halts to improve his balance.

Don't make the same kind of transition too many times at the same place, or your pony will start to anticipate. Practice transitions at different letters, in both directions, and in the middle of the ring.

Improving Bending

You already know that your pony should bend evenly through turns and circles so that his hind legs follow in the track of his front legs and he balances correctly. You should also know which side is your pony's stiffer side (the side on which he finds it harder to bend). Now you need to become more aware of the mistakes your pony makes when he finds turning and bending difficult. These problems are not hard to correct once you are aware of them.

When a pony bends correctly, his inside hind leg reaches well forward (engages) at every stride, his back comes up, and he stays balanced, without leaning. His hind legs follow in the tracks of his front legs, and he looks in the direction of the turn. He keeps the same pace, rhythm, and tempo, without speeding up, slowing down, or breaking gait. When he turns like this, he is well-balanced and can keep moving forward with energy and power (impulsion). However, this takes effort and good riding. It is harder work to bend correctly through a turn. If his rider is not alert, a pony may make mistakes that make him move and bend poorly.

Here are several common mistakes and ways to correct them:

- *Slowing down the tempo or breaking to a slower gait*: Use your legs in rhythm with the gait to maintain the rhythm and tempo.
- *Shortening stride*: Use your legs to ask him to keep the same length of stride through the turn. Be careful not to restrict him too much with your hands.
- *Speeding up the tempo or breaking to a faster gait*: Use half-halts in rhythm with the gait. Remember to breathe!
- *Falling in (leaning in)*: Use your inside leg more strongly to keep him out on the track of the turn.
- *Falling out with his outside shoulder*: Swivel your seat and use more outside supporting rein to prevent him from drifting outward. Don't pull him around with the inside rein.
- *Swinging hindquarters to the outside*: Use your outside leg behind the girth to keep his hind legs tracking behind his front legs.

Lengthening and Shortening Stride

Lengthening and shortening stride give you more accurate control of how your pony moves. Both are important for jumping and cross-country riding, as well as on the flat.

Lengthening stride is *not* just going faster. When a pony lengthens his stride, he uses his hind legs more powerfully with each stride. This makes him reach farther and cover more ground at each stride. He should keep the same rhythm (beats of the gait) and tempo (speed of the rhythm), and must stay in good balance as he lengthens his strides. Moving faster with short strides is not lengthening; it is more like scrambling. If a pony leans on his forehand too much, he may go faster and faster (called "running"). This puts him off balance and makes him hard to control.

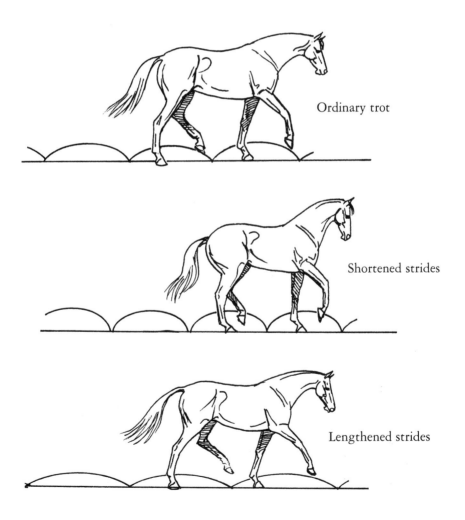

Ordinary trot

Shortened strides

Lengthened strides

Shortening stride is not just slowing down. To shorten stride correctly, a pony tucks his hindquarters under himself and shifts his balance back; it feels as if he "sits down" while going forward. When he shortens, his strides must stay lively, springy, and alert, with plenty of energy in the same rhythm and tempo. He should not let his energy "die" or drop down to a crawl. With shortened strides and good balance, a pony is ready and able to stop, go forward, turn, make transitions, or lengthen stride again whenever you ask him to. Shortening stride helps a pony keep his balance on slippery ground or when going downhill.

To shorten stride, use half-halts in rhythm with your pony's gait. With each half-halt you rebalance and sit taller. As your pony comes back to you, close your fingers to keep him from stretching out while you use your legs to keep him awake and lively. Remember to breathe so that you don't get stiff!

To ask your pony to lengthen his stride, both of you must be in good balance and in good working rhythm. Use half-halts in rhythm with his gait to prepare him and increase his energy so that he wants to go forward. Use your leg aids in rhythm with each stride, and keep a light, steady contact. Your hands allow him to stretch his neck and head forward a little more (an inch or two), but *don't* loosen the reins. As he responds to your legs, his strides should feel bigger and more powerful, and he may take a stronger contact with your hands. Remember to keep your balance, look forward, and ride straight.

Don't ask a pony to move with very short or very long strides for too long. Start by shortening or lengthening for only a few strides (three or four) at a time; then come back to a normal gait. It's more important to stay in good balance and rhythm than to try to lengthen or shorten for a long distance, especially at first. Always rebalance with half-halts before and after you lengthen or shorten stride.

Basic Lateral Work

"Lateral work" consists of exercises that involve moving sideways. These basic exercises can improve your pony's suppleness, balance, and reponse to your leg aids, and they are the foundation for the more advanced lateral work you will learn later. They also teach you to coordinate your aids and help you understand how they work.

To do lateral work, you must know about inside and outside aids. When doing lateral work, you use one set of aids to ask the pony to move sideways and the others to regulate the movement, telling him to stay in balance, how far to move, and when to stop moving sideways. You also use half-halts to keep him in balance so that he can step sideways. In each movement, you must be clear about how to use each aid, and what it does, and you must coordinate it with the other aids.

Lateral movements must be done correctly. If you overdo them or do them incorrectly, your pony may become confused and may resist your aids. It's important to maintain good rhythm, relaxation, and contact during any lateral movement. To keep your pony's free forward movement, always ride straight forward after each lateral movement. If your pony becomes tense, resists your aids, or hesitates to move freely forward, stop practicing lateral work until you get help with the problem.

Simple Quarter Turn on the Forehand   Your pony has already learned to move sideways from pressure, both on the ground and when you are mounted. The turn on the forehand is the next step in teaching him to move sideways in a more controlled way from leg pressure. The turn on the forehand described here is a basic turn, which lays a foundation for more advanced lateral work. You will learn more advanced turns on the forehand later.

QUARTER TURN ON THE FOREHAND AT THE RAIL

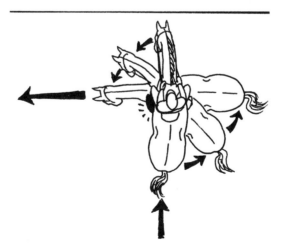

- ◆ Ride straight to the rail and halt.
- ◆ Inside leg behind the girth asks for each step.
- ◆ Ride straight forward after turn.

In the turn on the forehand, the pony's hind legs step sideways around his front legs, on which he pivots. As the pony turns, he moves his forelegs up and down but sets them down almost in the same spot. The pony bends slightly *away* from the direction in which his hind legs move; when his hind legs move to the right, he should be bent slightly to the left. (In more advanced turns on the forehand, the pony is bent in the opposite direction.)

At this stage, you should ask for only a quarter turn on the forehand (90 degrees). Your pony should take three or four steps to complete the turn. His inside hind leg should cross over in front of the other hind leg with each step. If the inside hind leg crosses behind the other hind leg, he is trying to back up. This is very awkward and makes it difficult to move forward after the turn.

Riding the quarter turn on the forehand at the rail of the ring helps the pony understand what you want him to do. The rail acts as a guide and keeps him from walking forward instead of turning. To start, ride across the ring and make a square halt facing the rail, leaving enough room so that your pony will not bump into the rail as he turns.

Bend the pony slightly *away* from the direction in which his hind legs should move. (To move his hind legs *right*, bend him slightly to the *left*. The left side is the inside, and your left seat bone, leg, and rein are your inside aids. The right is the outside, and your right seat bone, leg, and rein are the outside aids.)

Swivel your body and look slightly to the inside (*left*), and give a brief direct rein aid with your inside (*left*) hand. Use your inside (*left*) leg aid three or four inches behind the girth to ask the pony to step sideways with his hind legs. Your outside (*right*) rein and leg should be in contact with your pony but should remain quiet. Give a brief leg aid and direct rein aid to ask for each step, and relax your aids as your pony responds. At first, pause between steps and give him time to balance himself and prepare for the next aid. Later, you can ask him to make several steps in succession, but he should never hurry sideways too fast or out of control. When your pony takes the last step of the quarter turn, he will be facing straight down the track. Pat him and ride forward, to encourage free forward movement.

When performing a turn on the forehand, you must sit deep and tall and stay in balance in the center of the saddle. If you lean forward or shift your weight to one side, you confuse your pony, and he cannot make a good turn. Wait until he finishes one step before asking for the next. If you rush him or apply the leg aid too long, he may take too big a step sideways and hurry through the turn. Keep contact with your pony's mouth, but don't use too strong a rein aid. This can make him back up and spoil the turn.

When you can perform a turn on the forehand in one direction, try it the other way. This exercise is usually easier for a pony in one direction and more difficult in the other. He needs extra practice on his more difficult side.

Spiralling in and Leg-Yielding Out on a Circle To "yield" means to give, so "leg-yielding" means "giving" to a leg aid. Simple leg-yielding is a basic training movement in which a pony moves sideways from the rider's leg aid while going forward in a walk or trot. This builds on the simple forward-and-out exercise your pony has already learned.

Spiralling in and out on a circle is a good way to introduce leg-yielding. This exercise improves your pony's suppleness, balance, and bending, and makes you more aware of your inside and outside aids and how they work.

Start by riding a 20-meter circle at a walk. (It helps to ride the circle in the end of a dressage arena or to set up markers that show you the correct size circle.) Your pony must move forward in good rhythm, paying attention to your aids and bending correctly, with his hind feet following in the tracks of his front feet.

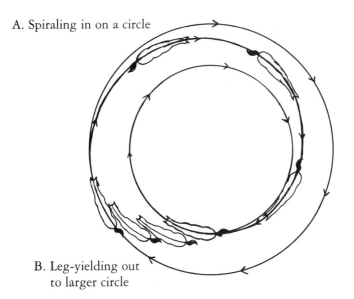

A. Spiraling in on a circle

B. Leg-yielding out
to larger circle

Spiralling in means gradually making the circle smaller by moving in a little more toward the center with each stride. To spiral in, sit deep and tall and swivel your body toward the center, using your outside leg on your pony's side behind the girth. Your inside aids maintain contact and keep your pony from cutting in too quickly, or falling in by leaning on his inside shoulder. Gradually spiral in until the circle is 15 meters in diameter (about three-fourths the size of the original circle). Use your inside aids to tell your pony when to stop spiralling in and to move forward on the smaller circle.

To spiral out, use your inside aids (inside leg near the girth and inside indirect rein) to ask your pony to move outward a little with each stride. Your outside aids should be in contact with your pony. You use them to keep him from moving sideways too much on any step, falling out (leaning on his outside shoulder), or rubber-necking (bending his neck too much to the inside). It should take several steps to return to the 20-meter circle. When the circle is large enough, use your outside aids (outside supporting rein and outside leg behind the girth) to stop moving sideways, and ride forward on the circle. Practice this exercise in both directions at the walk and later at the trot.

Simple Leg-Yielding from the Quarter Line to the Wall   Your pony has learned to move forward and out from your inside leg on a circle. Now you will ask him to move forward and sideways for several steps, first at a walk and later at the trot. When leg-yielding, your pony should be straight, with his head, neck, and body aimed at the end of the ring as he steps forward and sideways. He may bend very slightly at the poll away from the direction in which he is moving (when moving to the right, he looks slightly to the left). Neither his shoulders nor his hindquarters should get ahead of the other as he steps sideways, and he must stay in good balance. He should take regular, even strides, and should move freely forward after the exericse.

To prepare for a leg-yield, ride through the end of the ring (the short side) and turn down the quarter line (half-way between the center line and the rail). You will leg-yield forward and out for three or four strides from the quarter line toward the rail, keeping your pony pointed straight toward the end of the ring (see diagram).

When you turn onto the quarter line, ride straight for several strides while you give several half-halts (in rhythm with the walk), and make sure your pony is straight, on contact, and paying attention. Now you must notice the moment when his barrel swings out toward the rail. This is when his inside hind leg pushes off and

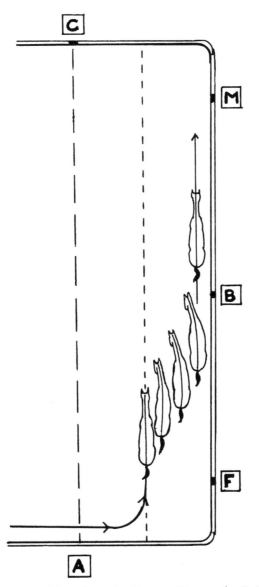

Leg-Yielding from the Quarter Line to the Rail

swings forward, and it is the time when he can respond to your aids and step sideways.

To ask a pony to leg-yield, use your inside aids (a short squeeze with your inside leg close to the girth, and a brief squeeze of your inside hand) just as his inside hind leg pushes off. Your outside hand may give a small opening rein aid to lead your pony in the right direction. Immediately after using the inside aids, give a brief half-halt to keep him straight and in balance so that he steps sideways instead of just going faster. Your outside aids should be in contact with your pony, ready to tell him "That's far enough" after each step.

Ask the pony to leg-yield toward the rail for three or four strides, and then ride straight forward and reward him with a pat. Practice this several times; then change directions and try leg-yielding from the other leg. You will probably find one direction easier than the other.

When you ride a leg-yield, you must keep your pony straight and rebalance him after each step. You must sit up straight and even, and you must not lean, twist, or squirm sideways to move him over. The inside rein must not pull your pony's head around, or you will make him crooked. If your pony doesn't pay attention to your leg aids or doesn't step sideways enough, you may have to tap him with a dressage whip beside your leg, or touch him gently with a spur. (Ask your instructor, to be sure you are using your aids correctly and not confusing your pony.)

When you can leg-yield easily at a walk, you may try the same exercise at a sitting trot. It's especially important to use good half-halts to get your pony straight, in balance, and paying attention, and not to trot too fast. Remember to half-halt after each step sideways, to keep the pony from going faster. After three or four steps, ride forward in a posting trot and reward him with a pat.

Aids for the Rein-Back (Backing Up)

In the rein-back, the pony steps backward with his legs moving almost in diagonal pairs. The right front and left hind, and left front and right hind move almost together, but the front foot may be raised and put down an instant before the hind foot. A correct rein-back requires obedience to all the aids and shows that the pony accepts the bit without resistance, moves straight, and is supple in his back and his hind legs.

Because the rein-back is a fairly difficult movement, you should not ask your pony to rein-back until he reaches the point in his training where he is ready to do it. He must respond to all your aids (seat, legs, and hands), go forward while accepting the bit, and respond properly to half-halts. You will need an experienced ground person to help you. If a pony resists the bit, is difficult to halt, or is not calm and cooperative, he is not ready to rein-back.

To ask a pony to rein-back, halt squarely, keeping contact with your legs and your hands. Give a brief, light leg aid; then relax your legs and squeeze your hands to apply a direct rein aid. It may help to tip your body *very slightly* forward (not enough for anyone watching to see). With each step, relax your aids. After two or three steps, sit deep and tall, close your legs, and ride your pony straight forward to encourage free forward movement.

Riding and Evaluating a Strange Pony

Riding different horses and ponies is a most important part of your riding education. Each horse is an individual, with something special you can learn from him. You may need to try out a new horse or pony for sale. To be safe, you must use good judgment and not try to ride a horse that is beyond your present ability.

Before riding a strange horse or pony, find out all you can about him. If possible, watch his owner ride him first, and compare the way he goes to your own pony. If he seems quicker in his reactions, more sensitive, or nervous, you will have to be especially quiet and smooth in the way you ride while you get to know him.

Before mounting, do a careful tack safety check, adjust the stirrups to fit, and check the girth. Don't wear spurs or carry a dressage whip on a horse or pony you don't know, especially without asking the owner first. Ride a strange horse in a ring, if possible, not in the open.

When mounting, be especially smooth and quiet. Some horses may be cold-backed (very sensitive in the back). Ask the horse to stand still while you mount and for a few moments afterward, while you get settled and get acquainted.

Try out a new horse or pony at a walk at first, making several halts and turns in each direction. Use the lightest and softest aids, increasing them a little at a time if necessary. Don't surprise a strange horse with sudden, strong aids. Remember to breathe deeply, which makes you feel more relaxed and natural to your horse. Give yourself and the horse time to relax and feel confident with each other.

Then ride as you would when warming up your own pony. It may take a little practice before you feel that you are in good balance with a new horse, especially during transitions, so be careful not to fall back onto his back or catch him in the mouth by mistake. Ride changes of direction and several transitions from trot to walk and walk to trot. Don't canter or jump until you feel that you know each other and are working well together. If you jump, start with ground poles or a low cross-rail and gradually work up to bigger fences with which you are both comfortable. As you ride, try to form your own opinion of this horse, his temperament, training, and way of moving.

Riding someone else's horse is a great privilege, so it is your responsibility to take the best possible care of him. Be tactful; never get rough or fight with him. Pay attention to his condition and bring him back calm and cool. After you have ridden someone else's horse, it is only polite to brush off and put the horse away properly, clean the tack, and re-adjust the stirrups to where they were. It's also important to be polite and tactful when giving your opinion of someone else's horse or pony. Even if you found him difficult to ride, find something nice to say about him and thank the owner for letting you ride him!

C-3 RIDING OVER FENCES

At C-3 Level, you are starting to make the transition from intermediate to advanced jumping. More than simply jumping bigger fences, this means jumping with better security, confidence, and control, and, especially, riding over fences in good form and classic style. This is not riding just to look pretty, but with the balance, smoothness, and control that allow you to ride different horses well.

Form Follows Function: Position and Stirrup Length

"Form follows function" is an old saying about riding style. It means that the "function," or the job you do, determines the "form," or the way you ride when you do it. You must have the right position, balance, and riding skills for the kind of riding you are doing. A classical dressage position is the wrong seat for show jumping, and a good cross-country galloping position won't help you ride a good dressage test. Good basics in the Balance Seat will adapt to special kinds of riding.

There are five basic positions and stirrup lengths for different kinds of riding:

1. *Dressage seat*: For dressage, schooling and riding on the flat, never for jumping. Rider sits tall and deep in the saddle, with legs long and hanging directly under his seat. Most work is done with rider sitting upright in the saddle. Long stirrups (bottom of ankle bone).

2. *General-purpose balanced seat*: For riding on the flat and over ground poles. Rider sits deep and tall, with legs directly under his seat. Stirrups are slightly shorter than dressage length (middle of ankle bone), with more bend in the joints of the legs. Seat is always close to the saddle.

3. *Balanced jumping seat*: For ordinary jumping, schooling over fences, and cross-country riding. Rider sits close to the

saddle, but shorter stirrups (top of ankle bone) cause sharper angles at ankle, knee, and hip joints. Rider's angles close (shoulders over knees) in jumping position. Seat stays close to saddle, but when rider jumps, his weight is carried on his thighs and legs, not on the pony's back.

FIVE BASIC POSITIONS AND STIRRUP LENGTHS

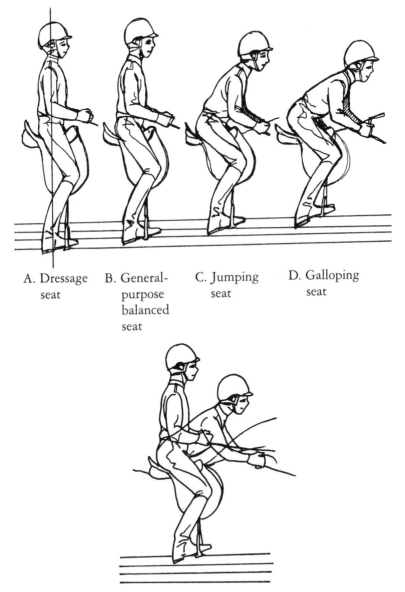

A. Dressage seat

B. General-purpose balanced seat

C. Jumping seat

D. Galloping seat

E. Show jumping seat

4. *Show-jumping seat*: For jumping larger fences and show-jumping courses. Rider sits close to saddle, but stirrups are shorter (just above ankle bone), causing deeper heels and sharper angles at knee and hip, especially during jumping. Because of shorter stirrups, the rider's seat is above the saddle and off the horse's back during the jump. Even shorter stirrups are used to jump extremely big fences.

5. *Cross-country seat*: For galloping and jumping cross-country. Shorter stirrups (just above ankle bone) cause deeper heels and sharper angles in rider's legs, and his seat is above the saddle and off the horse's back when galloping and jumping. The rider usually bridges his reins across the neck, keeping his balance over his feet and legs, riding in an "egg" position with a slightly rounded back. Shorter stirrups are used for fast galloping, steeplechasing, or racing.

Good Jumping Performance

A good jumping performance is more than just jumping higher, faster, or more difficult fences, or winning in competition. Good jumping is safer, smoother, easier for both horse and rider, and unites them. It feels wonderful and is beautiful to watch!

Here are some qualities of a good jumping performance:

In the Horse   During the approach, the horse moves straight and freely forward, in good balance. He meets the fence squarely at the center, in stride, and at the best takeoff spot. During takeoff, he engages both hind legs equally and pushes off powerfully. His shoulders rotate, bringing his forelegs up and folding them tightly. His neck and head stretch out and down, and his back rounds in an arc, or "bascule." His hind legs fold up tightly, and he lands lightly, in good balance. He goes forward smoothly, powerfully, and in stride.

Over a course, a good jumper moves freely forward with a steady, even pace, adjusting his stride as necessary for good takeoffs. He has extra "scope" (jumping ability) when needed. He is calm but willing, and his performance seems to flow smoothly.

In the Rider   A good jumping rider rides in balance with his horse, with eyes up, keeping a light contact with his horse's mouth. He lets the thrust of takeoff close his angles, bringing his shoulders just over his knees and toes, with his seat close to the saddle but slightly off the horse's back. His legs stay directly under him, with lower legs in contact with the horse's sides and heels down. His hands and arms follow the horse's mouth, keeping a light contact and a straight line from elbow to the bit throughout the jump. During landing, he stays in balance over his feet and absorbs the shock with his flexible joints.

A good jumping rider is effective and positive but rides smoothly and quietly, without roughness or extra movement. His seat and hands are independent, and he is in balance with his horse at all times, never interfering with his horse's efforts.

Common Jumping Faults in the Horse:

- *Taking off too close or too far away*: May be caused by a mistake by horse or rider. Often occurs when the horse is out of rhythm, unbalanced, or too much on the forehand during the approach.
- *Chipping in (extra stride)*: The horse puts in one or more short, quick strides just before takeoff. May happen when he is off balance, going too fast, loses confidence, or gets the wrong distance.
- *Jumping "inverted" (hollow back, high head)*: Usually seen in stiff, tense horses, or when rider interferes by sitting down on the horse's back or restricting him with the reins. Horse cannot jump with a good arc, or bascule, and cannot fold his front or hind legs well; this may cause him to hit the fence or knock down a rail.

Good Performance of Horse and Rider over a Jump

- *Hanging knees, trailing hind legs*: Hanging knees mean the fore-arms point down and the forelegs do not fold properly. It is dangerous, because hitting a fence with the forelegs can cause a fall. Hanging knees may be caused by getting too close to a fence, or poor jumping style. Trailing hind legs do not fold tightly and are likely to knock down rails, but they are not as dangerous as hanging knees.

- *Crooked jumping*: A horse who swerves across a jump, jumps at an angle, or twists sideways in the air is hard to control and to ride in a straight line. Horses that usually jump to one side may be trying to spare a weak or unsound leg and should be checked by a veterinarian.

Correcting Rider Jumping Faults

Nobody is perfect, so you undoubtedly will have some faults or mistakes in your jumping that need correcting. Rider jumping errors, however minor, don't just look bad; they handicap a rider and his horse, especially over bigger jumps. Most of these problems are unconscious habits that get started when a rider uses a wrong technique or tries to cope with a jumping problem.

The longer you have had a bad habit, the longer you will have to work to change it. The first step is *awareness*: realizing what you are doing. This may involve a timely comment from your instructor or seeing yourself in a photo or on a videotape. The next step is *correction*: learning a technique to correct the bad habit. This may mean changing your stirrup length or learning a new way of doing something. Then you must *practice* doing it the correct way so that it becomes a new habit. You will need to repeat an exercise that will help you learn a correct technique and make it a habit. At first, the new (correct) way will feel strange because your body is still used to your old (incorrect) habit. The more you practice, however, the more familiar the new procedure will become, and it will eventually turn into a good habit.

Here are some common rider jumping faults and ways to correct them.

Unsteady lower legs, heels up, lower legs swing: This makes you insecure over jumps, upsets your pony, and leaves you off balance during landing. Usually caused by tight, pinching knees that become a pivot point. This can happen if you jump big fences before your basic skills are solid. Too-long stirrups may contribute to the problem.

HORSE JUMPING FAULTS

Reaching: Taking
off too far away

Jumping crookedly, twisting   Getting under: Taking off too close

Hanging knees   Jumping inverted or hollow

Chipping in

RIDER JUMPING FAULTS

A. Good jumping position

B. Standing up ahead of the motion; hollow back

C. Behind the motion; leg rotates forward; round back

D. Looking down; pinching knees; leg pivots back; heel up

E. Ducking

Correction: Check stirrup length for jumping. Practice standing in the stirrups and half-seat at walk, trot, and canter, with weight sinking into your heels, and calves in contact with the pony's sides. Release your knees (relax the knee grip) until you feel your knees sliding up and down a little on the saddle flap as your pony trots. On takeoff, release knees and think "Sink": Let your seat sink closer to the saddle, your heels sink down and backward, and your legs sink into your pony's sides. Think of landing with your feet under you on the ground.

Jumping ahead of the motion, standing in the stirrups: This is a dangerous habit, as you can easily fall off. Stirrups too long for jumping can cause you to stand up instead of folding correctly. Some riders are afraid they will be left behind, so they stand up or get ahead of the motion, which is incorrect.

Correction: Check stirrups for correct jumping length. Practice folding at hip joint (shoulders over knees), keeping seat close to saddle. Instead of standing up, sink closer to the saddle and deeper into heels. Let pony close your angles as he takes off. Jumping low grids without reins and stirrups may help.

Jumping behind the motion; legs rotate forward: This is a serious fault because it interferes with the pony; you sit down on his back and catch him in the mouth. This can spoil your pony's jumping style and make him unhappy about jumping. This habit may get started if you jump a pony that is too strong for you, or if you jump cross-country fences that are too difficult or at too fast a pace for your level. It can also come from trying to get your heels down by shoving them forward, instead of letting them sink down and back as they should.

Correction: Ride in posting trot with the motion and in half-seat at trot and canter to help your balance. Jumping a quiet pony with stirrups but without reins (in a safely enclosed jumping chute) can also help. When you jump, think of landing with your feet on the ground—not sitting on your seat. If your pony is strong, work on half-halts and transitions to help make him easier to control.

Ducking: When you quickly snap forward into jumping position and fold too far, your chest comes too close to your pony's neck. Instead of letting the pony close your angles as he takes off, you put too much effort into the jump. Ducking disturbs a pony and may make him tense up and get quick. It often results from riding behind the motion during the approach, then trying to catch up on takeoff. Jumping with too-long stirrups can contribute to this habit.

Correction: Check stirrup length and balance. Exercises that help you ride in balance, with your pony during the approach, will help (see correction for getting behind the motion). Concentrate on keeping eyes on your target, feeling the pony's rhythm, and relaxing your seat and joints to allow him to close your angles. Breathing out as he takes off may help. It may help to practice a crest-release exercise, pressing hard with your forearms to keep your body from folding too far and coming too close to your pony's neck.

Round back; hollow back: A round back is too relaxed and floppy, folding at the waist instead of at the hip joints. Jumping with a round back makes it harder to control your hip angle and balance. It often goes with riding behind the motion or looking down. A hollow back is stiff, tight, and tense, with tight, locked hip joints. It can cause you to stand up instead of folding correctly, get ahead of the motion, and collapse forward on landing. Jumping with a hollow back can make your back sore.

Correction: Practice sitting deep and tall and stretching your spine. Practice riding in half-seat and folding into jumping position with a "long back"—keeping your back long and flat, folding at the hip joints, keeping your eyes up, and sinking your seat bones backward toward the saddle as you fold. Posting trot with the motion, riding bounces or no-strides, and simple gymnastics help you keep your back flat and fold at your hip joints.

Improving Your Jumping Seat

At C-2 Level, you learned to jump simple gymnastics and grids, and began learning to jump without stirrups. Now, jumping a grid (a series of fences in a jumping chute) without reins or stirrups will give you better timing and security over fences, and real confidence. Besides, it's fun! It is easier than it looks, as long as you are ready for it. However, to be safe, you *must* have help from your instructor, and you must ride a suitable pony—*not* a green pony, a rusher, or a problem jumper.

You have already learned to jump small, single fences without stirrups. To jump a series of fences without stirrups, you will need to build up strength in your legs and develop rhythm and balance. You do this by practicing posting trot without stirrups for longer and longer periods, cantering without stirrups, and practicing half-seat without stirrups often for short periods at the trot and canter.

Review riding a jumping grid of three or four bounces with stirrups but without reins, as you may have done at the C-2 level. When you can ride a jumping grid in good balance with your arms stretched out from your shoulders, you are ready for the next step.

The first time you ride through a jumping grid without reins or stirrups, the fences should be lowered to ground poles. This helps you keep your balance and rhythm as you develop confidence. Keep your eyes up, toes up, legs in contact with your pony's sides, and your seat close to the saddle. Let the pony close your angles as he canters over the ground poles in a steady rhythm. When you jump this grid with good balance, rhythm, and timing, it can be raised to low cross-rails, then later to small verticals.

Hands and Releases

The purpose of a release is to allow your pony to use his head and neck freely to balance himself as he jumps. The stretching of his head and neck when he jumps is called a "balancing gesture." This helps him raise his forehand, tuck up his front legs, round his back over the jump, and balance himself as he lands and canters on. If you restrict his neck or hurt his mouth, he will be handicapped in jumping and may lose his confidence. This can make a pony jump stiffly and awkwardly, make mistakes, tense up, and rush his fences, or refuse.

Excellent jumping form, with rider in balance, showing a straight line from elbow to the bit. *Photo: Ed Lawrence*

Releasing correctly does not mean abandoning control. Jumping riders say, "The approach belongs to the rider, but the jump belongs to the horse." This means that you can use all your aids to control your pony on the approach to a jump, but during the jump, you must allow him to use his head and neck freely. If you try to hold him back, slow him down, or discipline him during a jump, you interfere with his jumping efforts. After he lands, you may have to rebalance, correct a swerve, or even stop him.

Here are some problems with hands, reins, and releases, and what they do.

- *Reins too short*: Causes heavy hands that cannot follow pony's head and neck properly. Elbows get pulled out ahead of the body, and rider may get pulled forward.
- *Reins too long*: Results in poor contact and control, with hands unable to follow pony's head and neck properly. Elbows may stick out, which brings the hands back and prevents them from following.
- *Hands too high on approach or takeoff*: Makes pony raise his head; interferes with his jumping effort and can make him jump flat, with a high head and hollow back.
- *Hands too far up the mane, toward pony's ears*: Upsets rider's balance and contact. Often goes with throwing the upper body and arms too far forward and legs swinging back. Very insecure.
- *"Dropping" the pony*: Throwing the hands forward suddenly just before takeoff drops the contact without warning. You lose all control and may lose your balance. The pony is caught by surprise and may lose his balance, stop, or jump awkwardly. This is especially dangerous when jumping solid fences at a faster pace.
- *"Busy" hands that tug, pull, or interfere during approach*: This distracts a pony; throws his rhythm and stride off; and can cause him to make a mistake, lose his confidence, or even refuse. This is one of the worst habits a rider can have!
- *Restricting hands; stiff release*: Hands that are stiffly set against the pony's neck stop him from using his head and neck freely when he jumps. He will soon learn to jump flat, with a high head and hollow back.

Improving Your Hands and Release When Jumping

First, adjust the length of your reins so that you can ride with good contact. *Keep a straight line from the bit through your hands to your elbows.* During the approach, use half-halts, not pulls, to keep a steady rhythm, and maintain a light, steady contact until you feel your pony take off. Review the four basic releases (especially the long release) over ground poles and low, easy jumps; don't use the automatic release until your problems improve. Use trotting poles followed by a cross-rail or a simple gymnastic to steady your pony's stride while you work up to jumping without reins. (This will help restore your pony's confidence, too.) Jumping low but fairly wide spreads can help you feel how your pony stretches his neck during the jump, and learn to follow the motion freely with your hands and arms.

RIDER HAND AND RELEASE FAULTS

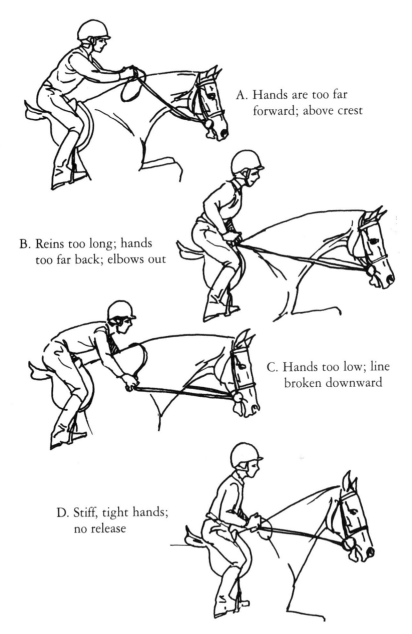

A. Hands are too far forward; above crest

B. Reins too long; hands too far back; elbows out

C. Hands too low; line broken downward

D. Stiff, tight hands; no release

Elements of a Stadium Jumping Course

Only four elements (basic parts) can be put together to make up a stadium jumping course. Each of these can include different kinds of obstacles and can range from easy to difficult. They are the following:

1. Single fences (or first fence in a line)
2. Related distances (line of two or more fences less than 85 feet apart)
3. Combinations
4. Turns and bending lines

ELEMENTS OF A COURSE

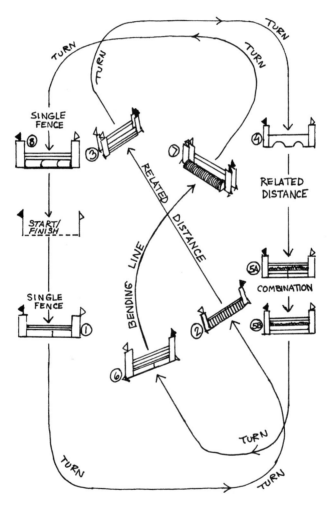

Single Fences   A single fence is a fence either set by itself or so far from the previous fence that it has little effect on how you jump it. The first fence of a course, a fence following a turn, or the first fence in a new line can be considered a single fence.

Good form and balance over a stadium fence, with eyes up and on a target. *Photo: Susan Sexton*

To jump a single fence, you must ride accurately and choose the right line. Be very positive when jumping the first fence on a course or a single fence, especially if it looks unusual or is placed so that you are going away from home.

Related Distances   A related distance is a line of two fences set close enough that the way you jump the first fence affects the number of strides and the way you jump the second fence. Most related distances are three to seven strides, or less than 85 feet.

The number of strides in a related distance depends on how the horse jumps the first fence (especially how much space he uses for landing), the length of his strides, and where he must take off for the second fence. Here is an example of a related distance that could be ridden in either four or five strides:

3' Vertical—60 feet—3' vertical

A. 12' canter stride: 6' landing, four 12' strides (48'), 6' takeoff = 60'.

B: 10' canter stride: 5' landing, five 10' strides (50'), 5' takeoff = 60'.

Related Distance: 3' vertical, 60' to 3' vertical.

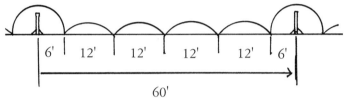

A. Ridden with 12' stride:

6' landing, four 12' strides, 6' takeoff

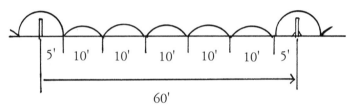

B. Ridden with 10' stride:

5' landing, five 10' strides, 5' takeoff

To ride related distances, you must know how long your pony's strides are at an average jumping canter. It's more important to keep good balance, an even pace, and the right length of stride for *your* pony than to try to get a certain number of strides in a line. For example, if your pony jumps safely and comfortably with a 10-foot stride, it may not be not sensible (or safe) to push him to try to take 12-foot or longer strides. The faster he goes and the longer his strides, the easier it is for him to lean too much on his forehand, get out of balance, and make a serious mistake. This is especially dangerous when jumping solid cross-country fences.

It is especially important to keep a steady rhythm and to keep your pony's strides even. If he keeps changing his balance and strides, you won't be able to tell when he is going to take off, and you both will have trouble.

Certain conditions can make a pony's strides shorter or longer than usual. This may change the way some fences or lines "ride."

Hard, slippery, or muddy ground; an uphill slope; and going away from home can make a pony shorten his strides or lose impulsion. A slight downhill slope, going toward home, or jumping a spread can make him lengthen his strides. You may have to steady him or encourage him to keep an even pace, with the length of stride that is best for him. Try to keep your pace even instead of making a big change in his stride close to the takeoff. This disturbs a pony and can result in a bad jump or a refusal.

Combinations A combination is two or more fences in line, placed so close together (with less than 39 feet between them) that there is room for only one or two strides. A double combination has two jumps or elements; a triple combination has three.

Combinations are really very short related distances. The way your pony jumps the first element, and how much room he uses during landing, determines how much space he has to take one or two strides and take off at the next element. Combinations must be set with distances that are reasonable and safe for your pony's strides and jumping ability. Large, long-striding horses and smaller, short-striding ponies should not be asked to jump the same combination unless the distance is adjusted for each.

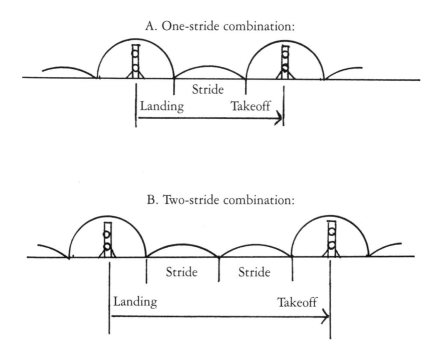

A. One-stride combination:

B. Two-stride combination:

In competition, a combination has the same fence number, but each element also has a letter (for example, Fence 10-A and 10-B). If your pony refuses the second or third element of a combination, you must re-jump the entire combination. (For instance, if your pony jumps 10-A but refuses at 10-B, you must go back and jump both 10-A and 10-B again.)

Here are some suggested distances for combinations:

One-Stride Combination

- Large horses: 24 feet
- Large ponies, small or short-striding horses: 22 to 23 feet
- Small to medium ponies (up to 13.2 hands): 20 to 22 feet

Two-Stride Combination

- Large horses: 35 to 36 feet
- Large ponies, small or short-striding horses: 33 to 34 feet
- Small to medium ponies (up to 13 hands): 30 to 32 feet

Turns and Bending Lines   Single fences and the first fence in a new line usually involve a turn. The turn, and the line resulting from the turn, can make a jump easy or difficult. A good turn brings you to the jump in good balance and sets up the right line to the next fence. A poor turn brings the pony in at an angle that can make him run out or misjudge the fence. It is usually best to try to jump a fence squarely in the center, as this makes a run-out less likely. However, there may be times when you must jump one side of a fence to save time, to get the best line to the next fence, or to take off from better footing. In this case, you must be especially careful to ride straight and avoid a runout.

A bending line is a line of two fences, the second of which is not in line with the first. To meet the second fence straight, you must ride the line on a curve. This takes clever riding and good control, and you must choose the best line to ride. If you ride a wider turn, you gain more room and take more strides. Riding a straighter line saves ground and takes fewer strides.

If you want to enter show-jumping competitions, you must know the rules and must enter the appropriate class and level of competition for you and your pony. You will need special coaching to safely prepare yourself and your pony for this type of competition and to help you during the show.

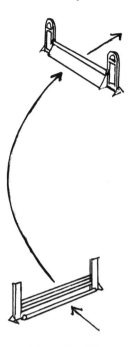

A Bending Line

C-3 RIDING IN THE OPEN

Galloping

As you become more experienced and knowledgeable about cross-country riding, you may do more riding at the gallop. This may include activities such as foxhunting, competing in horse trials or combined training events, and conditioning your pony for fast work. One thing that should *not* be included is racing your pony. This can ruin his training and endanger you both, and can cause serious injury. Racing requires special race training with an experienced, professional racehorse trainer.

Work at the gallop is fun, but it is a big responsibility. A pony can be injured much more easily during fast work than in ordinary riding. His tendons and ligaments are under more stress; they lose their strength and elasticity as they get tired. Galloping too fast, too long, or over the wrong kind of footing, especially when a pony is not fit enough, can injure muscles, joints, tendons, or ligaments, and can cripple a pony. Fast work also puts more demands on his heart and lungs, which can be damaged if overstressed. Many ponies get excited by galloping, and may become "hot" and hard to control.

They will keep on galloping long after they should have stopped, even if they are hurt or nearly exhausted. You must be responsible for knowing how much galloping is good for your pony; for knowing how fit he is and when he is tiring; and for deciding when and where to gallop, how fast to go, and when to stop.

This rider looks in the direction of her next fence as she rides a stadium jumping course. *Photo: Susan Sexton*

Check your galloping position. Your stirrups must be shorter than normal jumping length—at the top of your ankle bone. Shortened stirrups help you stay in balance and keep you from bumping your pony's back. They also make it easier to use your strength to control a strong pony at the gallop. In a galloping position, your seat should be above the saddle, and your body must be balanced over your stirrups. This means that your seat is *behind* your feet, and your shoulders are ahead of your feet, just over your knees. Your hands should be down alongside your pony's neck, with the reins in a bridge. *Don't* get so far forward that your crotch is over the pommel of the saddle, or you lean out over the pony's neck. Leaning too far forward is unsafe, makes it harder to keep control and stay in balance, and encourages your pony to lean too much on his forehand. This bad habit often shows up in riders who are tired, unfit, or riding with stirrups too long for galloping. On the other hand, you must not let your seat bump the saddle or fall back onto your pony's back, which can happen when you get tired. This makes you unbalanced, tires your pony out, and makes it harder for him to gallop and jump.

To gallop safely, you must be fit yourself. Riding in a galloping position takes fit muscles and good wind, and you may get surprisingly tired from galloping for only five minutes or so. When you get tired, you have difficulty staying in balance and in control. To get yourself fit for galloping work, practice riding in a galloping position at a trot (without posting) for five minutes at a time. You can do this around a ring or, even better, around a field, over rolling ground, or on a trail ride. Gradually increase the time until you can ride at a slow trot in galloping position for up to eight minutes. This exercise helps condition your pony, too.

Good galloping position: Horse and rider in balance

Poor galloping position: Rider leaning too far forward, horse on the forehand

Schooling Your Pony: Control, Safety, and Manners

When you gallop with others, as in foxhunting or riding cross-country with friends, you need especially good control. A pony's herd instinct makes him want to stay with other horses and not be left behind. The faster you gallop and the more horses there are galloping together, the more exciting it is. This may lead your pony to pull, to race other ponies, or to buck from excitement and high spirits. For safety, you must make him pay attention to *you*, and not get carried away by excitement and his natural herd instinct. You must be responsible for keeping him at a safe distance from other ponies, as he will not do this by himself.

To keep your pony's attention on you and to keep him balanced, you must ride with good balance and contact. Leaning too far forward or galloping with loose reins lets a pony lean on his forehand, become unbalanced, and get out of control. Every now and then, ask your pony to "come back" by shortening his stride and slowing slightly. When you can shorten his stride easily, you have good control at the gallop. If you ask your pony to "come back" and he does not respond, ask again with stronger aids. Sit up and use a pulley rein several times, if necessary. If he still does not respond, turn in a large circle, gradually making the circle smaller until he comes back under control. Always pull up gradually; pulling up suddenly can injure tendons or ligaments, especially when a pony is tired.

Before you can gallop with other ponies, your pony must gallop well under control on his own. At first, ride with only one other pony, who must be quiet and easy to control at a gallop. Practice keeping a safe distance (at least four pony lengths) behind the other pony at the walk, trot, and canter. If your pony begins to close up on the other pony, rock your shoulders back and use a brief pulley rein two or three times until he stays back and keeps his spacing. When you can keep your distance safely and easily at a canter, your leader can move into a gallop for a short distance while you practice maintaining spacing at a gallop.

Galloping beside another pony is exciting to both ponies. This can be a good exercise for a lazy pony, but a strong or excitable pony could turn into a runaway. When you gallop beside another pony, ride beside the other rider, not slightly ahead or behind. Riding beside another pony's hindquarters puts you in a position where you could get kicked.

Galloping over Natural Terrain

When you gallop cross-country, the ground is not always level, and you come across different kinds of footing. You must use good judgment and ride at a pace that is safe for the ground conditions. You must slow down to a canter or even a trot or walk to ride safely over some places, while in other places you can safely let your pony gallop on. It is easier for your pony if you set a steady, average pace suitable for your pony and for good control, and stay at that pace when conditions allow.

- *Rolling terrain*: Galloping over rolling terrain is fairly easy, as long as you remember to keep your balance. When going downhill, rock your weight slightly backward and slow to a balanced canter or a slow gallop. Uphill, keep your pony steady and stay up off his back; letting a pony run fast uphill tires him quickly. In steep places, slow to a balanced trot or walk when going down, and keep a slow, sensible pace when going up.
- *Narrow, twisting trails*: Keep to a slow gallop or canter, and be alert for low branches, tree roots, or sharp turns around trees. Your pace must be slow and balanced enough so that you can turn easily.
- *Heavy ground, deep sand*: Deep, soft ground such as deep sand or plowed fields is very hard on a pony's legs and tires him quickly. If you gallop into heavy ground suddenly, he can injure a tendon. If possible, stay to the edge of plowed fields and ride on the "headland" (the unplowed edge). If you must cross deep, soft ground, come back to a walk or trot.
- *Holes and rocks*: In some areas, you may find outcroppings of rock, groundhog holes, or prairie dog towns. Slow to a speed at which you and your pony can see a hole in time to avoid it, and stay in balance so that he can recover if he should stumble. Groundhog holes are usually on the side of a hill or near hedgerows. There will be two or more holes, and some holes may not have a telltale pile of dirt around them. Prairie dog towns have many holes scattered over a wide area around a central mound. Go around the whole area, if possible.
- *Hard ground, slippery ground, mud, and bog*: None of these conditions are safe for galloping. Slow to a trot or, at most, a slow canter. If the ground is very slippery or mud is very deep and boggy, walk. Beware of frosty ground, which may be frozen hard with a thin, very slippery layer of mud on top. The ground may stay frozen (and very slippery) in a shady area, in the woods, or behind a tree or wall, even after the ground in the open has thawed. *Never* gallop on or even alongside a paved road!

Improving Your Knowledge of Pace

Your speed at the gallop is called "pace," and you must be able to gallop at two standard speeds: a slow gallop and a faster cross-country gallop. An average cross-country pace for C Level is about 400 meters per minute, or 15 miles per hour. (If your pony is small or short-strided, 350 meters per minute—about 13 miles per hour—is a more reasonable pace.) A slow gallop is 250 meters per minute, or about 9 miles per hour, the speed of a strong canter.

To learn to recognize the two galloping speeds, you should work on a measured track 800 meters long (.5 miles, 874 yards, or 2,622 feet), as in learning to gallop at C-2 Level. Time yourself with a stopwatch. It may help to gallop alongside someone who can show you the right pace (for example, your instructor). If you ride the 800-meter (half-mile) track at an even gallop in the right time, you are going at the right pace.

Here are times for the speeds at the gallop:

- 250 meters per minute (9 miles per hour): 800 meters in 3 minutes, 20 seconds
- 350 meters per minute (13 miles per hour): 800 meters in 2 minutes, 20 seconds
- 400 meters per minute (15 miles per hour): 800 meters in 2 minutes

Recognizing Signs of Tiring

It is very important to be aware of your pony's condition and of how much energy he has left at all times. When a pony starts out, he may be fresh, eager, and full of energy, and he may want to run. You must save his energy early on in order to have enough left to finish your ride safely, in good condition, but without wasting time or going unnecessarily slowly. Save energy by going slowly up hills and over deep or difficult ground, and by keeping a steady, reasonable pace over good ground. Don't gallop all out; this tires a pony very quickly. Remember that heat and humidity will tire your pony much more quickly than normal weather conditions.

Stay aware of your pony's breathing. He will naturally breathe harder when he gallops, but if he begins to breathe extremely hard or loudly, he needs to slow down and catch his breath. Sometimes a pony will take an extra-large breath and then breathe more easily as he gallops. Irregular or very fast breathing means he needs to rest right away.

As a pony gets tired, he leans on his forehand, his strides feel heavier, and it becomes harder to keep him balanced. A tired pony tends to make mistakes when jumping, and may fumble his takeoff, jump flat, hit his fences, or land heavily. All these are signs that your pony needs to slow his pace, take a breather, or even stop.

While some ponies slow down as they get tired, many get caught up in the excitement and will keep going until they are exhausted, if you let them. Don't assume it's okay to keep going just because your pony is willing to go on. You must use good judgment to keep him safe. Never abuse his courage by letting him gallop on until he is exhausted or injured.

Jumping Different Types of Cross-Country Obstacles

In cross-country jumping, it is important to bring your pony into every fence straight, balanced, and "in front of your legs." This means that your legs have contact with his sides, and if you squeeze them firmly, he will immediately go forward. You must be positive (sure and strong), or he may lose his confidence. For most cross-country fences, it is more important to be in good balance and going forward with a positive attitude than it is to take off at an exact spot.

A good, bold jump over a cross-country fence. *Photo: Susan Sexton*

For safety's sake, never jump cross-country alone. Always have a knowledgeable person with you. You should school over any new cross-country fence, with the help of your instructor, before you gallop over it or ride it as part of a course. To give your pony confidence, it may help to follow a quiet, experienced horse over a new fence. The height and difficulty of the fences must be appropriate for both you and your pony. The way to build confidence is to school over many small cross-country obstacles of different types and never to overface your pony by asking him to jump a fence that is too big or difficult for either of you. To pass the C-3 rating, you must jump cross-country obstacles suitable for your pony, with a maximum height of 3 feet 3 inches.

Here are some new types of cross-country fences:

Banks   Jumping a bank requires you to jump up, then jump down. It is best to begin with a bank that is wide enough for you to jump up, take one or more strides, then jump down. Shorter banks, with only enough room to jump on, then off, are more difficult. Approach a bank with plenty of impulsion, but not too fast. You do not want your pony to jump too far and make the jump down difficult, or to try to clear the whole bank! Look up and ahead and keep your legs on so that he keeps going forward. Keep your balance in the middle, your eyes up, and sit up as he jumps down.

Steps   Steps are a series of banks, to be jumped up or down. You must keep going in rhythm, as a pony may lose impulsion when jumping up. When going down, find a central balance and keep your weight back, over your legs, and your eyes up.

One-Stride Bank

Jumping Down Steps

Drop Fences   Jumping a drop fence is like jumping down off a bank, except that you must jump the fence as well. This makes the landing steeper and the drop greater than those you experience when jumping off a bank.

Riding a drop fence is much like jumping off a bank, except that you must fold forward on takeoff as you would over a vertical fence. Use a short release and bridge your reins. As your horse begins to descend, open your hip angle and stay vertical to the ground, over your legs. Be careful not to get too far forward, which can pitch you forward on landing, but don't sit back so far or so hard that you drop your pony's hind legs down into the fence or hit his back as you land. You may have to relax your fingers and let your reins slip if your pony needs more rein as you land.

Riding a Drop Jump

Downhill Jumps   You have already practiced riding downhill approaches and small downhill jumps. Larger downhill jumps are ridden the same way, much like drop jumps. Good balance during the approach is most important. Be sure that your pony goes forward straight, in good balance, with his hocks well under him. Downhill sloping ground makes a jump lower, but the landing will be longer and steeper. Ride a downhill jump as you would a drop jump, staying back in a central balance, over your legs, and be ready to rebalance immediately on landing, especially if the downhill slope continues after the jump.

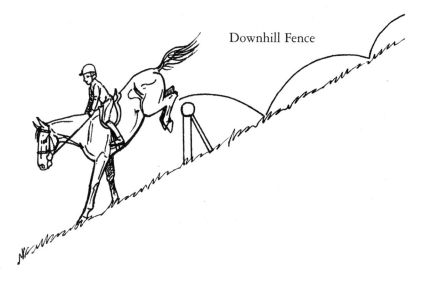

Downhill Fence

Uphill Jumps   Jumping an uphill jump is like jumping up a bank but is more demanding. The uphill sloping ground makes the jump bigger and may encourage your pony to take off too far away. Keep your pony in a lively, well-balanced canter, well in front of your legs. Never let him gallop uphill leaning on his forehand, with long, sprawling strides. Otherwise he could arrive at an uphill jump dangerously out of balance and without the power necessary to clear it.

When your pony takes off, you must stay well forward in order to free his back, loins, and hind legs, and let him use his head and neck freely. If you sit down or get left behind, he could drop his hind legs into the fence. Holding the mane or a neckstrap is a good precaution to be sure that you don't interfere with his mouth.

JUMPING UPHILL

A. An uphill approach must be ridden in a short, bouncy canter.

B. Wrong: Horse on the forehand, with long, flat strides; rider too far forward; takeoff too early.

Fences With Ditches and Water   Your pony has already learned to jump open ditches, but he must also learn how to jump an open ditch or water ditch that is part of a fence. Most horses are suspicious of holes in the ground, so you must ride positively, use your legs firmly, and look beyond the jump. If you look down into the ditch or drop contact, your pony may stop.

When the ditch is on the takeoff side, it acts as a ground line and encourages a horse to stand back and jump in good style.

A "trakehner" is a rail over a ditch or angled across a ditch. It is ridden as a jump with the ditch on the takeoff side.

When the ditch is on the landing side, your pony may not see it until the last moment. You must ride this jump strongly so that the pace and the thrust of the jump carry you well out over the ditch.

FENCES WITH DITCHES

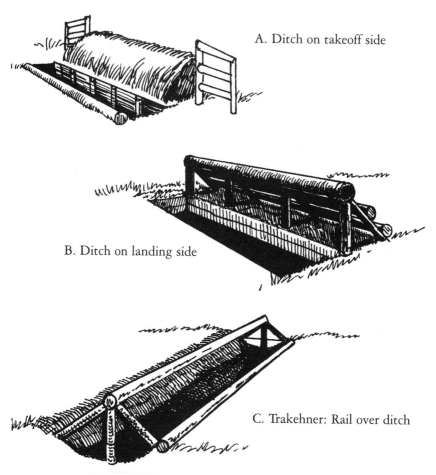

A. Ditch on takeoff side

B. Ditch on landing side

C. Trakehner: Rail over ditch

Coffin Jumps   A coffin jump is a combination of obstacles: a fence, followed by a ditch, then another fence. A more difficult type has a fence, a downhill slope to a ditch, then an uphill slope to the second fence. The distance from fence to ditch and from ditch to second fence may be a bounce or one or two strides.

To learn to jump coffin jumps, begin with a small fence or log two strides from a simple open ditch. Jump this in both directions—first the ditch and then the log, and vice versa. When your pony does this well, add another small log or fence and jump it as a triple.

When jumping a coffin, it's important to approach in good balance and rhythm, with your pony well in front of your legs. Stay in balance over your legs and let him rock you as he jumps, strides,

Coffin Jump

jumps, strides, and jumps again, just as when riding a gymnastic. Keep your eyes up and your legs on his sides, and don't drop contact with his mouth.

Combinations You may have to jump a combination of two or three fences placed less than three strides apart. The distance may require two strides, one stride, or a bounce. In competition, the elements of a combination are numbered A, B, and C. If your pony should refuse at the second or third element, you must go back and re-jump the whole combination.

You must be clear about the line you ride through a combination and about the exact spot in which you will jump each element. Drifting sideways or making an inaccurate approach may lead to a runout, or may change the distance enough to make it difficult to jump the second element safely.

When jumping combinations, you must jump the first element going forward in good balance and rhythm. If you meet the first element right and keep your rhythm, it helps you meet the next element right, too. Cross-country combination fences are usually set at slightly longer distances than those in stadium jumping, to allow for the longer strides your pony takes at a cross-country galloping pace.

Option Fences An option fence is an obstacle or combination of obstacles that can be jumped in more than one way. There is a difficult way, usually the fastest and most direct line, but with larger or more difficult fences, and an easier way, which often has more turns and a more complicated line, and takes longer, but may have lower or simpler fences. You must decide how to ride this obstacle while walking the course. When deciding which option to take, keep in mind your pony's abilities, experience, and length of stride, and which option would be easiest for him to jump well.

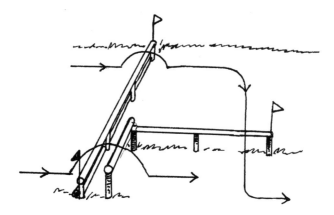

Option Fence with Short and Long Routes

Disobediences

Disobediences (refusals or runouts) must be handled correctly. First, stay in control. If your pony runs out, stop him as soon as possible and turn back toward the fence, *away* from the direction in which he ran out. In case of a refusal, you may correct your pony briefly in front of the fence with your legs, a cluck, and a tap of your stick, but you *must not* block the fence if others are waiting to jump. Move out of the way of any oncoming horse *immediately*; then try again when the fence is clear. If your pony is reluctant to jump a particular fence, it may help to follow another horse over it at a safe distance (at least six horse lengths).

Reasons for Disobediences

When a disobedience (a refusal or a runout) happens, you must discover the reason and correct the problem before asking the horse to jump again. Here are some common causes of disobediences:

Rider Problems:

- Getting left behind and catching the pony in the mouth
- Getting ahead of the motion and dropping the pony, or looking down
- Poor turn, crooked or disorganized approach
- Poor judgment: restricting a keen pony too much, or sitting passively on a pony that needs to be ridden positively
- Lack of nerve or determination (ponies can tell!)

Jumping Problems:

- Slippery ground
- Wrong takeoff distance
- Poor balance or lack of impulsion during approach
- Difficulty in seeing or judging the jump, especially when jumping from light into shadow

Fear, caused by:

- Unfamiliar or spooky-looking jump, or distractions
- Overfacing a pony (asking him to jump fences too big or too difficult for his stage of training)
- Bad experiences, such as a fall, hitting a fence, or a scare
- Pain or bad riding in the past, causing loss of confidence

Pain from:

- Lameness or sore back
- Improperly fitted saddle (pinching withers or jabbing shoulders during or after jumping)
- Too severe a bit or rough hands
- Bad riding, especially getting left behind or catching pony in the mouth

Cross-Country Courses

You may ride a cross-country course as part of a horse trial, combined-training event, or Pony Club rally, or just to learn and have fun. To ride a course, you and your pony must be fit and able to jump all the fences on the course, and to ride safely at an appropriate pace. The fences must be suitable for you and your pony—not just the height but also the degree of difficulty. In competition, you are not allowed to practice over any of the fences. At home, for practice, you should school your pony over each fence individually before you ride them all as a course.

Caution: Before you think about entering a horse trial, combined-training event, or Pony Club rally, you will need extra instruction and coaching to help you and your pony get ready to compete safely. This is not the kind of competition to enter "just for the experience"!

Riding a cross-country course demands more fitness and different riding skills than stadium jumping. You must be able to handle the galloping pace, the differences in terrain and footing, jumping into and out of shade, riding up and down hill, and different cross-country obstacles. You *must* be able to ride and jump with control at a safe pace, because galloping and jumping in the open can make some ponies very excitable, especially if they are allowed to go too fast. A cross-country course is much longer than a stadium-jumping course (usually more than a mile, with fifteen or more fences), so you must be fit, strong, and able to think and stay in control for a longer and more demanding ride. Your pony must also be fit enough to handle the pace and the length of the course as well as the jumps.

Walking the Course and Developing a Riding Plan

Before you ride a cross-country course, you must walk it at least twice and develop a riding plan. The official meeting and course walk gives you the official information about the course and a general idea of the layout of the course.

Pony clubbers walk a cross-country course. *Photo: Susan Sexton*

Always walk the course a second time, preferably with your instructor. Many good competitors like to walk it a third time, just to be sure. Plan your ride from start to finish, deciding what pace you will ride over each part and noting difficult terrain or places where you must slow down. Plan to save ground wherever you can, but be sure to stay on course. You must know exactly where the course starts and finishes, and the location of any flags that mark turns in the course.

Decide the exact pace, line, and angle at which you will jump each fence. Look for landmarks to keep you on the line you have chosen. Take note of anything that could make a fence more difficult, such as a slippery spot, places where you must jump from sunlight into shadow, or anything that might look spooky to your pony. Remind yourself about jumps that need extra balance, such as drop fences and downhill fences. For combinations or option fences, walk through all possible options and decide on the best way to ride the obstacle. However, once on course, circumstances may change so that you must change your plan. (For instance, if the ground is cut up or very slippery, you may have to jump a fence at a different spot.) Keep in mind the time of day you will ride and the position of the sun. This can create shadows that make the fences look different, and can change the way you ride them.

Tips on Riding a Cross-Country Course

- Your pony must be properly warmed up before jumping cross-country. Check your girth, stirrups, rein length, and chin strap before you start.
- Always ride strongly and positively to the first fence. Because it is going away from home, your pony may not want to jump.
- Keep a steady pace that allows your pony to move freely forward in good balance but under control. Slow down in plenty of time for downhill slopes or difficult ground, and don't race wildly up hills or on level ground.
- About 8 to 10 strides from each fence, steady your pony and be sure he is balanced and paying attention to your aids. It is better to come into a fence a bit slowly, increasing your stride as you get closer, than to gallop in too fast and have to check sharply.
- To keep your pony balanced and maintain a lively, steady canter during the approach, imagine that you are riding a gymnastic during the last few strides before each fence.
- Keep contact with your pony's mouth and keep him in front of your legs, but wait for the fence to come to you—don't anticipate and rush to get there.

- You make better time riding accurate lines and saving ground than by galloping fast and wide.
- Pay attention to your pony's rhythm, balance, and energy. If he feels tired, slow down and help him balance, especially on hills. Never risk hurting your pony by going faster or farther than he is fit to go.
- As you get tired toward the end of the course, stay in balance and don't lean on your pony's neck or let your seat bump down into the saddle. When you cross the finish line, slow down gradually. Ask for official permission to dismount. If you dismount before receiving permission, you could be eliminated.

It is very important to take care of your pony properly immediately after you finish a cross-country course, and later on. See Chapter 7 for more information on cooling out and caring for your pony after hard work.

CHAPTER 4

HORSE CARE AND MANAGEMENT

Horse management is the organized routine of caring for horses and ponies. Good management requires attention to detail, day by day, to ensure the safety, comfort, care, and health of the animal.

At the C Level, you are expected to be more responsible for your pony's daily care and to learn more about horse management. This involves more than just doing daily chores. It means looking at the big picture and planning ahead, learning what you need to take care of a horse, finding out how much it costs, and making intelligent choices. You will need to develop a system of account-keeping and to keep good records so that you know how you are spending your money and how to plan for the future. Good management means planning for your pony's needs (feed, veterinary care, deworming, shoeing) and maintaining your stable, pasture, tack, and equipment in good condition.

Schedules for each week, month, and year help you learn to budget your time and money. Use your record book to record deworming, inoculations, feeding and conditioning schedules, and veterinary and farrier work.

Plan to stick to a daily routine. Horses have a very good sense of time, and upsetting their routine can stress them. It's important to make up a schedule that you can keep, considering school and other responsibilities, and to be sure that it includes feeding your pony at least twice a day (three times is better).

Here is a sample schedule:

Early morning: (about 30 minutes)	Feed, water, check pony over, clean stall. Turn out for the day (or make pony comfortable if he stays in).
Noon (if possible):	Give hay to pony (if needed); check water. (This takes only a few minutes and could be done by someone else.)
Afternoon: (about 1 1/2 hours)	Groom and ride for an hour; cool pony out; wipe off tack. Feed and water.
Evening: (about 15 minutes)	Do a late-night check, water, give hay.

Some Pony Clubbers go to school later and can ride early in the morning. Some can only afford the time to ride three times per week and on weekends, for a total of five times a week. This is enough for most Pony Club activities, shows, and lower-level events. Pony Clubbers with this schedule must take time on weekends to do those things they couldn't do during the week.

During the summer or vacation times, you can spend more time with your pony. You may ride six days a week (but your pony should have at least one day off per week as a mental and physical break), and you may clean your tack every day or several times a week. Remember to set aside some time every week (perhaps on your pony's day off) for reading and studying Pony Club materials and books on the recommended reading list.

Care of a Stabled Pony

Facilities   A stabled pony should have a box stall that is big enough for him to turn around in and lie down in comfortably. (A good size is 12 feet by 12 feet for a horse or 10 feet by 10 feet for a pony.) The stall should have plenty of light and fresh air, be draft free, and have a window through which the pony can look outside. Feed tubs and water buckets should hang at about the height of the pony's chest, and there should be a salt block in the stall. Hay may be fed in a hay feeder or on the floor. The stall must be free of sharp objects and anything that could hurt a pony, as well as gaps that could trap his head or a hoof. Make sure that the pony cannot reach electrical wires and chew on them, and that the stall door fastens securely and cannot be opened by a pony.

A Well-Set-Up Stall

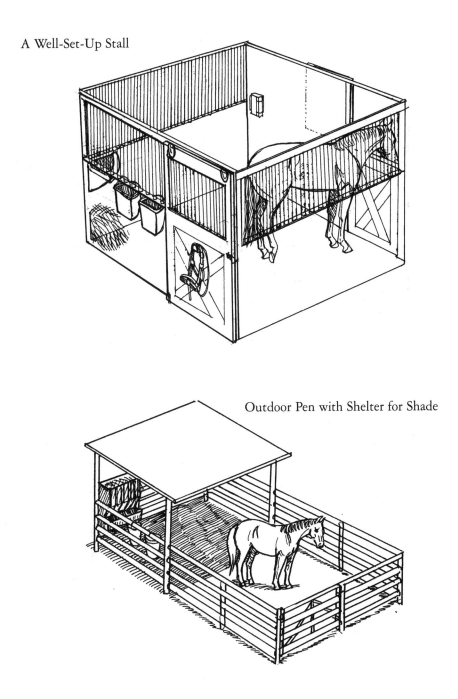

Outdoor Pen with Shelter for Shade

In some parts of the country, outdoor pens may be used instead of stalls. These are usually made of metal pipe fencing and are the size of a box stall or larger. There should be a roof over one section to provide shade.

Daily Care   A stabled pony must be fed at least twice a day (three times is better). His stall must be cleaned every day, and he should be groomed and have his feet cleaned daily, even if he is not ridden. If he is blanketed, his blankets must be kept clean, smooth, and comfortable. If possible, he should be checked late at night to be sure he has water and hay and is comfortable.

A stabled pony *must* have exercise every day, even if you cannot ride him. Turnout in a paddock for at least an hour a day is important for his health and mental attitude; he needs to play as well as exercise. To keep him fit for riding, he will need regular work.

Clean water must be available at all times, except when the pony is hot and sweaty. His bucket should be cleaned every day and filled up whenever it gets low. If he drinks a lot, he should have two buckets. Be sure that he has a full bucket before he is left for the day or the night. If you use an automatic watering system, you must keep it clean and be sure that it is working properly.

A horse or pony needs to eat small amounts frequently, never a big meal all at once. A stabled pony should be given hay at least twice a day (three times is better). Grain is usually fed early in the morning and in the evening. It is better to give three smaller feeds (an extra feed at lunch or late at night) than two large ones.

A stabled pony should have free access to salt, either a salt block or loose salt fed in a special salt feeder. You can feed him loose salt (about 30 to 60 grams, or 1 to 2 ounces daily) with his grain, but it is harder to be sure that your pony is getting as much salt as he needs.

Bedding and Manure Management   Bedding is used to keep a pony's stall clean, dry, and cushioned enough for him to lie down in comfortably. It protects his legs and feet from the strain of standing on a hard surface.

There are two types of bedding: drainage beddings and absorbent beddings. A drainage bedding (such as straw) allows urine to drain to the bottom of the stall. It should only be used over stall floors with good drainage, such as clay or stone dust floors. An absorbent bedding (for example, sawdust) absorbs the moisture from urine and manure and can be used over any kind of stall floor.

The kind of bedding you use depends on cost, what's available in your area, and how you dispose of manure and used bedding. In some areas, straw is preferred because mushroom growers will take it away. If used bedding is composted or spread on fields, it should be a type that breaks down quickly and makes good fertilizer.

No matter which kind of bedding you use, you must clean your pony's stall thoroughly every day. If you also pick the stall out later in the day, it keeps it cleaner, saves bedding, and saves work.

Following is a list of the various kinds of bedding:

- *Straw* is a drainage bedding. It makes a dry, comfortable bed but requires careful management. Also, some ponies will eat straw (especially oat straw).
- *Shavings* can be bought in bags or by the truckload. An absorbent bedding, they make a comfortable bed and are not edible. Most types of wood shavings are suitable, but black walnut shavings must *never* be used for horse bedding, as they can cause laminitis. (Check with your supplier about this.)
- *Sawdust* usually comes by the truckload. It is an absorbent bedding that makes a comfortable bed if bedded deeply, but it may be dusty. Check it for pieces of wood that may cause injury, and be sure that no black walnut sawdust is included.
- *Shredded paper*, an absorbent bedding, comes in bales or bags. It is inexpensive but must be bedded deeply, and requires frequent picking out. Shredded paper can be composted or spread on cropland, but it tends to blow around, so it is harder to keep the stable area neat.
- *Rubber stall mats* provide a cushion for the pony's feet and legs and are helpful if the stall has a hard surface (such as concrete). They do not absorb urine, so an absorbent bedding such as sawdust or shavings must be used over them.
- *Sand or dirt* is used in outside pens. It is not warm but absorbs moisture well. One problem with sand is that ponies swallow some sand along with their feed when they eat from the ground. The sand gradually builds up in their intestines and leads to "sand colic." If your pony's stall, pen, or corral has a sandy surface, feed hay and grain in a feeder and keep all feed off the ground. Never use sand from the seashore for horse stalls; it is salty, so ponies may eat it and get colic.

Good horse care means using bedding intelligently, without wasting it or using too little. Throwing out too much good, useable bedding along with the soiled bedding wastes bedding and makes your manure pile bigger than necessary. If you use too little bedding, your pony will be uncomfortable and all the bedding will get soiled and wet, so you will have to replace it all every day. Use enough bedding for a thick, soft, dry bed for your pony. If you clean the stall carefully, separate and save good bedding, and pick up manure frequently, you save bedding and have less soiled material to dispose of.

Manure and soiled bedding attract flies, so the manure pile should be at a distance from the stable. Manure and soiled bedding can be composted and makes good garden soil after it breaks down, or you may arrange with a farmer or a manure removal company to have it hauled away. Manure can be spread on cropland but should not be spread in horse pastures, as this contaminates the pasture with internal parasites. A manure pile generates quite a lot of heat, so it must not be piled against a wooden building.

Grooming   A stabled pony should be groomed every day, whether he is ridden or not. This clears the extra grease and scurf from his coat, which is especially important for ponies that work hard and sweat a lot. It also stimulates his circulation, which helps keep his skin and muscles in good condition. Grooming spreads the skin oils over the hair coat, making the coat shine. Finally, daily grooming is important because it gives you a chance to check your pony over carefully for injuries or minor problems.

While a pony should always be cleaned before he is ridden, the best time to groom thoroughly is after exercise, when his skin is warm. You will have to groom your pony especially well before riding in a Pony Club rally or any special event; he may need a bath or other special preparations. Only good, thorough grooming every day will produce a clean, shining, and healthy coat.

Clipping   During cold weather, ponies grow a heavy winter coat with extra scurf and grease to protect them against cold and wet. When a long-haired pony works hard, his coat becomes wet with sweat. The sweat mixes with scurf and grease, forming a sticky white lather that makes it hard for him to cool down and takes a long time to dry. A long, wet coat is heavy and uncomfortable, and he can get chilled if he stands around in a wet coat in cold weather. If a pony is worked regularly and usually gets so sweaty that he takes too long to dry, body clipping may help him. Body clipping shortens the coat to a length a little shorter than a summer coat, making a pony easier to groom and cool out and more comfortable during hard work. However, he must wear a blanket to make up for the loss of his winter coat, and you will have to be careful not to let him get chilled.

There are several types of body clips:

1. *A strip clip* is a minimum clip, like unzipping your jacket. A strip is clipped along the underside of the neck and the front of the chest, and underneath the belly. The pony still has most of his winter coat and usually does not need a blanket except in the coldest weather.
2. *A trace clip* is a partial clip. The sides of the neck, shoulders, and belly are clipped about halfway up. This clips the parts that sweat the most, leaving long hair on the legs and body. A trace-clipped pony may or may not need a blanket, depending on how much hair has been clipped off and how cold the weather is.

TYPES OF BODY CLIPS

A. Strip clip   B. Trace clip

C. Hunter clip

3. *A hunter clip*, often used on field hunters, includes the body, neck, and head. Long hair is left to protect the legs (called "stockings") and in a "saddle patch" (shaped like a saddle). Blanketing is necessary.
4. *A full clip*, used on show horses, includes the body, head, and legs. Warm blankets and sometimes a hood are necessary.

Blankets   Blankets, sheets, and turnout rugs are used to provide extra warmth and protection from the cold. If you clip your pony, if he is old or sick, or if his winter coat is too thin to keep him warm, he may need a blanket. A pony that has become used to blanketing needs extra daily care and attention and is more vulnerable to chills if he is not blanketed properly. It is healthier for the pony and easier for you if you allow your pony to grow a natural winter coat and avoid blanketing him unless he needs it.

If your pony wears a blanket, you must pay attention to the temperature. If it gets hot, he may need a lighter blanket or none at all, and when it is cold, a warmer one. The blanket must be kept smooth and properly adjusted, or it may rub your pony or slip around under him. A blanketed pony may need to wear a turnout rug (a sturdy, water-repellent blanket with leg straps to keep it in place when the pony rolls) when he is turned outdoors.

Caution: For safety's sake, you must handle blankets, sheets, and turnout rugs properly when putting them on, taking them off, or straightening them. If you are careless, they can pinch a pony and make him kick or act up. When straightening blankets, undo the leg straps or surcingles and lift the blankets into place; don't just tug on them. Always halter a pony before putting on, taking off, or straightening blankets. If he is loose in the stall with no way for you to control him, you could get hurt.

How to put a blanket on:

1. Place the folded blanket over the pony's neck and withers.
2. Fasten the chest strap.
3. Pull the blanket back over the pony's hindquarters and make it straight.
4. Fasten the front and back surcingles, or the leg straps if they are used.
5. Check to be sure that the blanket is straight and even, that there is room at the shoulders, and that the surcingles are not twisted.

BLANKETING

1. Place folded blanket forward on neck.

2. Fasten chest straps.

3. Unfold blanket over back, then fasten surcingles. Make sure there is enough room at shoulders.

4. Run leg straps through each other to prevent rubbing inside hind legs.

How to take a blanket off:

1. Unfasten the back and front surcingles or leg straps first.
2. Unfasten the chest strap.
3. Fold the front part of the blanket back over the top of the back portion and slide the blanket off backwards.

Caution: Don't undo the chest strap before unfastening the back and front surcingles or leg straps. If the blanket should slip back with the front undone, it can pinch the pony's flanks and make him kick.

Care of a Pastured Pony

Living in a pasture (also called "at grass") is the most natural life for a pony, and most ponies thrive on it. A pastured pony exercises himself enough to keep healthy, though not enough for riding fitness. (To be riding fit, he will need regular work, the same as a stabled pony.) Because he is not restricted to a stall, a pastured pony is less likely to be too fresh when you ride him. It may take less labor and cost less to keep a pony on pasture, but you must visit him every day and make sure that he is safe, comfortable, well-fed, and watered.

Pastured ponies must be checked at least once a day, whether they are ridden or not. If you catch your pony every day to give him his grain or a tidbit, he will learn to be easy to catch. Check him over for cuts, injuries, illness, or lameness. In fly season, he may need fly repellent and a fly mask to keep flies off his face and eyes. In some parts of the country, you must check for ticks.

Pasture Safety   A pasture must be checked for safety before you put your pony in it and as long as you use it. Here are some things to check:

The fence must be safe, secure, and easy to see, with no loose wires or broken boards, and the gate must open freely and close securely. An electric fence must be working properly.

The pasture must be free from hazards such as nails, holes, trash, sharp objects, and machinery. Water tanks must not have sharp edges.

Check for poisonous plants. Ponies are more likely to eat poisonous plants when the grass is poor. You must know which plants to watch out for in your area and when they usually appear. (See page 167.)

A pasture must not have sharp corners or places where one pony could corner another. Hazards such as telephone pole guy wires should be fenced off.

If there are several ponies in a pasture, they must be used to each other. A new pony usually gets chased and picked on at first, and there may be biting and kicking until they all get used to each other and settle down. Be careful when turning new ponies out with others, and avoid changing companions.

Fencing   Fencing must be high (at least 3 feet, 6 inches), tight, and secure, to keep ponies from getting out. It must also be a safe kind of fencing that will not cause injuries. Fencing is much safer if it is easy for a pony to see, even when he is running.

Some fence materials are:

- *Wooden fencing (boards or rails)*: Good, safe, and easy to see, but expensive to build; ponies may chew it.
- *Plastic fencing (vinyl-covered boards, plastic rails, or plastic strips)*: Safe and easy to see; not chewable; expensive to install.
- *Metal pipe fencing (welded pipe)*: Expensive to install but safe, nonchewable, and long lasting.
- *Woven wire (horse fence)*: Safe fencing, best used with a board along the top to keep ponies from leaning over the fence and bending it down. Hog fence or livestock fence, which has larger squares, is not recommended because a pony can put his foot through the squares and get hurt.
- *Electric (smooth) wire*: Sometimes used for pastures but is less secure than other kinds of fencing. It is also used with other fencing to keep ponies from leaning over or chewing on the fence. Requires an electric fence charger, which must be correctly installed and properly grounded. Fence must be checked daily to be sure it is operating properly. Ponies must be trained to respect electric fences.
- *Barbed wire*: Sometimes used for large pastures but can cause serious injuries, especially if a pony gets caught in loose wire. Must be strung tightly, with the bottom strand 2 feet from the ground, to discourage ponies from pawing over it. Not suitable for small pastures and paddocks; avoid using it if possible.

There are other types of fencing, including new high-tech materials and designs. Any type of fencing must be smooth, safe, easily visible, and properly installed.

Gates must open wide so that you can take a pony through safely, and they must close securely. Don't use a diagonal supporting wire on a gate; a pony can get his head caught between the gate and the wire.

Fence posts must be set deep and solid because ponies may lean against the fence. Metal fence posts can be a hazard, as they have sharp points and can injure a pony severely if he tries to jump over one. Board fences are safer if boards are placed on the inside of the posts, as the boards are less likely to come off if a pony leans against one.

Shelter   A pony must have shelter from wind, rain, and sun. This can be a building such as a "run-in shed" (a three-sided shelter), a stall, or part of a barn that is open to the pony. It also could be a natural shelter such as a stand of trees, or a windbreak such as a large hedge.

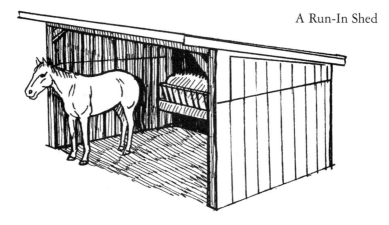

A Run-In Shed

There must be enough shelter for all the ponies in a field. If the shelter is too small or the doorway is too narrow, one pony may keep all the others out, and ponies may get kicked or hurt crowding through the doorway.

Sheds must be cleaned regularly.

Water   There must be a constant supply of clean water. This should be a running stream or a stock tank, not a stagnant pond. You must check the water supply every day, and stock tanks should be cleaned out weekly. It's especially important to check the water supply in hot weather, when it may dry up, and in winter, when you may have to break ice so that the pony can drink. A pony cannot get enough moisture to stay alive from eating snow, so keeping the water unfrozen is vital.

Minerals   Salt should be available free-choice, in a pasture-sized salt block, or in a salt feeder containing loose salt.

Supplementary Feeding   Whenever your pony cannot get enough feed to meet his nutritional needs by eating pasture grass, he will need supplementary feedings of grain, hay, or both.

If your pasture lacks good, nutritious grass (because it is small, weedy, overgrazed, drought-stricken, or snow-covered), you must provide hay. This can be fed in a hay feeder or on the ground, but if fed on the ground, some hay will be wasted and the pony may pick up sand or parasite eggs along with the hay. Ponies in a group may fight and chase each other away from the hay, so it should be placed in several piles at least 30 feet apart, away from gates, corners, fences, or places where one pony could corner another. Put out one or two extra piles so that each pony can get his share of hay even if he is chased away.

A pastured pony may need grain if he is ridden regularly and needs more energy for work, or if he needs to put on weight. If more than one pony is in the pasture, they should be tied up or brought into the barn and fed individually. Feeding grain to a group of loose ponies will cause fighting, and the more timid ponies will not get their share.

TOXIC PLANTS

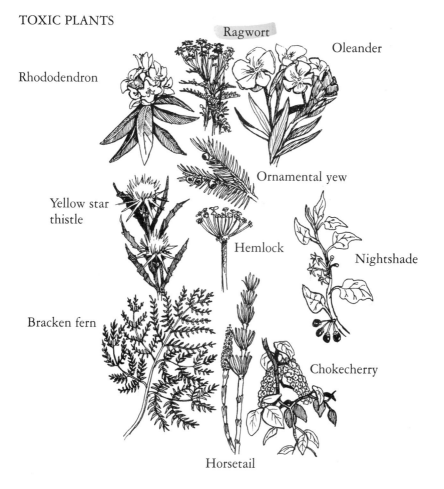

Rhododendron

Ragwort

Oleander

Yellow star thistle

Ornamental yew

Hemlock

Nightshade

Bracken fern

Chokecherry

Horsetail

TOXIC PLANTS

PLANT	WHERE FOUND	CHARACTERISTICS AND SYMPTOMS
Ornamental Yew Evergreen (red berries)	Northeast, Midwest	Landscaping shrub. Very toxic; even a mouthful can be fatal. Don't let pony nibble shrubs or eat clippings. *Symptoms:* Trembling, labored breathing, collapse.
Oleander (red and white flowers)	West coast, elsewhere	Ornamental house and garden plant. All parts of plant are very toxic: 4 ounces can be fatal. Plant clippings especially dangerous as they are sweet. *Symptoms:* Severe diarrhea, abnormal heartbeat.
Rhododendron (Mountain Laurel)	all over	Ornamental shrub. Leaves are most toxic. *Symptoms:* Depression, difficult breathing, collapse, and coma.
Ragwort Tansy Ragwort Groundsel Senecio	From Plains States to Southwest, Pacific Northwest	May be eaten in pasture when grass is poor; eating 20 lbs. at once or smaller amounts (per day) over several days or weeks causes liver damage. *Symptoms:* Yellow mucus membranes, liver failure, depression, lack of coordination.
Poison Hemlock	all over	Grows in low, wet areas. Roots harmless in spring but toxic rest of year. *Symptoms:* Loss of muscle strength, especially in hind legs; tremors, coma.
Horsetail	From Midwest to Pacific Northwest and Southwest	Grows in wet marshy or meadow areas. Poisoning occurs only when eaten in hay. Eating hay containing horsetail for 30 to 60 days causes thiamine deficiency. *Symptoms:* Lack of appetite, loss of coordination.

Plant	Region	Description
Chokecherry Wild Black Cherry	Southeast, Northeast, Midwest, and upper Midwest	Grows in fence rows and hedges. Especially dangerous when leaves are wilted (broken branches or after frost). Wilting releases cyanide and makes them sweet. 10 to 20 lbs. can be rapidly fatal. *Symptoms*: Heavy breathing, agitation, weakness, rapid death.
Black Nightshade Horse Nettle	all over	Vine with purple flowers, green and red berries; grows in fence rows, hedges, and pastures. Leaves are most toxic from early summer through late fall. Small amount (1 to 10 lbs.) can be fatal. *Symptoms*: Colic, lack of coordination, weakness, depression.
Yellow Star Thistle Russian Knapweed	California, Rocky Mountains, Plains States	Horse must eat large amount (50% to 100% of body weight, or 400–600 lbs.) before showing symptoms but by then damage is beyond help. Plant tastes good, so horses will continue to eat it. Poisoning makes horse unable to chew or swallow. *Symptoms*: Inability to chew or swallow.
Bracken Fern	Northeast, Pacific Northwest, upper Midwest	Fern found in wooded areas. Usually eaten in fall when pasture is poor. Horse must eat large amounts over 30–60 days before symptoms appear. Causes inability to use thiamine. *Symptoms*: Loss of appetite, loss of coordination; horse may stand with legs braced.
Frosted grass (especially clover, alfafa) lawn clippings	all over	Not a toxic plant, but can cause serious and even fatal problems for pastured horses. When first killed by frost, grass ferments. If eaten at this stage, it produces a lot of gas and can cause colic. Lawn clippings ferment after being cut and have the same effect. *Prevention*: Restrict horses from pasture right after first hard frost. Never feed lawn clippings. Once grass has dried, it is no longer a problem.

It's important to pay close attention to your pony's condition while at pasture, especially during the winter. A long coat may hide weight loss, which you may not notice if you do not check him carefully. You must also notice the condition of the pasture. If you see that it is becoming overgrazed (the grass is being eaten short in patches), start providing supplementary hay before your pony loses condition.

Toxic (Poisonous) Plants   There are certain toxic (poisonous) plants that grow in different parts of the country. Ponies are more likely to eat poisonous plants when the grass is poor, but some are attractive to ponies at any time. Different plants grow at different times of the year, so you must learn to recognize toxic plants and check your pasture regularly. Ask your local Cooperative Extension Service or your county agent about which ones to watch out for in your area. See illustrations and chart, pages 167–169.

Grooming   A pasture-kept pony does not need as much grooming as a stabled pony. He must be checked every day for injuries and for ticks, his hooves should be picked out, and fly repellent should be applied if needed. He should be curried and brushed clean before being ridden. It is normal for an outdoor pony to have more dust and grease in his coat than a stabled pony.

Pasture Management   A pasture is only as good as the grass it produces. To have good grass, a pasture needs good soil, the right plants, and good growing conditions. Cold weather, drought, flooding, too much horse traffic, and overgrazing can make it impossible to grow good grass. If a pasture doesn't grow good grass, it may need fertilizer, lime, or reseeding. Your county agricultural agent or Cooperative Extension Department can give you information about soil testing and pasture management in your area.

As horses use a pasture, they gradually change it (especially if it is small or has many horses). When the ground is soft, it gets torn up by horses' hooves, especially near sheds, water tanks, gates, and fences. Damage from hooves and overgrazing destroys the grass and can cause erosion. Horses prefer short, tender grass and will graze some areas until the grass is almost gone. They will not eat near where they have dropped manure, and usually use certain areas for this, which grow long, coarse grass and weeds. A pasture gradually becomes contaminated with parasite eggs, which are passed out in manure, so horses will become infested with worms. If you don't take care of a pasture, it will deteriorate.

The best thing you can do for a pasture is to give it a rest from horse grazing from time to time, to let the grass grow back. If possible, divide your pasture and paddock areas into smaller sections so that your pony can use one area while the other grows back. Large pastures can benefit by being used for cattle or sheep part of the year, as they eat different plants and do not carry the same kinds of internal parasites as horses. Rotating pastures "cleans" the pasture by breaking the life cycle of the horse parasites.

In some parts of the country, pastures grow better grass if they are mowed to keep the weeds down and the grass short and tender. In other places, the grass is sparse and easily uprooted; mowing would ruin the pasture. Your county agent or Cooperative Extension Service can tell you what pasture maintenance is best for your area.

If you have a small pasture or paddock, picking up manure every few days will greatly reduce the number of parasites your pony is exposed to, and will help preserve the grass.

Parasite and Fly Control

External Parasites   External parasites are those on the outside of the horse.

Lice sometimes are found on horses with long coats, usually when kept outdoors, especially if they are dirty and in poor condition. Lice can be controlled by applying medicated powder (ask your veterinarian).

Ticks are a problem in some parts of the country. They fasten themselves to the horse's skin and suck blood. Ticks irritate the skin and can cause running sores or infections; they can also carry dangerous diseases.

In tick-infested areas, you should check your pony every day for ticks, especially at the end of his dock. Yellow crusts show where a tick has been. If you find a tick still attached, pull it out with tweezers or use a special tick remover. Be careful to get all parts of the tick, including the head, not just the body. Drop the tick in a container of alcohol to kill it. Because ticks can carry human diseases, you should wear gloves and wash your hands after removing them.

Fly Control   Flies bother horses, bite and suck blood, and carry diseases. House flies and horseflies breed in manure, garbage, wet hay, and spilled feed, so keeping your stable area clean means fewer flies. You also can use fly traps, especially near the manure pile. Deerflies, greenhead flies, blackflies, and mosquitos breed in water, so these are more common where there are swamps, streams, or ponds nearby.

During fly season, your pony may need fly repellent (sprayed or wiped on). Before using it, you should test it first on a small area of your pony's skin to be sure that it doesn't irritate him. There are special fly repellents that are safe to use close to the eyes and ears, or you can use a fly mask to keep flies off your pony's face. When flies are very bad, horses need to be in the shade. It may help to keep your pony in during the day and turn him out at night.

Safety in and around the Stable

Nothing is more important than safety in and around the stable area. Nobody wants to get hurt or have a horse get hurt. Remember that horses are easily scared, even by things that don't bother people, and when a horse is upset, he may try to get away or may kick to defend himself.

To make your stable area safer, do your own safety check. Ask your parents and an experienced horseperson (such as your Pony Club D.C. or your instructor) to go through your stable area with you. Look around and ask yourself, "If I were a horse, what could I get hurt on here? How could a person get hurt?" Write down any safety problems you find, including anything that has caused an injury or a "near miss" in the past.

Once you have identified a hazard (a safety problem), you must decide how to deal with it. Some simple hazards can be taken care of immediately, such as removing a nail that is sticking out or picking up baling wire before someone trips on it. Other hazards may require repairs or improvements that may take some time, planning, and expense—for instance, replacing old electrical wiring or putting up a fence between your stable area and a busy road. Some hazards may have to be handled temporarily (or even permanently) by making a safety rule and seeing that it is *always* followed. For example, you may need to make a rule about keeping the dog tied up when you are riding, or always keeping a certain gate closed.

Most accidents happen through carelessness. People get careless when they are disorganized or in a hurry, and especially when they begin to think, "Nothing could ever happen to me," or "My pony would never cause an accident," or "I've always done it like that and nobody's been hurt yet." Too often, when an accident happens, everyone knows what was done wrong. Unfortunately, it is too late then to do it right and prevent the accident! If you are careless about safety, even if you don't have an accident yourself, other people (especially younger or less experienced Pony Clubbers) will follow your example and may get into trouble.

Safety requires the following:

- *Knowledge*: Knowing what can cause accidents, and the safe way to do things.
- *Planning*: Thinking ahead, making safety rules to prevent accidents, and being prepared for emergencies.
- *Responsibility*: Thinking of others (people and horses) and doing things the right (safe) way *every time*.

First-aid training, which is available through your local Red Cross, can help you avoid accidents and teach you what to do and what *not* to do in case of an accident. You should have human and equine first-aid kits in your stable and in your trailer, but you must know how to use them properly. (For more about first aid for horses, see Chapter 6, pages 227–232.)

Stable Safety Rules and Practices

- A neat stable area is a safer stable area. Keep trash picked up, tools hung up (sharp ends facing into the wall), and equipment such as wheelbarrows stored out of the way.
- Check stalls and aisles for nails or other objects sticking out where a pony (or a person) could bump into them and be hurt.
- When leading, grooming, or working with a horse, always handle him with a halter and lead rope. Never lead with just your hand on the halter.
- When handling a horse, keep your attention on him and keep his attention on you. Be aware of things that could spook him or that he could bump into or get hurt on, and keep a safe distance from other horses.
- No running, yelling, or rough play around the stable area; it upsets horses and can cause accidents.
- Keep other pets under control and out from underfoot. If a dog is tied on a long rope, it can wrap around a horse's legs and cause an accident. Teach your dog not to chase horses, or keep him away from the stable area.
- When leading a horse through a gate, into or out of a stall, open the gate wide and be sure the latch is not sticking out where it could catch him. If a gate closes on a horse or a gate latch catches on his blanket or tack, it may hurt or scare him.
- When turning a horse loose in a stall or pasture, close the gate and make him turn to face you before you let him go.

- The halter should usually be removed when your pony is left in a stall or in a pasture, with the halter and lead rope hung up close by. If a halter is left on in a stall or pasture, it must be of breakable leather or a safety halter with a breakaway crownpiece that would free him if he should get caught on something.

- Tie safely! (See *USPC D Manual*, pages 141–144, for more about safe tying.)

   Never tie or cross-tie to the bit or bridle—only to a halter.

   Tie with a quick-release knot, and use safety strings that will break in an emergency. Cross-ties should be equipped with safety strings.

   Tie in a safe place (not where the horse could catch his leg in a fence), to a solid, immovable object, at the height of the horse's back. When tying to a fence, tie to a solid post, not to a rail.

   Tie with about 18 inches from knot to halter. Don't leave so much slack that the horse could get his leg caught over the rope.

   Don't tie a horse at all unless you know he stands quietly while tied.

   Don't leave a horse unattended when tied or cross-tied.

Barn safety hazards: How many things can you find wrong?

Fire Prevention   Fire is the most serious danger around a stable. Stable areas are full of materials such as hay and bedding that catch fire easily and burn very fast. Everyone around a stable must take fire prevention seriously and must know what to do in case of fire. Post the fire department phone number in the barn and next to the telephone. It's important to work out emergency procedures (what you would do in case of a fire) and to have a fire drill.

Here are some basic rules for fire prevention:

- NO SMOKING in or around the stable area—by anyone, ever!
- Have adequate fire extinguishers (at least one inside and one outside the barn), know how to use them, check them regularly, and make sure they are properly charged. Have a faucet and hose outside the barn as well as inside.
- Keep aisles clear and doors free to open in case of an emergency. In winter, do not let snow or ice build up so that doors cannot be opened. Keep a halter and lead rope hanging on every stall.
- Keep aisles swept, trash picked up, and beams and rafters free from cobwebs. Don't leave piles of loose hay or bedding around.
- Cut down brush and weeds around the barn.
- Unplug electrical appliances when they are not being used and before leaving the stable. Avoid using hotplates or heaters in the stable.
- If possible, store hay in a building separate from the stable.
- Keep manure piles away from wooden buildings; they generate heat. Hay can cause a fire if it is baled or stored damp and packed too tightly.
- Never store gasoline, kerosene, flammable liquids such as paints and thinners, or oily rags in the barn. Do not park motor vehicles like tractors or lawnmowers in the barn.
- Have the barn wiring checked by an electrician to be sure it is safe and meets local fire laws. Wiring must be protected against being chewed by horses or by rats. Lightbulbs should be enclosed in explosion-proof glass cages. Never overload electrical circuits.

In case of fire:

1. First, sound the alarm. Get people out first!
2. Call the fire department (see "Reporting an Emergency").

3. Evacuate the horses only if you can do so safely.
4. Fight the fire (using fire extinguishers or hoses) only if you can do so safely.

Reporting an Emergency   It is EXTREMELY IMPORTANT to know how to report an emergency (such as a fire or a serious accident to a person or a horse). Thinking clearly and doing the right things promptly could save a life. If you have planned ahead, you will know what to do, which helps a lot.

To report an emergency, you must know where the telephone is and whom to call. Post important emergency phone numbers next to the telephone: 911, or numbers for your local fire department, ambulance, and police department, and also numbers for the veterinarian and an adult who could help in an emergency.

When reporting an emergency, always tell the person who answers *where you are* (the address), *what the trouble is* (a fire, an injured person, a pony with colic), and *what kind of help you need* (fire department, an ambulance, a veterinarian, etc.). Be prepared to give directions to your location, and *do not hang up until the other person does*, as they may need to ask important questions.

Grooming

You already know how to groom a horse or pony thoroughly, and why it is important for his health and condition. Nothing takes the place of good daily grooming, especially for conditioning the skin and hair coat. Some special grooming tasks are necessary for your pony's health and comfort, or for improving his appearance for special occasions. You can find more information on special grooming procedures (including step-by-step instructions) in *Grooming to Win* by Susan Harris, or in the other books listed in Appendix B.

Removing Bot Eggs   Bot eggs are tiny yellow eggs laid by the botfly on the hair of the pony's legs, shoulders, and mane. You should remove them in daily grooming, because every bot egg you remove is one less internal parasite to end up in your pony.

To remove bot eggs, lubricate them with a dab of shampoo and scrape them off with a piece of sandpaper, a styrofoam bot block, or a special bot knife.

Bathing a Pony   Bathing is no substitute for good daily grooming, as shampoo removes some of the natural skin oils that make the coat shine. A bath, however, may be necessary to get a pony really clean for a special occasion, especially if he is light colored. (For step by step instructions, see *Grooming to Win*.)

Removing Stains   Here are several ways to remove stains from white markings or a light-colored coat (groom thoroughly first):

- A cactus cloth, made from cactus fibers, helps to rub out stains and sweat marks and has natural oils that help make the coat shine.
- Shampoo the stained area. Apply stain-removing shampoo full-strength on the stain for five minutes, then rinse the spot thoroughly.
- Bonami scouring powder can be applied with a wet sponge to make a thick paste. Rub the paste into the stain and let it dry; then brush away the powder, and the stain will come out. (Only Bonami should be used, as it does not burn the skin).

Shampooing the Tail   A pony's tail should be shampooed if it gets muddy or dirty, or before a special event. The normal procedure is to wet down and shampoo the entire tail, paying special attention to the skin of the dock. In cold weather, wet only the hair below the dock.

For safety, always stand to the side when washing or rinsing the tail.

Coat Dressings   Silicone coat dressings bond to the hair, making it slippery and shiny. They help hair resist stains for several days and can be used on white markings to prevent staining. They can also be used on the tail hair, to make it easier to remove bedding, burrs, or tangles without breaking off hairs. Don't use coat dressing on the saddle area; it can make the saddle pad slip.

Don't rely on coat dressings instead of good daily grooming to create an artificially shiny coat. Judges and examiners can tell the difference! Coat dressings are discouraged in Pony Club rallies, rating tests, and inspections.

Hot-Towel Cleaning   Hot-towel cleaning can be used to clean the head and face, the roots of the mane, the rump, and other places that are especially dusty, greasy, or hard to clean. It is a good way to get a pony clean when it is too cold to give him a bath.

For hot-towel cleaning you will need rubber dishwashing gloves; a large bucket of very hot water with one-half teaspoon of shampoo added; and a large, light-colored towel. The water must be steaming hot—so hot that you need rubber gloves to dip your hands in it.

Dip one end of the towel in the hot water, and wring it out nearly dry. Rub the towel quickly over the skin in a side-to-side motion, and follow it by rubbing with the dry end of the towel. The dirt and scurf sticks to the towel instead of the hair, leaving a dirty handprint on the towel. Shift to a clean area of the towel and continue. When the towel is dirty or begins to get cold, rinse it and wring it out again.

Cleaning the Sheath or Udder   The sheath or udder should be cleaned regularly for the pony's comfort and health. A sticky substance called smegma collects in this area (in mares, between the folds of the udder, and in geldings and stallions, inside the sheath). A strong odor or streaks of smegma (a black, or reddish, sticky substance) on the insides of the hind legs or outside the sheath show that the pony needs cleaning. A buildup of smegma can make it uncomfortable for a gelding or stallion to urinate, and can lead to infection and a swollen sheath.

For Pony Club inspections, C-1s are expected to clean the area around the sheath or udder; C-2s' and C-3s' ponies must be clean inside as well as outside. (For step-by-step instructions on how to clean the sheath or udder, see *Grooming to Win*.)

Caution: Don't try to clean your pony's sheath or udder without help from an experienced horseperson. Most ponies do not mind this procedure, but some may try to kick.

Trimming the Head and Legs   Ponies grow long hair on their legs, ears, and faces for natural protection. For competition or special events, this hair may be trimmed to make the pony look neater and to make his head and legs look finer. This is usually done with electric clippers but can also be done with hand trimmers or with scissors and a comb.

Before you trim your pony, think about how he is kept and whether he needs his natural protection. If he lives outside, especially in cold weather, he should be trimmed very little or not at all. Never cut the long hairs near the eyes; these protect the pony from bumping his eyes against objects in the dark.

Different breeds have different trimming styles. You should know the style that is appropriate for your pony before you trim him or pull his mane. Trimming is not required for Pony Club inspections (as long as the pony is neat and tidy), and any trimming style appropriate for the pony's breed is allowed. Braiding is not allowed in most Pony Club activities and competitions. Check the rules for the activity or competition you are participating in.

Step-by-step instructions for trimming the legs, head, ears, and bridle path can be found in *Grooming to Win* and in the other sources listed in Appendix B.

TRIMMED PONY

- Head, ears, muzzle, and jaw trimmed
- Legs and fetlocks trimmed
- Short bridle path cut in mane
- Mane pulled
- Tail banged

Manes and Tails   The mane and tail provide important protection against flies, and warmth in the winter. During the winter, the skin of the mane and tail produces more dandruff and grease, which protects against cold and rain.

During grooming, you should carefully untangle the mane and tail, brush the skin clean, and check for ticks. To keep from breaking off and pulling out too many hairs, avoid using dandy brushes, currycombs, or metal combs on mane and tail hair. You can use a hairbrush, a body brush, or your fingers to carefully untangle the long hairs.

Pulling the mane is a way of shortening and thinning a long, thick mane in order to make it neater and easier to braid. The mane must always be shortened by pulling or thinning, *never* by cutting with scissors.

The manes of hunters, jumpers, event horses, and dressage horses and ponies are usually pulled to a short, even length (about 4 inches). The tail may be "banged off" (cut off square at the bottom, at the height of the fetlocks) or left natural. Before pulling or trimming your pony's mane or tail, know what style is appropriate for his breed. Any trimming style is acceptable in Pony Club, as long as the mane and tail are neat and clean.

For step-by-step instructions for pulling manes and trimming tails, see *Grooming to Win* or one of the books listed in Appendix B.

Tack

As a C Level Pony Clubber, you are expected to take extra good care of your tack. This requires good daily tack care, regular cleaning and conditioning, and checking your tack regularly for condition and any necessary repairs.

You are also expected to know the name of each piece of equipment you use (including type of bit) on the flat and over fences, and to be able to explain its proper adjustment, how it works, and why it is used on your pony. C Level Pony Clubbers must use a smooth snaffle bit for dressage; kimberwickes and pelhams are permitted for jumping and cross-country riding. Rough, twisted, or severe mouthpieces are not permitted in Pony Club activities, and no Pony Clubber will be permitted to ride with any bit or control device that is considered unsafe, inhumane, or detrimental to good riding and training. A running martingale is permitted for jumping and cross-country, but martingales are not allowed in dressage tests. Review the Tack chapter of the *USPC D Level Manual*, especially the section on bits and how they work. (More information on bits and bitting can be found in the *USPC B/A Manual*. Check the rules for any rally or competition you participate in, so that you know what is and is not permitted.

Make it a habit to check the fit and adjustment of each piece of tack before you mount. Be aware of your pony's comfort. You may have to move a buckle, loosen or pad a strap to avoid rubbing or pinching his skin, or change girths to prevent a rub from developing into a girth sore.

Each time you untack, rinse off and dry the bit. Wipe off all leather parts with a damp sponge; then go over the leather with a sponge moistened with a little saddle soap. At least once a week (more often if possible), you should take apart your tack and clean it thoroughly, with special attention to stress points such as the bit and rein fastenings, girth, billets, and stirrup leathers.

For special occasions like inspections at rallies, it's important that your tack show the effects of good daily care. If you neglect your tack and try to do a special cleaning right before the rally, it will not feel or look as good as tack that has been cleaned and conditioned regularly.

Metal parts such as the bit, stirrup irons, spurs, and buckles should be cleaned and polished. A pot scrubbing cloth will remove dirt and stains, and metal polish should be used on all metal parts except the mouthpiece of the bit.

Saddle pads, girth covers, and washable girths should be freshly laundered. Rinse twice to remove all traces of detergent and bleach, which can irritate the pony's skin when he sweats.

For more information on cleaning tack and preparing for rallies, see the *USPC Horse Management Handbook.*

Turnout

"Turnout" means the way you present yourself and your pony, especially for lessons, clinics, rallies, or competitions. Good turnout means being neat, clean and workmanlike, not fancy. "Workmanlike" means ready to work—to do the job. This means having the right clothes, tack, and equipment, with everything clean, in good condition, and properly fitted, and having your pony clean, properly prepared, and in good condition. When riding in a lesson or clinic, neat and proper attire make it easier to sit correctly and helps the instructor see how you ride. It is also a courtesy to the instructor or examiner to appear neatly turned out. Good turnout is important for safety and for the comfort of your pony.

At C Level, you are expected to be neatly and correctly turned out for ordinary lessons and practice sessions, as well as for rallies and competitions. Before a rally or special event, find out what kind of attire is required. Don't mix formal and informal attire (so, don't wear a turtleneck shirt, which is informal, with a formal black coat).

Neatness, cleanliness, and proper fit of your clothes matter far more than newness or cost. Here are some tips for keeping your clothes clean and appearing at your best at Pony Club inspections and competitions, even when grooming and tacking up:

- Hang your coat and other riding clothes in a garment bag. Pack a kit for clothing care and turnout with the following items:

Clean sponge, washcloth, towel, and clothes brush

Stock pin, extra safety pins

Small sewing kit, extra buttons, spot remover

Comb and brush; for girls, extra hair nets, hairpins, rubber bands

Small mirror

- Clean and polish boots and spur straps. Keep boot trees (wooden, plastic, or homemade) in your boots. Boot dye will cover scuffs that polish alone won't cover (but don't use it on the inside calf, as it will rub off on saddle and horse). Boot dye will make rubber boots shine. Pack a kit with the following boot-care items:

  Castile soap, sponge, towel, and boot brush

  Boot polish, leather dressing, black boot dye

  Boot pulls, boot jack, knee-high nylon hose, baby powder (for pulling on tight boots)

  Rubber boots or rubbers for muddy conditions

- Black boot dye can restore faded velvet on helmets.

- A stock tie should be tied in a square knot, with the ends fastened to the shirt with safety pins. The stock pin should be plain (no decoration), pinned horizontally through the knot.

- To protect your riding clothes when grooming, wear a coverall or a large apron.

- Your coat, stock, and gloves will stay neater if you remove them and hang them up as soon as possible after riding. Touch up any spots with a clean sponge and clothes brush.

- Keep a clean towel with you when tacking up, and wipe off any dirt or dust before touching your clothes.

- Make sure your shirt is tucked in; your belt in place; your stock, choker, or collar is straight; and your hair is neat (for girls, in braids or a hairnet). Spurs must be put on correctly (see page 11); long ends of spur straps should be cut off. For Pony Club rallies and activities, remember to wear your Pony Club pin.

Handling Your Pony during Tack and Turnout Inspections

When presenting yourself and your pony for inspections, you must demonstrate safe handling and horsemanship. Your pony must be taught to stand still (see Chapter 10 on ground training), and you must handle him in a way that keeps you and the examiner safe and the pony under control. While you are paying attention to the examiner, be aware of your pony's attitude and behavior, because ponies may get excited. Safe, correct handling must be a habit that you practice all the time, at home as well as during inspections.

Lead your pony to the inspection point, in correct leading position, holding the reins correctly (see *USPC D Level Manual*, page 155). Halt the pony, turn to face him, and give him a voice command to "Stand" as you change to the rein hold for standing, which is described below. While the examiner checks your tack, stand facing your pony so that you can keep him under control and see what the examiner is doing.

POSITION FOR HOLDING PONY FOR INSPECTION

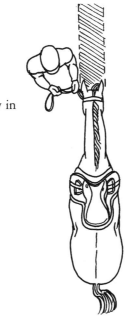

Don't stand directly in front of pony.

Stand on one side (usually the left side), beside the pony's head and neck, facing the pony so that you can see all four legs. Hold the reins in your left hand about six inches from the bit, with the end of the reins folded in your right hand. While it is more usual to handle a pony from the left side, there may be times when it is better to stand on his right side. In this case, change the reins to the other hand.

Pony Clubbers undergo a tack and safety inspection before riding in a rally. *Photo: Susan Sexton*

You may need to change your position in order to follow the examiner's instructions, such as picking up your pony's feet or looking at some part of the tack. Remember to keep control of your pony while following instructions.

CHAPTER 5

FEEDING, WATERING, AND NUTRITION

Ponies are grazing animals. They were designed by nature to live on grass and water, moving freely and eating small amounts almost constantly. Their digestive systems are made to handle large amounts of grass, hay, and other plant material, a little at a time.

Like people and other animals, ponies need all the basic types of nutrients: carbohydrates, proteins, fats, vitamins, minerals, and water. Good feeding practices are based on a knowledge of your pony's digestive system and his nutritional needs.

The Pony's Digestive System

Digestion is the process of breaking food down so that the pony can absorb it and use it. The digestive tract is a long tube reaching from the pony's mouth to under his tail. This tube is about ten times as long as the pony (more than 100 feet long in a full-sized horse); some parts have many loops and folds. It is designed so that different nutrients (types of food) are broken down and absorbed in special places.

Mouth The lips, front teeth (incisors), and tongue pick up food and bite it off. The molars (back teeth) chew the food, breaking it into smaller pieces, which is very important for good digestion. The food is mixed with saliva, which makes it easier to chew and swallow. Saliva contains enzymes that change plant starch into animal starch, which the pony can absorb. Since a pony eats mostly dry food, a great deal of saliva is necessary to soften the food and help with digestion. This is one reason a pony needs plenty of water.

PARTS OF THE DIGESTIVE SYSTEM

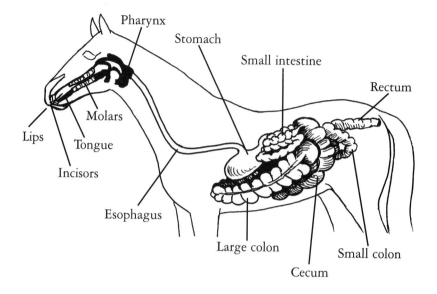

Ponies are normally slow eaters. They need fifteen to twenty minutes to eat a pound of hay, and five to ten minutes for a pound of grain. If a pony eats too fast, he may not chew his food thoroughly and cannot digest it as well, and he could choke. If your pony gobbles his food, try one of these remedies:

- Feed small amounts of grain more often. Feed hay first so that he will not be so hungry.
- Spread his grain out in a thin layer in a large feeder so that he can pick up only a small amount at a time.
- Place large, smooth stones, the size of a softball, in the feeder so that he must take longer to pick up each mouthful.

Pharynx   The pharynx makes sure that the food goes into the esophagus, not the windpipe, as it is swallowed.

Esophagus   The esophagus is a long, muscular tube that takes the food down to the stomach. It is designed to move food only one way, toward the stomach. Ponies cannot vomit. Because they cannot get rid of bad or spoiled food, it is extremely important they be fed only good, clean, and mold-free feeds that are safe to eat.

Stomach   The stomach is a small, muscular sack where food is mixed with digestive juices, and where proteins and minerals begin to be absorbed into the bloodstream. It holds only about 2 to 4 gallons and works best when it is about two-thirds full. Too much food all at once results in poor digestion, and can cause pain (colic). It is important to feed small amounts at least two to three times per day.

Some horse owners used to believe that if a pony was allowed to drink after eating, the water would wash the food out of the stomach and cause poor digestion. This is not true, and ponies should have water available all the time, except when they are hot and sweaty.

Small Intestine   The small intestine is a tube about 70 feet long, with many loops and folds. Here nutrients, especially proteins, carbohydrates, fats, and minerals, are broken down and absorbed into the bloodstream. The pancreas and the liver supply digestive juices. The digested food is absorbed into the bloodstream and carried to all parts of the body.

Large Intestine   The large intestine is a tube about 25 feet long, where the remaining food is broken down and absorbed and solid wastes are collected. The large intestine does most of the work of digesting grass, hay, and bulky plant material. "Friendly" bacteria living in the large intestine break down cellulose (plant fiber) into fatty acids that can be used by the pony. They also manufacture certain essential vitamins and amino acids.

The large intestine has four parts:

1. *Cecum* (also called the water gut): A large pouch about 4 feet long, where roughage (plant fiber) is broken down through fermentation, by helpful bacteria.
2. *Large colon*: A tube about 12 feet long, where the last of the nutrients are broken down and absorbed.
3. *Small colon*: A smaller tube about 10 feet long, where water is absorbed and solid waste is formed into manure balls.
4. *Rectum*: The end of the digestive tract, about 1 foot long.

It takes about seventy-two hours (three days) for food to pass all the way through the digestive tract and to be completely digested. Digestion can be affected by exercise and by excitement. This is why a pony should not be worked hard right after being fed.

Nutrients Needed by Horses

There are six types of essential nutrients. These are provided in water, sunlight, and different kinds of feed.

NUTRIENT	SOURCES	WHY NECESSARY
Water	Water (12 gallons or more per day)	For life and for vital functions; an essential part of every cell.
Carbohydrates	Grass, hay, grain. Plants make carbohydrates during a process called photosynthesis.	Starches and sugars are used for energy. Cellulose (plant fiber) is necessary for digestion.
Proteins	Oilseed meals, oats, barley, corn, alfalfa.	For growth, repair, and maintenance of body; the "building blocks" of cells.
Fatty Acids, Lipids	Corn oil, wheat-germ oil.	Produce extra energy especially when carbohydrates are not enough. Small amounts are used in digestion, especially of vitamins.
Vitamins	Hay, grain, sunlight, vitamin supplements.	For vital body functions.
Minerals	Hay, grain, salt, mineral supplements.	To build and maintain tissue, especially bones. Also act as triggers for body functions.

Types of Nutrients

Water   Water is the only nutrient that does not need to be broken down or changed by the body in order to be used. Fifty percent of a pony's body weight is made up of water.

Water is an essential part of every cell and of all vital fluids (including blood), which carry nutrients to all parts of the body, pick up waste products, and help to eliminate them. Water in the body serves as a built-in cooling system in hot weather and helps keep the body warm in cold weather.

Lack of water in the body is called "dehydration." This is very serious and can weaken or even kill a pony. Most ponies become dehydrated because they are not given enough clean, pure water often enough. A horse or pony needs at least 12 gallons of water daily. He should have as much water as he wants at all times, except when he is hot and sweaty. It is important to know how much your pony is drinking, and if he is not drinking a normal amount, to find out why.

Carbohydrates　Carbohydrates (plant starches) make up most of the fuel a pony uses for energy. They are are found in hays, grains, and pasture grasses. Carbohydrates are the cheapest and most abundant source of energy for a pony. The energy generated by carbohydrate metabolism (the chemical process of breaking down and using carbohydrates) keeps a pony's body temperature up to normal, which is especially important in the winter. It also gives him the "go-power" for fast hard work. Excess energy is stored as fat.

Carbohydrates are made of carbon, hydrogen, and oxygen. These are turned by plants into plant starch or carbohydrates during a process called "photosynthesis." Ponies cannot make carbohydrates themselves. They must eat plant material (hay, grain, or grass) to get them.

As a pony digests carbohydrates, he breaks them down into several useful components, which are the following:

- *Starches and sugars*, which are used for energy
- *Cellulose*, which makes up most of the fiber in the pony's diet. Fiber or bulk is necessary to keep food moving along through the digestive tract. Cellulose comes from the woody parts of plants (stems, leaves, and hulls) and is found in grass and hay. It is digested by bacteria in the large intestine.

If you feed your pony more energy food than he needs, he may get frisky and hard to handle. He will also gain weight because he stores up extra energy as fat. Feeding excess fiber (especially large amounts of coarse, stemmy hay or weeds) can give a pony a hay belly (a big belly caused by the digestive tract being full of coarse fiber).

A serious problem related to metabolism (the chemical process of breaking down, absorbing, and using food) and carbohydrates is Azoturia. The milder form of this ailment is called "tying up." Azoturia and tying up usually occur in horses that work hard on full-feed rations all week but are kept in the stall for one or two idle days while still being fed the same amount of grain (which is loaded with carbohydrates). Because it often occurs when a horse starts to work after a weekend off, it is sometimes called "Monday Morning Disease." When he starts to exercise, the horse shows signs of discomfort and distress, and his hindquarter muscles go into severe cramps, until he cannot move.

A horse that is "tying up" may show some or all of these symptoms:

- Stiffness and a short stride in one or both hind legs, which may get worse until he cannot move at all
- Hard, tense, and sometimes quivering large muscles of the hindquarters
- Dark-colored urine
- Elevated temperature
- Sweating, restlessness, and an anxious expression

Pony Tying Up

If you see signs of azoturia or suspect that your pony may be tying up, stop work immediately and do not move him. Azoturia is very serious and requires immediate medical attention by your veterinarian. Offering him feed, water, or electrolyte supplements *will not help* this condition.

It is not known what causes the big hindquarter muscles to cramp and to be unable to relax, but when this happens, muscle damage occurs and a protein called myoglobin is released from the damaged cells. This is carried to the kidneys and excreted in the urine, which may be very dark. In severe cases, kidney damage can result.

Good stable management with proper conditioning, balancing feed and exercise, and cutting the grain ration on rest days can help prevent azoturia. Once a pony has had an attack, he is more likely to have another one. Azoturia and tying up are serious problems; it is better to prevent them than to have to cope with them!

Proteins Proteins are the building blocks of life. They are essential components of every cell in the body and are needed for growth, maintenance, and repair of the body's tissues.

Proteins are made of amino acids, which break down plant protein (from feed) into animal protein, or "building blocks" that the body can use. There are 24 amino acids, 10 of which are essential to horses; lysine and methionine are the two most important. Without enough of these two, no other amino acids can be used by the horse. It's important to feed the right kinds of feed, with high-quality protein, to make sure that your pony gets the right amino acids and especially enough lysine and methionine.

A horse's protein needs are expressed as a percentage of his total ration (the total amount of feed he gets in twenty-four hours). A fat, mature pony needs about 8 percent protein; a young foal that is growing fast needs about 14 percent. If your pony doesn't get enough protein, he may be too thin and will not be able to build muscle. Feeding more protein than he needs causes him to waste energy excreting the excess protein, and could lead to kidney or liver damage. Overfeeding protein is a waste of money because high-protein feeds are the most expensive.

Oilseed meals such as linseed meal, cottonseed meal, and soybean meal are rich in protein. Soybean meal, which is about 44 to 50 percent available protein, is the cheapest, most available, and most commonly used in this country. Oats and barley each have about 13 percent available protein, and corn about 10 percent. The available protein in hay and pasture grass varies greatly, depending on the plants that make up the pasture or hay, and on the condition and time of year. High-quality alfalfa can contain as much as 21 percent available protein, while dead grass and weeds may have less than 5 percent.

Fats (Lipids) Fats are also called "lipids." There are four essential fatty acids, which are used to carry certain vitamins through the bloodstream and are necessary in small amounts for the horse's metabolism. Fatty acids also affect the condition of the skin and hair coat, and rate of growth in young horses.

Fats produce about two and one-half times as much energy as carbohydrates. They act as an emergency energy source. When a horse needs more energy than he can get from carbohydrates (because of hard work, stress, illness, or cold weather), he can burn fat.

Horses (especially small ponies) need only small amounts of fat in their diet. Old animals may need a little extra fat because their metabolism slows down. One half to one cup of corn oil added to the feed each day will help keep their skin and hair coats in good condition and will aid in energy production.

The best sources of fatty acids are wheat-germ oil and corn oil (which is less expensive). Feeds with high fat content spoil easily and become rancid, especially in hot weather. They lose essential fatty acids, smell and taste bad, and are no longer good for horses. Feeds high in fat should be kept away from heat and light, stored in small quantities, and used up quickly.

Vitamins   Vitamins are organic (non-mineral) substances that are required in small amounts to regulate certain chemical reactions in the body.

There are two types of vitamins: those carried in liquid fat (fat-soluble vitamins) and those carried in water (water-soluble vitamins). Fat-soluble vitamins can be stored in the liver and in body fat, and called up for use when the body needs them. They include vitamins A, D, E, and K. Water-soluble vitamins are produced in the intestine from natural plant sources and cannot be stored in the body. Water-soluble vitamins are vitamin C, thiamine, riboflavin, B_{12}, niacin, pantothenic acid, B_6, choline, folacin, biotin, and aminobenzoic acid.

Here are the basic vitamins needed by ponies:

Fat-Soluble Vitamins

Vitamin A   Made from carotene by the horse. Carotene is found in green pasture grasses and good-quality hay. Keeps eyes, skin, hair, nerves, and hooves healthy.

Vitamin D   Comes from sunlight or sun-cured hay. Helps the body use calcium for development of strong bones.

Vitamin E   Closely tied to the mineral selenium. Necessary for fertility, production of red blood cells, and their ability to carry oxygen in the blood. Vitamin E is lost when feed is heated during processing, or stored for long periods of time.

Vitamin K   Responsible for proper clotting of the blood, which stops the bleeding when a horse is cut.

Water-Soluble Vitamins   These are produced in the intestine by friendly bacteria but cannot be stored in the body. A horse must be healthy and must eat good-quality plant food to be able to produce these vitamins as he needs them.

Vitamin C   Healthy horses produce an adequate amount of vitamin C (ascorbic acid) in their intestines.

Thiamine   Helps carbohydrates release energy. Necessary for appetite.

Riboflavin   Related to energy release and the nervous system.

Vitamin B_{12}   Helps in metabolism of protein, carbohydrates, and fatty acids. Also helps to prevent anemia.

Niacin   Necessary for metabolism.

Vitamin B_6   If vitamin B_6 is low, tryptophan (an essential amino acid) cannot be used by the pony.

Folacin   Aids in formation of red blood cells.

Biotin   Necessary for metabolism. May be deficient if pony eats moldy feed, because mold "ties up" this vitamin.

Choline, pantothenic acid, folacin, and p-aminobenzoic acid (PABA) are other water-soluble vitamins.

Only a small amount of each required vitamin is needed, but if a horse does not get enough, he may develop a vitamin-deficiency disease. If certain vitamins are lacking, he may not be able to use other vitamins.

Horses get most of the vitamins they need from good-quality hay and green, growing pasture grass. During the winter, or when pasture grass is poor, it may help to feed a vitamin supplement. Ask your veterinarian before adding any supplement to your pony's feed.

Follow the manufacturer's directions, and don't mix supplements or feed more than one.

Minerals   Minerals are inorganic elements (substances not produced by living things). Like vitamins, they are necessary in small amounts in a horse's diet. Their main job is to build and maintain bones and, second, to act as a trigger for certain body functions. Minerals are essential to the metabolism of every cell in the body. Ninety percent of a horse's skeleton is made up of minerals, especially calcium and phosphorous.

There are six major minerals: salt, calcium, phosphorous, magnesium, potassium, and sulfur. "Trace minerals," which are just as important to horses but needed only in very small amounts, include iodine, iron, cobalt, copper, zinc, and manganese.

Plants pick up minerals from the soil in which they grow. If the soil is low in a certain mineral, the feed from plants grown in that soil will be low in that mineral. In different areas of the country, the soil may be high in certain minerals and deficient in others. It's important to know where your feed comes from and which minerals it contains. This can be determined by having hay or soil tested, or by checking the ingredients tag on bags of feed.

Here are the minerals that are most important in feeding horses:

Salt   Lost in sweat, so horses need more salt than other animals. All horse feeds are low in salt. Your pony should always have free-choice salt in his stall and in the pasture, either in a salt block or as loose salt in a feeder.

Calcium and Phosphorous   Essential for sound bones, especially in young, growing horses. Ninety-nine percent of the calcium and 80 percent of the phosphorous in the body is found in the bones. Magnesium is closely associated with calcium and phosphorous. Vitamin D is also important because without it a horse cannot absorb calcium.

To use calcium and phosphorous, a horse must have the right amount of each mineral, but they must also be in balance. If he has too much of one, he cannot use either mineral properly.

Mature horses need approximately twice as much calcium as phosphorous in their diet (two parts calcium to one part phosphorous). Growing horses need equal amounts of calcium and phosphorous (one part calcium to one part phosphorous) in their diet.

Hays and grasses are good sources of calcium but are low in phosphorous. Grains are high in phosphorous but low in calcium.

Potassium Important in maintaining the pH (acid-base balance) and fluid level in the cells. Horses that work hard and sweat heavily may lose potassium, especially in hot weather. Giving the right mixture of electrolytes, containing potassium, may help, but this must be done under the supervision of a veterinarian.

Iodine A trace mineral that helps regulate thyroid activity. Only small amounts are necessary. In some areas, the soil may be deficient in iodine, and any feed grown in it will be also. Feeding iodized salt will take care of your pony's iodine needs.

Other Trace Minerals Most trace minerals are supplied by a horse's normal diet. Some salt has trace minerals added.

If your feed is too low in certain minerals, you may have to give your pony a mineral supplement. Feeding too much of certain minerals, however, is likely to cause more harm than overfeeding vitamins will. Ask for your veterinarian's advice before adding any mineral supplement to your pony's diet.

Types of Hays and Grains

Hay Hay is a kind of roughage made of dried grass and plants. It is a substitute for the grass a horse would eat if he were in pasture. Good hay provides bulk as well as energy, protein, vitamins, and minerals, and plenty of fiber, which is necessary for good digestion. Hay is the cheapest source of energy, and hay (or good pasture grass, if available) should make up the major portion of a horse's diet.

Of the several kinds of hay, some are more nutritious than others.

Grass hays Include timothy, brome, orchard grass, ryegrass, prairie hay, Coastal Bermuda, and others. They have more fiber and are less concentrated than other kinds of hay.

Legume hays Include alfalfa, clover, and lucerne. Legumes are plants that produce seeds in a pod, take in nitrogen from the air, and produce protein. Legume hays have more protein, calcium, and vitamins than grass hays.

Oat hay Contains both oat stalks and some grain.

The higher the quality of hay, the better nutrition it offers. Look for green color, leafiness, and fine stems, which mean that the hay was cut early. If hay is cut too late, the stems become coarse and woody, there are fewer leaves, and much of the nutrition is lost. Good hay smells sweet, like a newly cut lawn. Moldy or musty hay can give a horse colic; dusty hay can cause a chronic cough and permanent lung damage. Check each bale as you open it and sniff the hay before you feed it. *Never* feed hay that smells moldy or musty or that has gray or white patches. If the hay is good but only a little dusty, you can wet it down to get rid of the dust or, better still, avoid feeding it.

Grains   Grains are concentrates, which means they have more nutrients (especially energy) packed into a smaller amount than bulk foods like hay or other roughages. Grains usually have about 50 to 60 percent more digestible energy per pound than hay.

A healthy diet for a horse consists of at least 50 percent roughage—bulk feeds such as hay and grass. Grains and other concentrates should be fed when a horse needs either more energy or nutrients other than those he gets from the roughage he eats.

Grains may be in kernel form or processed to make them easier to chew and digest. Some grains such as oats and barley may be crimped (slightly crushed) or rolled (slightly flattened). Barley and corn are sometimes flaked (crushed into flakes, like cereal).

Oats   Have more fiber in their hulls and are less concentrated than other grains. This makes them the safest grain to feed, because it is harder to overfeed oats than other grains.

The best oats have plump, heavy kernels and weigh at least thirty-two pounds per bushel. This means they have plenty of starch and not too much fiber.

Corn   Has the most energy (calories) per pound of all the grains. It must be fed carefully because it is more concentrated. One quart of corn provides as much digestible energy as two quarts of oats, so it is easier to overfeed corn than oats.

It is not true that corn is a "hot" food, as some horse owners believe. If you overfeed your pony with corn, he may become too fat, which can cause him to sweat when he works. Digesting fiber (found in hay or roughage) is what actually produces a higher body temperature.

Corn may be fed on the cob (ear corn), as whole or shelled corn, or may be cracked, rolled, or flaked. It's important to feed only good-quality corn that is not moldy. Toxins found in moldy corn can cause brain damage and death.

Barley   Similar to oats, barley is a good compromise between oats and corn because it has more energy than oats but not quite as much as corn. Barley has more fiber than corn but not as much as oats. It is easier to overfeed barley than oats.

Barley should be rolled or flaked (slightly flattened) to get rid of the outer husk so that it is easier to digest.

Bran   The ground-up hulls of wheat. This bulky feed is sometimes mixed with other feeds or fed as a bran mash. Bran should not be fed in large quantities, as it contains large amounts of phosphorous and can upset the calcium-phosphorous balance. This can cause serious bone problems.

Sweet Feed   Mixed grain with molasses added. Molasses makes the feed less dusty and more tasty. Be careful when storing and feeding sweet feed in hot, humid conditions, as it can spoil. Sweet feed attracts flies, so it is important to keep feed tubs clean.

Pelleted Feeds   Feed that is ground up and pressed into pellets. There are four types of pellets: those made of a single ingredient (such as alfalfa meal), mixed-grain pellets, feed supplements, and complete feed pellets (those containing both grain and hay).

One problem with feeding pelleted complete feeds is that horses may chew wood just to satisfy their need to chew. Supplying some grass hay keeps them busy, provides necessary bulk, and helps prevent wood chewing.

Beet Pulp   Beet pulp is a by-product of processed sugar beets. It may be used as a form of roughage, especially for horses with heaves or allergies. It usually is shredded or made into pellets. Beet pulp is more digestible than hay but bulkier than grain. The calcium content of beet pulp is higher than that of timothy hay but less than that of alfafa. Beet pulp is very low in phosphorous and B vitamins, and contains no carotene or vitamin D.

Dry beet pulp swells as it absorbs water or saliva. It must always be fed wet; eating dry beet pulp may cause choking.

Pasture Grass   Good pasture is not only an open space where horses can exercise freely in fresh air but also their most natural food source. Pasture can be an inexpensive source of good nutrition. It is especially important for broodmares, foals, and growing horses.

Not all pasture grass is equally good to eat. Pastures with weeds, swamps, sparse grass, or coarse, tough grass don't provide much nutrition. Neither do pastures that have been overgrazed. In the winter, the grass may be dead and have little nutritional value, or may be buried under deep snow. A horse will get thin and can starve on poor pasture unless he is given enough hay and, possibly, grain.

In the spring, the grass grows fast and contains lots of water. This lush grass can upset a horse's digestion, especially if he gets too much new grass when he is not used to it. Small ponies and fat horses or ponies are in danger of contracting laminitis (see pages 222–224 for more information) if they eat too much rich grass.

It's important to know what kinds of grass and other plants grow in your pasture, and how to keep it in good condition. For information and advice about pasture management where you live, contact your local cooperative extension, county agent, or agricultural college.

Horses are hard on pastures. They eat the grass close to the ground before moving on, and their hooves tear up the turf in high-traffic areas around gates, fence lines, and feeding and watering areas. Horses will not graze where they have dropped manure, and these areas tend to become increasingly larger, with long grass. To produce good grass, pastures may need to be seeded, fertilized, treated with lime, and cleared of weeds. Pastures also need a rest from time to time so that the grass can grow back. If you divide your pasture into two sections, your pony can graze in one section while the grass grows back in the other.

A paddock is a small area in which a horse can be turned out to exercise or graze. For a paddock or small pasture to have good grass, more upkeep is required than would be necessary in a large pasture, because horses graze more and leave more hoofprints and manure in paddocks and small pastures (relative to their size). In a small paddock, droppings should be picked up every couple of days, to control parasites. Weeds should be cut down so that good grass can grow.

Don't overgraze a pasture by keeping too many horses in it for too long, or the grass will get eaten right down to the ground. Try not to put horses out in a pasture or ride in it when the ground is soft and muddy and the grass is very short. If the turf gets cut up, you will soon have a mudhole with very little grass.

Watering Water is the most essential part of your pony's diet. Without enough water, he will become dehydrated and distressed, and could die. You *must* make sure that your pony has plenty of fresh, clean water available at all times, except when he is hot and sweaty and has not yet been cooled out.

A horse needs at least 12 gallons of water a day. His water must be checked twice a day (more often is better). In the winter, you must keep the water from freezing over. This may mean chopping a hole in the ice on a stream or pond, or using a stock tank heater. A horse cannot get enough moisture to live on from eating snow.

If the water is dirty or scummy; smells bad; has hay, grain, or manure in it; or is very cold (colder than forty degrees Farenheit), a horse may not drink enough to keep himself healthy. Water buckets, automatic waterers, and water tanks must be kept clean.

The source of water must not be polluted by fertilizers, pesticides, or other harmful chemicals. A natural water source should be a clean running stream or spring, not a stagnant pond.

Weighing and Measuring Feed

You need to weigh and measure your pony's feed to make sure he is getting enough to eat without wasting any. Feed should be measured by pounds, which is more accurate than counting scoops of grain or flakes of hay.

Nutritional recommendations are given in pounds, so you must know the weight of the hay and grain you feed your pony. You can weigh feed on a household scale or baby scale.

To measure grain, use a small coffee can (one-pound size), a large can (two and one-half-pound size), or a grain scoop. Weigh each kind of grain you feed and find out how much grain equals one pound. Also find out how many pounds of each kind of grain your can or scoop holds. A pound of corn takes up less space than a pound of oats, whereas a pound of bran occupies more space. You may want to label your grain can to remind yourself how much of each kind of grain equals one pound.

Hay comes in bales weighing from 40 to 75 pounds or more, so you can't just feed "half a bale a day"—you must know how many pounds of hay your pony gets. Weigh an average-size flake of hay, and find out how much hay it takes to make 5, 10, or 15 pounds.

WEIGHING AND MEASURING FEED

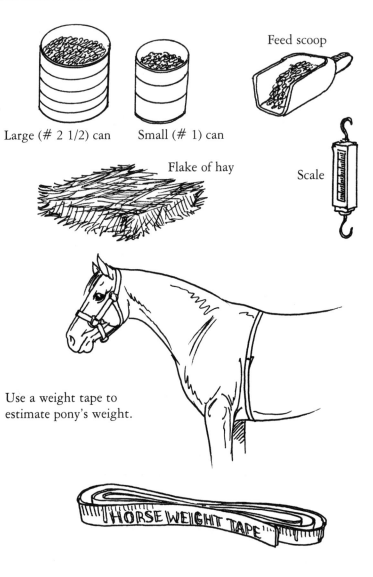

Large (# 2 1/2) can   Small (# 1) can   Feed scoop

Flake of hay   Scale

Use a weight tape to
estimate pony's weight.

HORSE WEIGHT TAPE

To figure out how much feed your pony should get, you need to know how much he weighs. You can get a horse-weight tape at a feed store. Stretch the tape around his heart girth so that you can read his approximate weight from the tape. Write down his weight. It's a good idea to check his weight every couple of weeks to see whether he is gaining or losing weight.

A good rule of thumb is that a horse should be fed about 2 to 3 pounds of feed for every 100 pounds he weighs. This is his *total ration*, which is everything he eats in a day, including both hay and grain. (For example, a small pony weighing 500 pounds might eat 10 to 15 pounds a day; an average-size horse of 1,000 pounds would eat 20 to 30 pounds a day.)

To keep their digestion working properly, horses and ponies should be fed mostly roughage, with smaller amounts of grain as needed. Most small ponies (and some larger animals) do well on all hay or grass, with little or no grain.

Feeding Ponies Versus Feeding Horses

In Pony Club and in this book, the word "pony" is used for any mount used by a young person. However, this can cause some confusion when it comes to feeding, because horses and ponies often need to be fed differently.

True ponies are small, hardy animals that developed to live in harsh conditions. They use food more efficiently and do not require as much food for their size as horses do. They especially should not be overfed with grain and other concentrates, which can make them too frisky and hard to control, and can cause serious problems such as laminitis. Many small ponies can easily founder if kept on too-rich pastures.

Most nutrition guidelines are made with the average horse in mind. Some horses need more food for their size than ponies do. Naturally "chunky" horses can easily become overweight; they should be fed according to pony guidelines.

How Much Should You Feed?

The amount of food, especially grain, that a horse or pony needs, depends on many things. It can change from day to day. You need to consider the individual animal—his size, type, and condition; whether he is kept stabled or in a pasture; how much work he is doing and how he behaves; how experienced his rider is; and his age and health. You should also look closely at the pony himself and use common sense when you feed him. If he tires easily, is run down, or starts to lose weight, he needs more feed—probably more grain. If he is too fat or too frisky, he should have it cut back. Ask your veterinarian for his advice. (For more information on feeding, see the Nutrition section of the *USPC B/A Manual.*)

Different Rations for Different Purposes

Your pony may need special feeding at certain times, depending on what he is doing. Here are some suggested feeding plans for different purposes.

Maintenance Ration   A ration that keeps the horse just as he is—not gaining and not losing weight. This is a basic ration for maintaining ordinary health and fitness. It should not be too high in energy or protein. Extra grain may be added for extra energy when the horse does more work.

Conditioning Ration   A ration for developing fitness. As a horse's work increases, he needs more concentrated feed (more grain) for extra energy.

Rest-Day Ration   When a horse has a day off, his grain should be cut to half or less of his normal amount. In some cases, the grain could be cut out entirely. This helps to prevent Azoturia, or tying-up syndrome, which can happen if you forget to cut back his grain on a rest day. He should get some extra hay or roughage to make up for the missing grain: about three pounds of grass hay for every one pound of grain cut from his regular ration.

Roughing Off   Taking a long vacation from work (for instance, if your pony isn't ridden in the winter) is called "roughing off," or "laying up." When you stop working a fit horse, let him down gradually. As his work is cut down, his grain should be gradually cut back and his roughage increased until he is at a maintenance level. If he has been stabled and is going out on pasture, he should start with a short period of grazing (about an hour) each day, which should be increased gradually over several weeks, until he is used to being on grass all day.

Feeding a Sick Horse   A sick horse or pony needs food that is nutritious but easy to digest. Since he is inactive, he may need a more laxative diet. Bran mashes are good for this. He may not feel like eating much, so he should be offered small meals of the feed he likes best. Do not leave leftover feed in front of him all day; rather, offer him a little bit at a time as often as you can. Fresh grass, good hay, and the addition of sliced carrots and apples or molasses to his feed may tempt his appetite. Be sure he has plenty of fresh, clean water, and notice how much he drinks. If your pony is sick, ask your veterinarian what kind of diet is best for him and whether he recommends any special feeds or supplements.

A Feeding Schedule for Your Pony

You should prepare a feeding schedule for your own pony that shows how much of each kind of feed he should get at each feeding and what times he should be fed. Then it is up to you to follow it. Here is a sample schedule:

MY PONY'S RATION

(   ) POUNDS OF HAY PER DAY, WHICH EQUALS (   ) FLAKES.
KIND OF HAY:

(   ) HOURS OF PASTURE GRAZING PER DAY.
PASTURE GRASS IS: (Poor, fair, average, good, very good)

(   ) POUNDS OF GRAIN PER DAY, WHICH EQUALS (   )
MEASURES.
KIND OF GRAIN:

Make two copies of the feeding schedule, and post one copy in your feed room and the other on his stall.

CHAPTER 6

HEALTH CARE AND VETERINARY KNOWLEDGE

Your veterinarian is your best source of advice on your pony's health. He or she should see your pony at least twice a year to perform a routine health check and to bring his immunizations up to date.

It is best to talk with your veterinarian about health care and first aid before you have a problem. Ask him or her how to treat minor wounds and what medications he or she recommends. Following your veterinarian's advice makes treating your pony easier and may keep you from making a mistake. Veterinarians often go to Pony Club meetings and talk about horse-related first aid, wound care, and other health-care subjects.

Before you call the veterinarian, have all your information in order. Write down your pony's vital signs (temperature, pulse, and respiration rates), the symptoms you have noticed, and any questions you need to ask. Have your pony inside, and be on hand to help when the veterinarian comes. Write down the diagnosis, treatment, and recommendations in your horse record book.

Health-Care Records

Preventive health care is meant to prevent disease or problems. It includes immunizations, regular deworming, and dental care.

To keep your pony's health care up to date, you need a calendar and a record book. Mark the dates when immunizations, deworming, and farrier visits are due, and call for appointments at least a week ahead. Veterinary visits and other health care should be recorded in your record book; write down the date, what was done for the pony, and any notes or instructions. Shoeing and hoof trimming appointments should also be recorded in your record book.

Immunizations

Immunizations (also called inoculations, vaccinations, or "shots") protect horses against certain diseases. A product used to immunize a horse is called a "vaccine." Vaccines work by stimulating the body to produce substances called "antibodies," which can fight off a particular disease. As long as the horse has enough antibodies, he has "immunity," or protection against that disease. Not all vaccines can provide 100 percent protection, but they give a horse a much better chance of avoiding a disease, and, should he get it, he will have a milder case.

When a horse is first inoculated against a certain disease, two to three weeks may pass before he develops enough antibodies for immunity. Immunity may last for as long as a year or as little as three months, depending on the product. It's important to know how long the immunity lasts for each inoculation, and how often your pony needs a "booster shot" to keep up his immunity.

Every horse should be inoculated against the most common and serious diseases at least once a year. Some diseases are more common in certain areas; if your pony goes to rallies or competitions away from home, he may be exposed to different diseases. Ask your veterinarian which diseases are common in your area, which inoculations he or she recommends for your pony, and how often booster shots are needed.

Following is a list of the basic inoculations all horses should receive:

1. *Tetanus*: All horses should have a tetanus shot once a year. A booster shot may be necessary if a horse gets a serious wound or a puncture wound.
2. *Equine Encephalomyelitis (sleeping sickness)*: There are three types of encephalomyelitis: Eastern, Western, and Venezuelan. All horses and ponies should be inoculated against the Eastern and Western types. In some parts of the country, they should also be protected against the Venezuelan type (VEE). In the North, one shot is usually given in the spring. In the South, shots may be needed every six months or even every three months because the mosquitoes that spread the disease are active all year.

3. *Influenza (flu)*: If your pony goes to rallies, shows, or events away from home where he is exposed to other horses, a flu shot is especially important. Immunity lasts for only three months, so booster shots should be scheduled.
4. *Rabies*: If there is rabies in the wildlife in your area, all horses and ponies *must* have a rabies shot every year. Pets and barn cats should also have rabies shots.

You may need to protect your pony against several other diseases, for example, strangles, rhinopneumonitis, Potomac fever, and leptospirosis. Combined vaccines are available that inoculate against two, three, or even four diseases in one shot. Ask your veterinarian what he or she recommends.

Health Care Schedules

For a New Pony

+ Prepurchase exam by a veterinarian, check for health and soundness, and a Coggins test for Equine Infectious Anemia (see pages 218–219).
+ Inoculations (for first-time inoculations, two shots two weeks apart may be required, and two to three weeks to develop immunity).
+ Have teeth checked by a veterinarian or equine dental specialist.
+ Have a farrier check feet and shoes and trim or reset if needed.
+ Keep isolated from other ponies for two weeks to prevent exposing them to possible disease.
+ Deworm at least twenty-four hours before turning out in pasture.
+ Start a health-care record book.

Annual Checkup Spring is when veterinarians usually perform annual checkups and give the following inoculations or booster shots:

+ Tetanus
+ Encephalomyelitis (Eastern, Western, and/or Venezuelan)
+ Rabies (if needed in your area)
+ Coggins test (if required for travel or events)
+ Any other inoculations he or she recommends

Every Six Months

- Check the teeth and float, if necessary (veterinarian or equine dental specialist)
- Encephalomyelitis booster shot (some areas of country)
- Any other booster shots recommended by your veterinarian

Every Three Months

- Deworm (or every two months or every six weeks if recommended by your veterinarian). Rotate deworming products as he or she recommends.
- Encephalomyelitis shot (in the South or if your veterinarian recommends it)
- Influenza booster shot (if your pony travels a lot or if your veterinarian recommends it)
- Any other booster shots recommended by your veterinarian

Every Six Weeks

- Farrier visit: trim feet, reset shoes, or replace shoes as needed
- Deworming (if your veterinarian recommends it)

Internal Parasites and Deworming

Ponies are exposed to internal parasites, or "worms," all the time. Ponies must be dewormed on a regular schedule, or they will get thin and unhealthy. Worms cause damage to the pony's blood vessels, intestines, heart, and lungs, which can lead to fatal colic. Ninety percent of all cases of colic are believed to be caused by the damage done by parasites, especially by large strongyles.

The Life Cycles of Parasites   Each type of internal parasite or worm has its own life cycle. Most lay large numbers of eggs in the pony's intestines; the eggs then are excreted in the pony's manure. The eggs hatch into tiny larvae, too small to be seen with the naked eye. These larvae take several weeks to develop into "infective larvae," which crawl onto blades of grass. When the pony eats the grass, he eats the larvae, too.

Once inside the pony, different parasites live and develop in different places. Some parasites live in the lining of the intestines; others migrate through the blood vessels to other organs. Most adult horse parasites live in the digestive tract, where they suck blood or live off the digestive juices. Internal parasites damage a pony's digestion, making him unable to absorb nutrients from his food properly; these parasites can also damage blood vessels and other internal organs.

LIFE CYCLE OF INTERNAL PARASITES

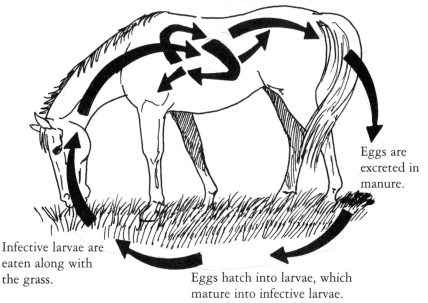

Larvae migrate through bloodstream to various organs, then mature and lay eggs in intestines.

Eggs are excreted in manure.

Infective larvae are eaten along with the grass.

Eggs hatch into larvae, which mature into infective larvae.

Types of Internal Parasites (Worms)   The most common types of internal parasites are the following:

- *Large strongyles (bloodworms)*: These invade the blood vessels of the intestines and cause serious damage to blood vessels, the digestive tract, and other vital organs. Damage from large strongyles is the most common cause of colic and can be fatal.
- *Small strongyles*: Another type of bloodworm that also causes severe damage to the blood vessels and internal organs. An infected pony may have a pot belly, dull coat, anemia, diarrhea, or colic.
- *Ascarids (roundworms)*: Large worms that live in the small intestine, they are found most often in foals and young horses. These parasites can cause coughing, inflammation of the lining of the intestine, and even a rupture of the intestine.

- *Bots*: The larvae of the botfly lays its eggs on the hair of the pony's legs, shoulders, and chin. As the eggs hatch, the larvae enter the pony's mouth and are swallowed. They mature into "bots," which attach themselves to the lining of the stomach and can cause ulcers. The larvae eventually are excreted in the manure and hatch into botflies.

  Bot eggs (small, yellow eggs attached to the hair) should be removed, as this prevents them from being swallowed and infesting the pony.

- *Pinworms*: These live in the end of the large intestine. They irritate the rectum and can cause the pony to rub his tail. A dry, gray or yellow discharge is a sign of pinworms.

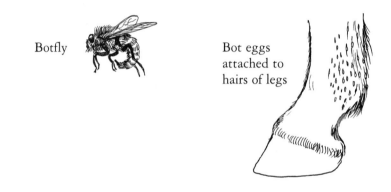

Botfly

Bot eggs attached to hairs of legs

Testing for Worms   Your veterinarian can perform a "fecal parasite count" (a simple test on a single manure ball) that tells what kind of parasites your pony has and how many. This test can help you decide which kind of dewormer to use. Ask your veterinarian how often you should have this test done.

Deworming   Dewormer (usually a special medicated paste) must be given to horses on a regular schedule (usually every eight to twelve weeks) to kill the worms. Different dewormers work against different types of parasites and at certain stages of development, so you should read the label when choosing a dewormer. Some parasites can develop resistance to a dewormer if it is used over and over again, so rotating the types of dewormer you use is important. Your veterinarian will advise you on how often your pony must be dewormed and what kind of dewormer is best to use.

Dewormers also can be given in powder or pellets added to the grain, or by stomach tube (which must be done by a veterinarian), but today most are given by mouth, using a deworming paste. When deworming your pony, it's important to know how much he weighs so that he receives the proper dose. (You can estimate his weight by using a weight tape.) Your veterinarian can show you how to measure the right dose for your pony and how to give him the deworming paste.

Parasite Control   Parasite control aims at keeping horses as free from parasites as possible by breaking the parasites' life cycle. This involves regular deworming, good pasture management, and keeping feed and water from becoming contaminated by manure and the parasite eggs it contains.

Worms, their eggs, and their larvae are carried in the pony's intestines and excreted in manure. A single pile of manure can contain thousands of parasite eggs and larvae. To keep your pasture from becoming contaminated, you should deworm a new horse twenty-four hours before you turn him out on pasture.

To reduce worm problems, follow these good-management practices:

- Deworm your pony on a regular schedule, following your veterinarian's advice on how often to deworm and which products to use.
- Avoid keeping too many horses in small pastures; otherwise a heavy infestation of worm eggs may result. Horses in very large pastures or on rangeland are less exposed to worms.
- Avoid overgrazing. Horses will not eat grass near droppings (which is heavily contaminated with parasites) unless the rest of the grass is gone.
- Rotate pastures to give them a rest from horse grazing. Horse parasites cannot live in sheep or cattle; when these animals graze a pasture, the worms' life cycle is destroyed.
- Manure should be picked up from paddocks and small pastures at least once a week, and from small paddocks and corrals every couple of days. This is the most effective way of reducing your pony's exposure to worms.
- Keep hay, feed, and water from becoming contaminated with manure.

Teeth and Dental Care

A horse must have a healthy mouth and teeth in order to chew his feed properly, to stay in good condition, and to be comfortable with a bit in his mouth. You must know enough about your pony's mouth and teeth to keep him healthy and comfortable and to recognize problems. Your pony's teeth need regular care from a veterinarian or an equine dental specialist.

Anatomy of the Mouth   The horse's teeth and mouth are designed for grazing. His lips pick out the grass he wants; the front teeth tear it off, and his tongue passes the grass back to the back teeth, which grind it up before it is swallowed.

Here are the teeth and the parts of the mouth you should know about:

THE MOUTH

A. Skull, showing teeth and roots of teeth in jaws

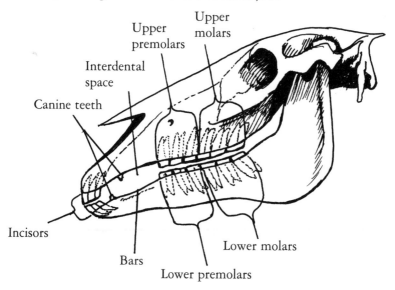

B. Cross-section of mouth, with bit

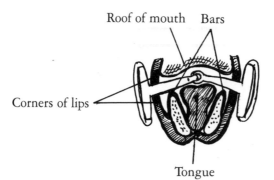

- *Incisors (12):* Front teeth, used to tear off grass. There are 6 in the upper jaw and 6 in the lower jaw.
- *Premolars and molars (24):* Back teeth, used to grind food. Molars are found at the back of the jaw and premolars in front of them. There are 12 (6 on each side) in the upper jaw and the same number in the lower jaw.
- *Canine teeth, or tushes (4):* Smaller, pointed teeth, found in the upper and lower jaw just behind the incisors. Usually found only in male horses (although a few mares have them).
- *Wolf teeth (some horses may have 1 to 4):* Small, extra premolars (*not* canine teeth, or tushes) found in some horses, located right in front of the first premolars. They may cause discomfort if the bit touches them, and can be removed easily.
- *Interdental space:* The toothless space between the front and back teeth, where the bit rests.
- *Bars:* The upper surface of the lower jawbones, in the interdental space. The bit rests on the bars, which are quite sensitive.

Number of Teeth   A horse has either 40 teeth (in males, counting the 4 canines) or 36 teeth (in mares, who usually have no canine teeth).

Baby Teeth and Permanent Teeth   Horses start out with baby teeth, just as we do. A foal is born with both sets of teeth (baby teeth and permanent teeth) in its jaws. First the baby teeth grow out through the gums, in pairs, between birth and about nine months of age. The permanent teeth are also growing, and, when the horse is about two and one-half years of age, they begin to appear and push the baby teeth out. Usually all the baby teeth have been lost and all the permanent teeth have appeared by the time the horse is five years old. The horse is then said to have a "full mouth."

Tooth Growth and Wear   Horses' teeth are constantly growing and wearing down. Each tooth has a long root that reaches deep into the jaw. As a tooth grows, it breaks through the gum, then grows until it is long enough to meet its opposite tooth. As these grind together, the surface of each tooth keeps wearing down at about the same rate as it grows. As each tooth grows out and wears down, its appearance changes (especially on the "table," or grinding surface) as new parts of the tooth appear. This makes it possible to tell a horse's age by the shape and markings of his teeth, but only up to about the age of eight. After the horse turns eight, the changes in his teeth are not as constant, and his age can only be estimated.

A horse's upper jaw is wider than his lower jaw, in the back where he grinds his food. His teeth grind sideways, in one direction. As his teeth wear down, sharp edges, or "hooks," can form on his upper and lower teeth. These hooks can make his mouth sore and make chewing difficult, which can cause him to lose weight. This is common in older horses but can occur in a horse of any age.

JAWS AND SURFACES OF TEETH

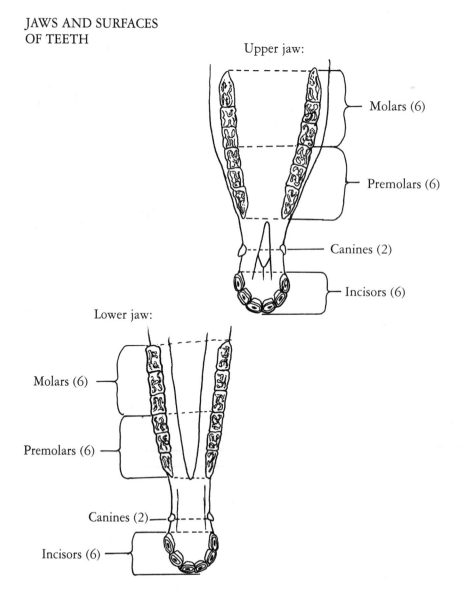

Upper jaw:

Molars (6)

Premolars (6)

Canines (2)

Incisors (6)

Lower jaw:

Molars (6)

Premolars (6)

Canines (2)

Incisors (6)

Hooks, or sharp edges, on upper and lower molars

Upper and lower molars made smooth by floating or rasping

Dental Care Your pony's teeth should be checked by your veterinarian or an equine dental specialist every six months. If your pony has sharp edges or uneven teeth, they should be "floated," or filed down, with a special rasp. This procedure doesn't hurt the pony, though he may not like the sound of the rasp, and will make his mouth much more comfortable.

Besides scheduling regular checkups, you should watch out for signs of mouth or tooth trouble. If a horse loses weight or fails to eat normally, his teeth should be checked. A horse whose mouth is sore may let feed fall out of his mouth as he eats, and may become touchy and difficult to bridle, or may not want to accept contact with the bit when you ride him. "Quidding" means dropping chewed-up wads of grass or hay out of the mouth. A horse does this to protect a sore place—a clear sign that his mouth needs attention.

Diseases and Prevention

There are two kinds of diseases: communicable diseases (such as colds and flu), which can be passed from one horse to another, and non-communicable ailments (for example, colic and laminitis), which occur when something goes wrong with an individual horse. As a horse owner, you should know what causes diseases, how to prevent them, and how to recognize their symptoms. They must be treated by your veterinarian.

Preventing the Spread of Diseases Communicable diseases are transmitted in different ways, but horses are more likely to become infected when they are exposed to many other horses at a show, rally, or competition, or when a new horse brings a disease into the stable. Inoculations can protect against certain diseases.

Here are some management practices that help you protect your pony against communicable diseases:

- Follow your veterinarian's advice about which diseases to inoculate your pony against, and how often to give booster shots.
- A new horse should have a Coggins test and up-to-date inoculations, and should be isolated for two weeks before being brought into a stable with other horses.
- Avoid letting your pony mix with strange horses that could expose him to diseases. Don't let him touch noses with other horses.
- Never share buckets at a show or rally, and don't let your pony drink from a water trough used by many different horses. Don't borrow or lend bits, saddle pads, blankets, or grooming equipment unless they are thoroughly disinfected first.

Communicable Diseases

TETANUS (LOCKJAW): Tetanus is not passed from horse to horse, but all horses are exposed to tetanus when they suffer a deep cut or a puncture wound. Horses are especially susceptible to tetanus; it is very serious and often fatal.

Tetanus is caused by clostridium tetani, an organism found in soil and manure, which can grow only where there is no oxygen. When a horse suffers a deep wound (especially a puncture wound), tetanus germs are carried deep inside the body. Away from oxygen, they reproduce, throwing off "tetanus toxin," a poison that attacks the nerves, causing severe spasms of the jaws and other muscles.

Puncture wounds are especially likely to cause tetanus because they carry the tetanus organism deep inside the tissues and close up around it.

Symptoms: The horse is unusually tense and jumpy, cannot eat or drink normally, and stands stiffly in one place. His third eyelid, which is usually hidden, is exposed.

Prevention: Every horse and pony should have a tetanus shot once a year. If a horse suffers a deep wound or a puncture wound, he may need a tetanus booster shot.

Caution: People can get tetanus, especially if they get a cut while working around horses or a stable area. Anyone working around horses should keep his or her immunity up by having a tetanus booster shot when his or her doctor recommends it.

STRANGLES (DISTEMPER): A respiratory infection caused by streptococcus equi bacteria (not the same as cat or dog distemper). It is spread by mucus from infected horses and is highly contagious; it can even be carried to other stables on boots or clothing. Horses often are exposed to this disease at competitions or horse sales, or if they are shipped in a trailer used by many other horses. Young horses are more vulnerable, but horses of any age can get this infection.

Strangles can be followed by serious complications, including heart disease, pneumonia, and internal abscesses.

Symptoms: Loss of appetite, sore throat, fever, and a runny nose. The mucus turns white, then becomes thick and yellow. Later, the lymph glands of the throat swell, and abscesses form that eventually break and drain.

Prevention: A vaccine is available but is not 100 percent effective for all horses. Avoiding exposure to large numbers of strange horses and isolating new horses are important preventive measures.

INFLUENZA (FLU): An upper respiratory infection caused by a virus. There are several strains of equine influenza. It is spread through the air by sneezing, coughing, and contact with infected horses, especially where large numbers of horses are gathered, such as at shows, sales, and racetracks.

Symptoms: Depression and loss of appetite, fever, runny nose with white mucus, coughing. The cough may hang on after other symptoms are gone.

Prevention: Influenza vaccine is available; immunity lasts for only two to three months, so periodic booster shots are necessary.

RHINOPNEUMONITIS: An upper respiratory infection caused by a virus (Equine herpesvirus 1, or EHV 1). It is quite contagious and is spread by sneezing, coughing, and contact with infected horses. Young horses are especially susceptible, but horses of any age may get it. Because rhinopneumonitis causes pregnant mares to abort, it is a serious problem for breeding farms.

Symptoms: Similar to those of a cold, or upper respiratory infection (coughing, runny nose, fever, sometimes swollen glands).

Prevention: Two types of vaccine are available; your veterinarian should decide which is best for your pony and how often he should have booster shots.

EQUINE ENCEPHALOMYELITIS (SLEEPING SICKNESS): A serious disease caused by a virus, which causes brain damage and can be fatal. Encephalomyelitis is carried by birds and is transmitted when a mosquito bites an infected bird and then bites a horse. There are three major types of encephalomyelitis: Eastern, Western, and Venezuelan.

Symptoms: Early symptoms are fever and excitability, then depression and drowsiness. The horse may walk in circles or stand with his head pressed against a wall. Eventually he becomes paralyzed and may die within two to four days.

Prevention: Vaccines are available for all three types. In the North, inoculating once a year is usually enough. In the South, booster shots may be necessary every three to six months because the mosquitos that spread the disease are active all year. Ask your veterinarian which types your pony should be inoculated against, and how often.

RABIES: A virus disease that affects the brain and nervous system. It is very serious because it is always fatal in horses and because people can get it. Rabies is transmitted in saliva by the bite of a rabid animal, often a wild animal such as a skunk or a raccoon.

Symptoms: Rabies takes a long time (up to two months) to develop, so you may not know that the horse was bitten. The site of the bite may itch or become inflamed. Other symptoms are depression, inability to eat and drink normally, lack of coordination, personality change or unusual behavior (excitement or aggressiveness for no apparent reason), and paralysis. Symptoms can vary and may be confused with those of other diseases, such as encephalomyelitis.

Caution: If there is any possibility that a horse could have rabies, *do not handle him.* Call the veterinarian immediately.

Prevention: In areas where there is rabies in the wildlife, a rabies shot should be given every year to horses and ponies, dogs, pets, and barn cats.

EQUINE INFECTIOUS ANEMIA (EIA OR SWAMP FEVER): A blood disease caused by a virus. It is usually transmitted when a fly or mosquito bites an infected horse and then bites another horse, transferring infected blood. It also can be transmitted by needles used on more than one horse. EIA is incurable and often fatal.

Some cases of EIA are "acute" (a fairly short, severe case that usually is fatal); others are "chronic" (a long-term case that weakens the horse and may flare up into an acute case). Some horses are "carriers"; that is, they show no signs of the disease but may transmit it to other horses.

The Coggins test is a blood test that detects the antibodies formed when a horse is infected with EIA. A negative Coggins test is required for Pony Club events and by most competitions and stables. Some states have laws requiring testing. Horses that test positive for EIA must be quarantined, or kept separated from healthy horses.

Symptoms: Fever, depression, sweating, loss of appetite, increasing weakness, jaundice, frequent urination, staggering gait, and paralysis. A positive Coggins test confirms the diagnosis.

Prevention: Because there is no effective treatment and no vaccine to prevent EIA, it's important to keep healthy horses away from those infected with EIA. Horses and ponies should have a negative Coggins test as part of the pre-purchase exam. Negative Coggins tests should be required by Pony Clubs, stables, and competitions; and animals that test positive for EIA should be quarantined.

Non-Communicable Diseases and Ailments   Ailments that are not transmitted from one horse to another are called non-communicable diseases. You should recognize their symptoms and know what to do if they occur. It's important to know what causes these ailments because they usually can be prevented with good horse management.

COLIC: "Colic" means belly pain and can range from a minor upset to very severe. Colic should always be taken seriously because it can be fatal.

Colic pain may come from gas, spasms or cramps, irritation of the bowel, excessive fullness of the stomach or intestines, obstruction (blockage) of the bowel, or a twisted intestine.

There are several types of colic:

Spasmodic colic: Caused by spasms (or cramps) of the bowel. This colic often is the result of a horse eating spoiled feed, overeating, or drinking cold water when he is overheated.

Flatulent (gas) colic: Caused by a buildup of gas in the intestines, often is the result of eating spoiled feed, frozen grass, or lawn clippings, which ferment and produce gas.

Impaction colic: Caused when indigestible material collects and blocks the bowel. This kind of colic usually develops more slowly than other colics, over several days, and often is caused by lack of water or by swallowing sand along with the feed.

Thromboembolism: Caused by worm larvae that invade the blood vessels that supply the intestines. A large clot may form, blocking off blood supply to part of the bowel, causing severe damage. This type of colic can be prevented by regular deworming.

Obstruction (twisted gut): Occurs when the bowel becomes twisted or "telescopes" on itself. This can happen during other types of colic, especially if a horse rolls violently while his intestines are distended with gas. This type of colic is very serious, and surgery is usually necessary to save the horse.

Many colics can be prevented by good management. Here are some of the most common and most preventable causes of colic:

+ Overeating (especially grain)
+ Spoiled or unsuitable feed (especially grass clippings or frozen grass)
+ Sudden change of diet
+ A horse drinking large amounts of cold water when he is overheated
+ Working horse hard right after he has eaten
+ Swallowing sand along with feed
+ Damage to intestines caused by worms

Symptoms of Colic:

Mild or early colic: When a horse has mild colic or is just starting to feel discomfort, the symptoms are fairly mild. Some of the first signs you might notice are that the horse stops eating or moving and looks at his barrel. He acts restless and may paw, curl up his upper lip, or stretch out as if he wants to urinate. He may lie down and get up again. His pulse rate will be slightly higher than normal.

More serious colic: As the pain becomes more severe, the horse tries to lie down and roll. (Rolling should *not* be allowed because it increases the danger of twisting the intestines.) He may look anxious, paw, kick at his belly, and break out in a sweat. His pulse rate is higher, and he may breathe heavily. In severe colic, the horse may roll and thrash violently.

The color of the horse's mucus membranes (his gums) is an important sign that the veterinarian will want to know about. In serious cases, the gums may become bright red or bluish.

COLIC

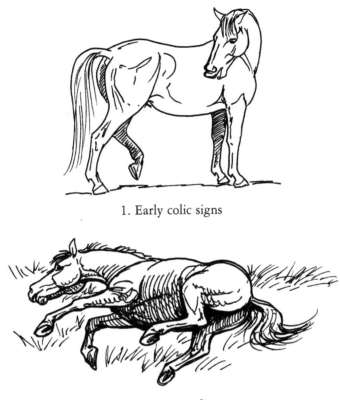

1. Early colic signs

2. Severe colic

What to Do: If you see signs of colic, take the horse's vital signs, note the color of his gums, and write everything down. Call your veterinarian, and walk the horse slowly while you wait; don't let him lie down or roll. Record his vital signs every fifteen minutes. If he seems to be feeling better after walking for twenty minutes or so (he passes gas and manure, is interested in eating, and seems more alert), you can put him in his stall or paddock and check on him every fifteen minutes. If his symptoms are severe or if he seems to be getting worse, keep him from lying down and rolling, and cover him with a blanket if he is in danger of getting chilled. Don't give food or medication to a horse with colic unless your veterinarian tells you to.

AZOTURIA (TYING UP, OR MONDAY MORNING SICKNESS): Azoturia (also called "tying up") is a serious metabolic disorder. It usually occurs when fit, hard-working horses that receive a full daily ration of grain are kept idle in a stall for a day or two with no corresponding cutback in their grain ration. When the horse begins to work again, he shows signs of distress, and the muscles of his hindquarters go into spasms (cramps), until he cannot move. Horses that have had one attack of azoturia are more likely to have another.

Symptoms: Symptoms usually appear shortly after exercise begins, usually after one or two days of rest. They include the following: stiffness and short stride in the hind legs, which may get worse until the horse cannot move at all; hard, tense, and sometimes quivering muscles in the hindquarters; dark-colored urine; elevated temperature, pulse, and respiration rates.; and sweating, restlessness, and an anxious expression.

What to Do: Stop the horse as soon as you suspect he is tying up; continuing to move can make him worse. Call the veterinarian. If the horse is sweating and the weather is cold, blanket him to prevent chilling. (Do not blanket a horse in hot weather.)

Prevention: Proper management and conditioning, especially the balancing of feed and exercise, is the best prevention. Always cut the grain ration to half or less on days when a horse is idle, especially if he must remain in the stall.

LAMINITIS: Laminitis is a serious metabolic disorder that can cripple a horse. It is an inflammation of the sensitive laminae inside the feet. During an attack of laminitis, the laminae begin to tear loose from the rest of the hoof, and the coffin bone (the bottom bone of the foot) may sink down. This makes it terribly painful to bear weight on the feet and can lead to permanent damage. Laminitis develops when toxins (poisons) that are released into the horse's bloodstream damage the circulation in the feet. These toxins usually come from overeating grain or too much lush grass, but they can also be a side effect from other diseases or a reaction to a drug.

LAMINITIS

A. Normal laminae
   attach wall of
   hoof to coffin
   bone.

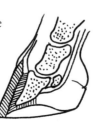
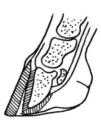

B. Laminitis:
   Laminae
   separate,
   coffin bone
   rotates, sole
   drops.

Ponies tend to be more prone to laminitis than horses, and overweight horses or ponies with fat deposits on their rump, back, and crest are especially at risk. Concussion from hard work on hard ground can also be a cause. Horses that have had one attack of laminitis are more likely to have another.

Symptoms: Laminitis may affect both front feet or all four feet (not just one foot). The horse is in severe pain and does not want to walk; he may lie down and refuse to get up. He stands with his hind legs drawn up under his body and his front legs forward, to keep as much weight as he can off his painful front feet. The feet feel hot, and there is a hard, pounding pulse in the digital artery at the back of the pastern.

Laminitis Stance

A horse that has had laminitis is said to be "foundered." His feet may have dropped soles and may show wavy, irregular rings. His toes may curl up, and he may have "seedy toe," a condition in which the wall separates from the sole at the toe, with soft, rotten horn in between.

What to Do: Call the veterinarian immediately. Remove any grain, and take the pony off pasture. Hosing the legs and feet with cold water may help ease the pain (but ask your veterinarian; some veterinarians believe that soaking with hot water is better).

The pony will need treatment to reverse the effects of the toxins, and painkillers so that he can walk, which will help the circulation in his feet. Later, he may need special shoeing to correct hoof problems that result from founder.

Prevention: Laminitis usually can be prevented by careful feeding, management, and conditioning. Here are some ways to prevent laminitis:

- The most common cause of laminitis is overeating. Keep grain locked up so that your pony cannot get into it. If your pony should get into the grain, try to estimate how much he has eaten and call the veterinarian immediately.
- Ponies and some horses may develop laminitis if they eat too much lush grass, especially in the spring.
- Never feed horses feed meant for other livestock. Some cattle and pig feeds contain additives that can cause laminitis.
- Don't let your pony get fat. Overweight animals are especially prone to laminitis.

HEAVES (EMPHYSEMA): Heaves is a breathing problem caused by eating dusty or moldy hay, by allergies, or by living in dusty conditions. The alveoli (small air sacs) in the lungs lose their elasticity, and the horse must use his abdominal muscles to push air out of his lungs. Horses with heaves have a chronic cough and lack stamina. Heaves cannot be cured, but good care and management may help relieve the symptoms. Many horses with moderate heaves can be used for light riding, but they are not able to do strenuous work.

Symptoms: A chronic cough, especially during exercise, and a noticeable double lift of the flanks and belly as the horse breathes out.

HEAVES

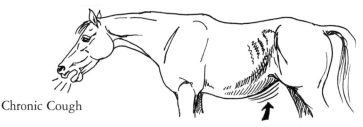

Chronic Cough

Abdominal jerk when exhaling

Prevention: Never feed horses moldy or dusty hay. If you choose to feed a horse hay that is only slightly dusty, you should wet it down before giving it to your horse (but it is better to avoid feeding horses *any* dusty hay). Keep bedding as free as possible from dust. Do not keep horses in an environment where they are constantly forced to breathe dusty air. Horses with heaves should be kept at pasture as much as possible, and their hay and feed should be wet down. Some horses do better on a special non-allergenic feed or when fed beet pulp instead of hay.

CHOKING: Choking in horses means obstruction (blockage) of the esophagus; it is not the same as choking in people. It happens when something gets stuck and the horse cannot finish swallowing it. The horse can still breathe, but he becomes quite distressed, and he needs a veterinarian's help without delay.

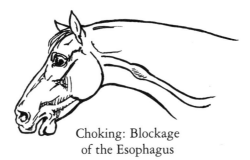

Choking: Blockage
of the Esophagus

Choking is most common in horses fed coarse hay or pelleted feed, especially if they are not given enough water. Large chunks of apple or carrot may cause choking, which is why they should be cut into small slices before they are given to horses. A serious case of choking can cause scarring, which narrows the esophagus, making choking more likely to recur.

Symptoms: The horse stops eating, keeps trying to swallow, and becomes distressed. He may drool, and chewed food may come back through his nostrils. You may be able to feel a hard lump in the esophagus (along the jugular groove).

What to Do: Call the veterinarian. Keep the animal quiet. Remove feed and hay, but let him drink if he wants to (water may soften the mass and help it pass on down the esophagus).

Prevention: Make sure your pony has plenty of water available at all times, especially in cold weather. Slow down greedy eaters by placing large, smooth stones (softball size) in the grain feeder or by spreading the grain out in a thin layer. Feed small amounts often, and feed good-quality hay. Cut apples into small slices, and slice carrots lengthwise before feeding them to your pony.

Skin Diseases   Some skin diseases are highly contagious; others are not. To avoid spreading skin diseases, a pony should have his own equipment, which should not be used on other animals. Laundering saddle pads and washable girths once a week helps prevent the spread of skin diseases. Grooming tools should be washed and disinfected weekly.

Skin diseases should be diagnosed and treated by your veterinarian.

RINGWORM: This is a fungus infection that produces round, painless crusts on the horse's skin. These fall off, leaving round, hairless patches. Ringworm is very contagious and can be spread to and from other animals such as cattle, dogs, cats, and people. You can get it from your pony, and he can get it from you!

Treatment   If you see signs of ringworm on your horse, isolate him from other animals and keep his blankets, grooming tools, and tack separate. The horse should be sponged daily with a fungicide (for example, Captan), and an iodine solution may be painted on the skin lesions to kill the fungus. The tack and grooming tools must be disinfected with a fungicide solution.

RAINROT: This skin infection is caused by an organism that lives in dirty, ungroomed coats, especially during wet weather. Rainrot appears as many small, scabby crusts that adhere tightly to the skin. When the crusts are removed, the spots underneath are wet and raw. Rainrot appears on the horse's body wherever the coat stays wet, especially on top of the back and croup. It is most common in the spring and fall, in horses kept outdoors; it rarely occurs in horses that are stabled and groomed daily. Rainrot does not seem to be contagious, although several horses living in the same conditions may develop it at the same time. To prevent rainrot, check pastured horses daily, especially in wet weather.

Treatment   Rainrot is treated with antibiotics (usually penicillin). The horse should be protected from the weather while he is being treated. Washing with a mild shampoo helps to soften the crusts so that they can be removed without hurting the horse. A mixture of mineral oil and 2 percent tamed iodine can be used to treat the affected areas.

SCRATCHES (ALSO CALLED MUD FEVER OR "GREASE"): A painful, chapped condition of the pasterns, which crack open, ooze serum, and may become infected. It results from the loss of skin oils through contact with urine, manure, or harsh detergents, or long exposure to wet, muddy conditions. Scratches is most common in "mud season": fall, winter, and spring.

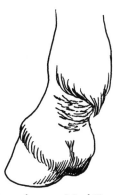

Scratches, or Mud Fever

If scratches develops, the area should be washed gently with mild soap and patted dry, but repeated washings and harsh chemicals should be avoided. Trim the long fetlock hairs to keep them from irritating the area. Apply an antibacterial ointment (like Nitrafurazone), cover with a non-stick dressing, and bandage the area. The horse must be kept out of wet, dirty conditions to allow the pasterns to heal.

To prevent scratches, avoid letting horses stand in wet, dirty conditions. Don't wash the horse's legs in cold weather or use harsh detergents. It may help to protect the pasterns with hand cream or Vaseline before riding or turning out the horse in muddy conditions.

First-Aid Kit

It's essential for all horse owners to have at least a basic first-aid kit in case of accidents and emergencies. You must know how to use the items you have in your first-aid kit. A first-aid kit should contain the following items:

- Absorbent cotton
- Gauze roll, stretch type, at least two inches wide
- Crepe bandage (Vetrap or similar type)
- Sterile non-stick gauze dressings, 4 x 4 inches
- Sterile gauze "sponges" (smaller squares for cleaning wounds)
- Adhesive tape, at least one inch wide

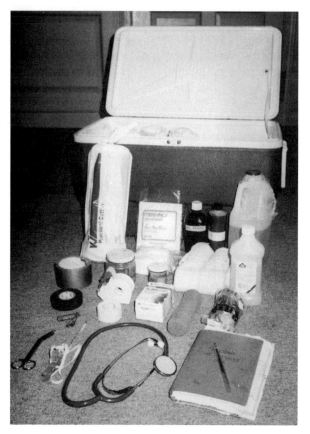

EQUINE FIRST-AID KIT:

Top: Cooler, containing four sheet cotton leg pads.

Back row, left to right: Cotton, 4" x 4" gauze squares, leg brace, Betadine, saline solution.

Second row: Duct tape, petroleum jelly, wound-dressing salve, four bandages, alcohol.

Third row: Plastic tape, adhesive tape, Kling gauze, 6" Ace bandage, Vetrap bandage.

Front row: Bandage scissors, bandage pins, veterinary thermometer with string and clip, stethoscope, and notebook and pen. *Photo: Ruth Harvie*

- Pressure pads (non-deodorant-type sanitary napkins work well)
- Bandage scissors (with blunt ends, capable of cutting bandages)

- Saline solution or bottled water for cleaning wounds
- Betadine, Phisohex, or antibacterial soap for cleaning wounds
- Wound dressing (Nitrafurazone or antibiotic ointment or powder, or wound dressing recommended by your veterinarian)
- Veterinary thermometer (with string and clip)
- Vaseline
- Rubbing alcohol
- Liniment or body wash
- Four leg bandages and four leg pads (sheet cottons)
- Bandage pins and masking tape
- Notebook and pencil

A plastic picnic cooler or a large plastic bucket with a snap-on lid makes a good container for a first-aid kit and keeps the items inside clean. The contents should be checked every week or two, and items should be replaced when necessary.

First Aid for Serious Wounds

Ponies sometimes get cuts, bumps, and scratches, just like people do. You can take care of minor "Band-Aid" cuts yourself, but serious wounds must be seen by a veterinarian. These include the following:

- Major bleeding
- Deep wounds
- Wounds on a leg, a joint, or an eye
- All puncture wounds
- Wounds that need to be sutured (stitched)

Wounds that go right through the skin or that gap open may need sutures; they should be seen by a veterinarian within six hours or it may be too late to suture them successfully. If a veterinarian is going to treat a wound, do not put any antiseptic or ointment on it. You may clean it with sterile saline solution (the best choice because it stings less), bottled seltzer water, or plain water, and cover it with a non-stick, sterile dressing and a bandage. Keep the pony quiet and away from dust and dirt until the veterinarian arrives.

Serious Bleeding Serious bleeding occurs when a large blood vessel is cut. You may see either spurting of bright red blood (from an artery) or a steady flow of darker blood (from a vein). The first thing to do is to control the pony and keep him quiet so that you can control the bleeding.

To control bleeding, apply pressure directly on the wound. Use a thick pad (several clean gauze pads, a sanitary napkin, or a folded cloth), and press down firmly. Keep the pressure on until the bleeding stops or the veterinarian arrives. If the wound is on a leg, you can apply a stable bandage to hold the pad in place. Do not take the pads or bandage off, even if blood soaks through, because this can start the bleeding again. Let the veterinarian remove the covering.

Kinds of Wounds

- *Incised wounds*: Clean cuts made by a sharp object, like glass. Incised wounds may bleed a lot; if they are deep or gap open, they may need stitches.
- *Lacerations*: Torn cuts, where the skin is ripped (often made by barbed wire). If they are deep or very big, they may need stitches. Lacerations on the legs or over joints can be serious and should be seen by a veterinarian.
- *Abrasions*: Scrapes or sores caused by rubbing. They are not usually deep but may be full of dirt. They should be cleaned thoroughly by running a stream of clean cold water over the wound.
- *Puncture wounds*: Deep, narrow wounds such as those made by a nail or splinter. Sometimes a piece of splinter may be left in the wound. Puncture wounds can be serious because they may go deep into a muscle, tendon or joint, and they can easily get infected. There is more danger of tetanus with puncture wounds than with other types of wounds, so the pony may need a tetanus booster shot. All puncture wounds should be seen by a veterinarian.
- *Bruises*: Often caused by a kick or a blow. The skin may not be broken, but the tissues and blood vessels underneath are damaged. There may be swelling, and the area will be tender. Sometimes bleeding under the skin causes a hematoma (a swelling filled with blood). Applying cold (an ice pack wrapped in a towel, or cold water from a hose) for fifteen to twenty minutes will help reduce the pain and swelling.

Treating Minor Wounds

1. If a wound bleeds quite a lot, press a pad (several gauze pads; a sanitary napkin; or a clean, folded cloth) firmly against the wound. In a minor cut, the bleeding may stop on its own within a few minutes.

2. Hose the wound and the area around it with a gentle stream of cool water for ten minutes, letting the water float away dirt and particles that stick to the surface. This method works well for abrasions and dirty wounds.

3. Next, clean the wound gently, using saline solution, sterile water, or bottled water (if available), and an antibacterial soap like Betadine or Phisohex. (If these are not available, use any gentle soap.) To clean the wound, use gauze pads (not cotton, which leaves fibers in the wound). Discard each cleaning pad as it becomes soiled; don't dip it back into the cleaning solution. Clean the area above the wound first, and work down.

4. Gently blot the wound dry with a sterile gauze square, or allow it to dry without touching it.

5. If the wound is small, dust it with antibiotic powder (Nitrafurazone powder, or whatever your veterinarian recommends), or apply a small amount of antibiotic cream. Don't use peroxide, alcohol, iodine, Vaseline, or strong antiseptics on wounds; these can damage the tissues and may interfere with healing. Some veterinarians prefer that you not put anything at all on a wound.

6. If the wound is in a place that may get dirty and can be bandaged (a leg, for example), the wound should be protected with a dressing and a bandage. Use a large, sterile, non-stick gauze dressing over the wound; then apply a stable bandage over it.

7. If the area cannot be bandaged, you may apply antibiotic powder or ointment (some veterinarians prefer that you put nothing on the wound), and check the wound frequently to be sure that it is not contaminated with dirt or bedding. If the wound gets dirty, clean it gently with running water. Don't scrub the wound itself, or you may damage the healing tissues.

Proud Flesh   Proud flesh (also called "excessive granulation") is a healing problem. It can occur in wounds that do not close properly, especially on the legs, or in wounds that are irritated by improper treatment, strong antiseptics, or too much movement (especially near a joint). The wound forms too much granulation tissue (a tissue that normally helps wounds to heal), which bulges out from the surface of the wound. Proud flesh appears pink or pinkish-white and bunchy, like the surface of a cauliflower, and is wet and raw. If a wound seems to be developing proud flesh, your veterinarian should see it.

Proud Flesh, or Excessive Granulation

Cold Hosing   Cold hosing means running a stream of cool water over a wound or a leg. This method is used to clean wounds, to reduce swelling, and to treat bruises and sprains. The steady stream of water acts like a gentle massage, and the cold helps to reduce pain and swelling.

Here is the procedure for cold hosing a wound or a lame leg:

1. Grease the heels and the back of the pastern with Vaseline to protect them from becoming chapped.
2. Start with a slow, steady stream. Wet the hoof first, and slowly work up the leg until the water flows down from above the injured area.
3. Run the water over the leg for five to ten minutes to clean a wound; for fifteen to twenty minutes, to treat a bruise or cool a lame leg. Dry the leg carefully afterward. For a lame leg, repeat this procedure twice a day.

Note: It's important to realize that we are always learning more about horse health care, diseases, injuries, and first aid. As more research is done, recommended treatments and medications may change. As a horse owner, you must stay up to date on the best methods of horse health care. Your veterinarian is your best source of advice on what is best for your pony.

CHAPTER 7

CONDITIONING

"Conditioning" is the process of getting a pony fit (it can also apply to you!) so that he can go longer and faster and work harder without getting tired. Through conditioning, he also becomes tougher and stronger and is less likely to hurt himself.

Conditioning could be called "body building." The body has a wonderful ability to respond to work. When it works a little harder than it is used to, it becomes stronger. Muscles get bigger and stronger, blood carries more oxygen and nutrients, and the heart and lungs pump better. If the body gets more work than it is ready for, it can suffer damage and start to break down. If the body works less than usual, it gets lazy and becomes weaker and softer. Conditioning only works over time, so exercise must be repeated and increased gradually, day by day, over weeks and months. If you try to do too much exercise in one day, not only are you not conditioning, but you are running the risk of injury. The only way to build a strong body (in you or your pony) is to give it just enough exercise every day, along with the right nutrition and enough rest.

Conditioning also involves knowing how to ride your pony safely, cool him out, and care for him properly when doing strenuous work, especially in hot weather. You can seriously overstress your pony if you do not know enough about conditioning and care.

SAFETY, HEALTH, AND SOUNDNESS CONSIDERATIONS

Before you start to condition a pony, have your veterinarian check him for overall health and soundness. No pony can be in good condition if he is unhealthy or unsound. If you work an injured pony, you could make the injury much worse.

When you ride or compete (especially in strenuous activities), you must know how to evaluate your pony's fitness, use good judgment while riding, and care for him properly afterward. To do these things, you must understand what happens to your pony's body when he works hard, and how to help him cool out safely. In North America, competitions and rallies are often held in hot weather, so you need to know how to keep your pony safe and comfortable in these conditions.

One of the most important things you can do to keep your pony sound is to warm him up gradually and cool him out carefully each time you ride. Another is to know your pony so well that you quickly notice any small change that points to something wrong.

Each day, take time to jog your pony in hand and notice how he moves, especially before he is warmed up. Clean his feet and check his shoes before and after you ride. Run your hands over his back and muscles and down each leg when you first bring him out, and when he is cooled out after work. If you find tenderness, heat, or "filling" (swelling that "fills up" the spaces around the tendons), or if he is lame or slightly "off," get help from your veterinarian *right away*. Don't work your pony or put off doing something about a problem, hoping it will go away!

Vital Signs: Temperature, Pulse, and Respiration Rates

Vital signs are important indicators of a pony's health, fitness, and condition. During work, his temperature and pulse and respiration rates go up; they come back down as he returns to normal. The time he takes to return to normal (recovery time) is an important indicator of fitness. A fit pony recovers quickly; an unfit pony takes longer to recover.

These are average temperatures and pulse and respiration rates, but individual ponies vary. A temperature reading that is normal for one pony could be above normal for another. It's important to know what your pony's normal temperature, pulse, and respiration rates are, and to keep a record of this information. This is important for evaluating your pony's condition, spotting trouble, and for your veterinarian to know when he or she is diagnosing illness.

Take (and write down) your pony's vital signs at rest (when he has not been worked) and after exercise (after he is cooled out). This gives you a record, or "base line," of what is normal for him. You can use these figures for comparison when you check his recovery rate during conditioning, or if you believe he is sick. Abnormal vital signs (such as a temperature one or two degrees above normal in a resting pony) can be a symptom of illness.

Taking Temperature A pony's temperature is taken rectally, using a veterinary thermometer (which has a ring on the end, with a string and clip to fasten it to the pony's tail).

TAKING THE TEMPERATURE

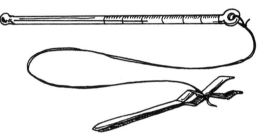

Veterinary thermometer with string and clip

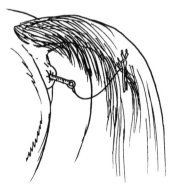

Taking a pony's temperature

Caution: Do not try to take a pony's temperature yourself until an experienced person has shown you how to do it safely.

Shake the thermometer until the mercury is below 97° Fahrenheit, and grease the thermometer with petroleum jelly. Stand to one side of the pony, lift his tail, and gently push about two-thirds of the thermometer into the rectum. Clip the string to the pony's tail, or hold the end of the thermometer firmly so that it cannot be drawn into the rectum. After one to two minutes, withdraw the thermometer, wipe it clean, and read the temperature.

A pony's normal temperature at rest is about 100.5° Fahrenheit, but this can vary slightly from one animal to another.

Taking the Pulse (Heart Rate)   The pulse rate tells how fast a pony's heart is beating. It can be felt on an artery that is close to the surface, or heard by listening with a stethoscope over the heart.

You can feel the pulse at the facial artery, at the inside bottom edge of your pony's jawbone. The facial artery (which feels like a thick string) crosses the jawbone. If you rest your fingertip lightly on the artery, you will feel it twitch—this is the pulse, or heartbeat. Check your watch and count how many beats you feel in ten seconds. If you multiply that number by six, you will have the beats per minute or heart rate.

There are other places to take a pony's pulse; one easy way is to use a stethoscope to listen to his heart. (Ask your veterinarian to show you how to take the pulse and where to listen with a stethoscope.)

A pony's normal resting pulse rate is between thirty and forty-five beats per minute, but this rate varies in individuals. The pulse rate goes much higher during work and when a pony is excited or stressed.

TAKING THE PULSE

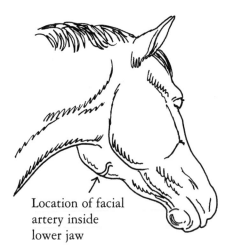

Location of facial
artery inside
lower jaw

Taking Respiration (Breathing) Rate   Watch the pony's flank as it goes in and out with each breath, or watch his nostrils. One "in and out" is one breath. Count his breaths for fifteen seconds and multiply by four; this gives you the breaths per minute, or respiration rate.

A pony's normal breathing rate at rest is between eight and sixteen breaths per minute. Ponies breathe faster when stressed, excited, ill, or very hot.

Thermoregulation: Temperature Control

The body's temperature-control process is called "thermoregulation." This is the process by which a horse keeps himself warm in cold weather, and cools himself in hot weather and during and after hard work.

As the body burns fuel to produce energy, the body gets hotter. (You feel this yourself when you exercise.) A small rise in temperature helps the muscles to work at their best level, which is why "warming up" before strenuous work is important. However, hard work produces a great deal of extra heat, which the body must get rid of. Hot, humid weather or standing in a hot, enclosed place such as a closed stall or trailer can also cause a horse's temperature to rise.

A horse can get rid of excess heat in the following ways:

- By radiation: When the horse's temperature is higher than the air around him, he radiates heat into the cooler air. Radiation does not work when the horse is covered by tack or a cooler, or when the air temperature is hotter than the horse.
- By heat transfer from a hotter surface to a cooler one (for example, pouring cool water over a hot horse)
- By a current of air passing over the skin—for instance, standing in a breeze or using a fan
- By evaporation: As sweat or water evaporates from the skin, the temperature of the skin goes down.

The body must be able to get rid of excessive heat; otherwise, serious problems such as muscle cramps and heat exhaustion result. Getting rid of excessive heat is more difficult for horses and ponies than for some other animals because horses and ponies have large bodies and thick, dense muscles that hold in the heat. Overweight horses and ponies and those with thick hair coats overheat more easily and are more difficult to cool out. Some horses cool more easily than others, depending on their body type and condition, and whether they are used to working in heat and humidity.

Heat Index   When the heat and humidity are high, horses must be worked with caution. In extreme conditions, horses should not be worked at all because they can become dangerously overheated. This applies to people, too!

The heat index is the temperature plus the humidity level. You can find out the temperature and humidity by checking the local weather report. To find the heat index, add the two numbers. For example, if the temperature is 80 degrees Farenheit and the humidity level is 60 percent, the heat index is 140.

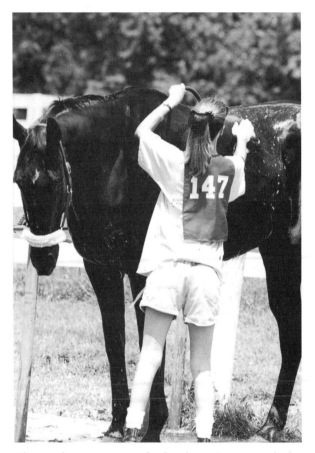

The quickest way to cool a hot horse is to pour large amounts of cold water over him. *Photo: Susan Sexton*

High humidity makes it harder to cool down. Horses can work well and cool down effectively when the heat index is around 125 (for example, a pleasant seventy degrees with 55 percent humidity). At a heat index of 140 or above, a horse must sweat heavily to cool himself down. At 150 or above, horses have great difficulty cooling themselves down naturally, and special measures are necessary to help them. When the heat index is 180 or higher, horses should not be worked at all, as they can become dangerously overheated.

Special Measures for Cooling Out in Hot Weather   A very hot pony needs to cool down rapidly. It was once believed that cooling should be done slowly, but recent research shows this is not true.

Note: Rapid cooling of very hot horses does *not* cause muscle cramps or tying up, but staying overheated too long can be dangerous!

Sponge or hose down the pony with plenty of cool water, all over his body, and scrape him as you go. Keep sponging and scraping until the water that you scrape off his skin is no longer hot. When the water running off is cool, the pony will have cooled to a normal temperature.

In severe conditions, use *cold* water with ice. (This should be done under supervision of a veterinarian or an experienced person.)

In these conditions, *do not* cover a pony with a cooler or an anti-sweat sheet. This holds the heat in and keeps him from cooling down as quickly as he needs to. Coolers and anti-sweat sheets are meant to keep a pony with a wet coat from becoming chilled in *cold* weather.

Exercise and Care in Cold Weather

Ponies can work quite well in cold weather, but there are some special problems to watch out for.

Footing and Shoeing   During cold weather, you must choose a safe place to ride that has the best footing possible, especially if you must ride outdoors. You may be able to keep a track or area open for riding, or you may cushion hard ground by spreading used bedding over it. (**Caution**: Ice will stay frozen underneath straw or used bedding. This should be used only in areas where the ground is frozen but dry.) Icy places, often found in low areas where water collects, should be blocked off.

When the ground freezes, the footing becomes very hard, which increases the concussion on a pony's feet and legs. The ground may be slick and icy, or frozen with a thin layer of slick mud on top; both footings are very slippery. Rough ground with frozen hoofprints is very hard on a pony's feet and legs, and he can easily stumble. For your pony's safety and your own, avoid riding on slippery or uneven frozen ground, and, if you must cross it, keep to a walk. To make winter riding easier, your farrier can add borium (a super-hard substance that bites into ice and frozen ground) to your pony's shoes.

Snow can be a good footing to ride on if it is light and not too deep. (For more about riding in snow, see page 81).

Warmup and Exercise   Warming up is especially important in cold weather, when a pony's muscles may take longer to warm up. You may not be able to ride as regularly in cold weather as you do in warm weather, so you should avoid overworking your pony when you do ride him.

If a pony has a long coat, he may get hot and sweaty quickly, especially when the weather is not very cold. If he sweats and dries, he is cooling himself normally. However, if his coat gets soaked through and he stands in a cold wind, he can get chilled. Be aware of how hot and wet he is; keep him moving enough to keep warm, but don't overwork him.

If your pony is clipped or has a thin coat, don't let him get chilled while you are riding. Keep a cooler or cover over him until you are ready to mount, and keep him moving. If he must stand still for a while, he should be covered with a cooler. A clipped pony doing slow work in cold weather may need to wear a "quarter sheet" (a special blanket that covers his back and hindquarters, made to be used under the saddle).

Cooling Out in Cold Weather   Cooling out is easier in cold weather because the air is cooler than the horse's body and he loses heat more quickly. After hard work, he should "warm down" gradually at a walk. Once his temperature returns to normal, it's important to keep him from getting chilled, which can lead to illness.

If the weather is cool but not breezy, a horse may cool out and dry off while walking slowly. If it is cold or windy, he should be covered with a cooler or an anti-sweat sheet. Be careful not to let a horse get overheated under a waterproof rain sheet.

If your pony has a long coat, he may be damp long after he has cooled down to a normal temperature. If he is exposed to cold air, wind, or drafts while his coat is damp, he will get chilled, which can make him ill. A cool but damp pony must be kept out of drafts and should be covered with an anti-sweat sheet, a wool cooler, or other "breathable" cover while he dries. His coat cannot keep him warm until it is dry and fluffy. (See page 248 for more on drying a wet coat.)

Basic Conditioning: From Unfit to Ordinary Riding Fitness

An unfit but healthy pony needs a gradual conditioning program to bring him into shape for ordinary riding. This usually takes about four to six weeks, depending on the pony's age and condition.

To get a pony fit, you should ride him at least four times a week (five or six times a week is better). He should have at least one day off on which he is turned out. Soft ponies easily get rubs and sores, so make sure your pony is groomed clean each time you ride, and that his tack fits well. You must also pay attention to his feet and legs, and adjust his feed for the amount of work he is doing.

When you start out, you should do most conditioning work at the walk. As you progress, your riding sessions should gradually get longer, instead of going faster. This is called "long, slow distance work," and it is what makes a pony sound and strong.

Start out by leading your pony at a brisk walk for ten minutes. If you can, lead him at a jog for one minute. (This will get *you* fit, too!) Then mount up and ride at a brisk walk for another ten to fifteen minutes. He should work enough to sweat a little. Cool him out, and sponge or brush him clean after riding.

Each time you ride, increase the length of your ride a little, until your rides last about forty minutes. After a week of walking, you can begin to add short trots—about a minute at first, gradually working up to three-minute trots. Always walk for the first fifteen minutes, and walk for five minutes after each trot. Walk the last fifteen minutes to cool out.

Watch your pony's breathing to know when he needs a break. At first, he may breathe hard when he trots even a little. He should return to normal breathing when you walk for five minutes.

Next, begin walking up gentle hills. As your pony gets fitter and doesn't breathe as hard going uphill, start trotting slowly up gentle hills. Walk down hills; trotting downhill is hard on a pony's legs.

Each week your riding sessions can become a little longer (forty-five minutes to an hour), and you can add more trotting until you are trotting for five minutes at a time, with five minutes of walking in between. Riding conditioning trail rides is more fun for both of you than going around a ring.

When your pony can do forty-five minutes to an hour of walking, including hill work and five-minute trots, you can add short canters.

Most fitness work, however, should be done at the walk and trot. When a pony can do a one-hour ride, including several five-minute trots and short canters, without getting too tired, he is ready for regular riding lessons and can start cavaletti work and jumping. For fast work, long-distance trail rides, foxhunting, or eventing, he will need further conditioning.

As a pony becomes more fit and does more work, he burns more energy. His grain should be increased gradually, a little each week.

Caution: To prevent Azoturia, *always* cut your pony's grain back to half or less of his regular amount on any day he is not ridden.

Further Conditioning

Once a pony has reached basic riding fitness, he will need further conditioning in order to be ready for more strenuous work such as Pony Club rallies, combined-training events, foxhunting, and competitive trail rides.

Trotting   To increase your pony's endurance and ability to go for longer distances, gradually increase the length of your trots from five minutes to eight minutes, then ten minutes. Always walk for at least five minutes after each trot. Eventually, your work should be approximately 50 percent walking and 50 percent trotting, and you should be able to trot a mile in ten minutes; this is a pace of 6 miles per hour. Spend half the time posting and half in half-seat; this will get you fit, too! As your pony gets fitter, you can trot up longer and steeper hills. (But remember to *walk* downhill.)

Galloping   To develop wind and fitness for activities such as eventing or foxhunting, which require a faster pace, you will need to add slow galloping to your conditioning work once or twice a week. This strengthens a pony's muscles, improves his wind, and teaches him to work at a comfortable galloping pace.

You should gallop on a measured course 1/2 mile (800 meters) to 1 mile (1,600 meters) long, and only on good footing (see page 82 for more about galloping and pace). You *must* warm up your pony for twenty to thirty minutes at the walk and trot before you gallop.

When you start, your gallops should be fairly short (about 800 meters, or 1/2 mile) and not too fast (about 250 meters per minute, or 10 miles per hour, which is really just a strong canter). After a gallop, slow down gradually, and walk until your pony's breathing returns to normal. Then do a second slow gallop at the same distance and speed. A fit pony should recover his normal breathing in five minutes or less. After the last canter or gallop, check your pony's recovery rate, and walk him until he is completely cooled out—at least twenty minutes.

In all your work, but especially in galloping, you must increase the level of the work gradually, and you must use good judgment about how much work is best for your pony. This means keeping track of how he is feeling and acting. If he is lively, eager, and strong, you may increase his work (but be careful not to gallop so much or so fast that you make him "hot" and excitable). If he shows signs of being overworked (acting tired or cranky; having stiff, sore muscles; showing swelling in his legs; or not eating well), you *must* slow down and give him less work. Don't follow any conditioning program too rigidly—pay attention to how your pony is doing, and use your common sense! You may find that factors such as bad weather, a minor injury, or loss of a shoe may force you to alter your conditioning schedule.

Conditioning for Special Activities

Different activities such as show jumping, competitive trail rides, combined-training events, and foxhunting require special conditioning after your pony has reached basic fitness.

Conditioning for Showing, Dressage, and Show Jumping   A pony that is being shown must be in show condition, with the right weight, muscle development, and a shiny coat. His legs and muscles must be able to handle the work he does, but he does not need to be as fit as for eventing or distance riding. In fact, when some ponies get too fit, they get too strong and excitable. Feed him just enough to keep him in good flesh, with a shiny coat, but don't overfeed him so that he gets too frisky and hard to handle, or overweight.

Ordinary riding of one to two hours a day, six days a week, is usually sufficient to get a pony fit for showing. Remember to warm up gradually and cool down carefully after work. A pony should not be jumped every day because this is hard on his legs; two to three times per week is plenty.

Conditioning for Competitive Trail and Distance Riding   A competitive trail ride is a test of conditioning and horsemanship. A pony is expected to cover a distance of 20 to 50 miles, including hills and natural terrain, within a time limit. You might have 4 to 4 1/2 hours to complete a 20-mile ride, or 7 to 7 1/2 hours to complete a 50-mile ride. You are penalized if you finish too early or too late. At

several checkpoints, veterinarians and judges check your pony's condition. A pony may be eliminated, or "pulled," from the ride if he shows signs of fatigue, stress, or lameness. The object is to finish the ride within the time allotted, with your horse in the best condition possible. You will need specialized conditioning under expert supervision in order to condition your pony for these distances.

Conditioning for Combined-Training Events   Combined-training events are sometimes called "the complete test of a horse and rider." For a one-day horse trial or Pony Club rally, a pony must be fit enough to do a dressage test, ride a cross-country course, and jump a stadium course. A typical Novice cross-country course is about 2,000 meters, and the speed required is 350 meters per minute. At Training level, the cross-country course is about 2,500 meters, at 400 to 450 meters per minute.

Caution: Eventing is a demanding sport that requires proper conditioning and training for both horse and rider. Before entering an event at any level, you must get advice and instruction from someone who is an expert in conditioning and preparing horses and riders for combined-training events—not just anyone who may have competed in combined training. Most injuries (and a great many jumping falls) are related to fatigue, lack of proper conditioning, and ignorance of pace.

You and your instructor should review your conditioning plans daily, evaluating your pony's condition and deciding how much and what kind of work you should do with him.

Here is a typical weekly work schedule:

Monday   Flat work and dressage
Tuesday   Jumping (gymnastics and stadium jumping)
Wednesday   Fitness work (distance and hill work)
Thursday   Flat work
Friday   Jumping (school cross-country fences)
Saturday   Fitness work (gallop)
Sunday   Rest day

Conditioning for Foxhunting   Conditioning for foxhunting is a combination of conditioning for distance riding and galloping work. You may be out hunting as long as four hours or more, hacking across country from one covert (wood lot) to another, and galloping to stay up with the hunt during runs. Since you don't know how long you will be out, how often you will run, or how long a run may be, you must have a fit pony, and must ride so that you save his energy. Most hunts start out fairly slowly at the beginning of the season, and go harder and stay out longer as the season goes on.

The most important part of conditioning for hunting is plenty of long, slow, distance work, which gives your pony a good "base" of fitness. Most foxhunters begin conditioning at least three months before the start of the hunting season, starting with walking trail rides and gradually riding longer and farther, adding trotting and hill work (as described in Basic Conditioning). Sometimes riding out for hound exercise is possible, which is an excellent way to learn about hounds while getting a pony fit. (However, this is the business of the hunt staff and you *must* have permission.)

Care of Your Pony during Hard Work or Competition

Riding in a competition, horse trial, competitive trail ride, or hunt makes extra demands on your pony. He will need good preparation, thoughtful riding, and special care before, during, and after a day of hard work. Strenuous riding activities such as eventing are a big responsibility, because galloping, jumping, and riding for longer distances put a pony under more stress than ordinary riding. You could hurt your pony if you do not know how to take care of him properly, or if you do not use good judgment when riding him.

Following are some tips on preparing for a strenuous day's work, and caring for your pony before, during, and after the event.

Two to Three Months before the Event:

- Get advice and instruction from an expert in the kind of event you wish to enter. Ask whether you and your pony are qualified to take part in the event, and at what level. What instruction and training will you need?
- Begin a regular conditioning program to get your pony (and yourself) fit for the event.

During the Week before the Event:

- Have pony's shoes checked and reset if needed.
- Check tack carefully; have any necessary repairs done.
- Give pony his last gallop (a fairly fast gallop) three days ahead. On the last two days, do mostly flat work.
- Have trailer and vehicle checked and serviced.

The Day before the Event:

- Exercise pony lightly (flat work).
- Clean, check, and pack all tack and equipment.
- Do any last-minute trimming, bathing, or special grooming.
- Have trailer hitched, packed, and ready to go.

Day of the Event (Early Morning):

- Feed and water early, and give hay. Groom thoroughly, pick out feet, and remove any stains from coat.
- Wrap legs and tail for trailering.
- Check that all equipment is packed in the trailer. Load pony and tie up a hay net so he can eat hay during the trip.

On Arrival:

- Park in a safe place (off the road), in the shade, if possible, not blocking a driveway or parking too close to another rig. Unload pony and store your equipment neatly.
- If using a stall, check carefully for nails, splinters, and other hazards before putting down bedding or putting your pony in the stall. Hang water buckets and hay net safely, and store equipment neatly.
- Tack up, checking adjustment of all tack carefully.
- When you are away from your trailer or stall, leave equipment locked up, but leave a halter and tie rope where you can reach them easily when you return.

During the Event:

- Warm up gradually, with fifteen minutes of walking before more strenuous work. Check your girth after riding for ten minutes. Keep a safe distance from other ponies.
- Keep your pony's condition in mind as you ride. Don't work him longer or faster than he is used to. Check his breathing to know when he needs a rest.
- Hot, humid weather, deep footing, and hills are very stressful. Even a pony in good condition can get overtired quickly in such conditions. If you must ride in these conditions, go slower than usual and let your pony slow down and take a breather whenever you can. Be prepared to pull out early if he is having a hard time.

- Cold, wet weather, especially if it is windy, can chill your pony as well as you. Keep him moving, and cover him whenever he has to stop (as long as he is not overheated). Try to keep him sheltered from the wind.
- Be aware of your pony's way of moving. If he feels sluggish or clumsy, or starts to stumble or jump carelessly, he is seriously tired and needs to stop. If you feel him moving unevenly, stop and check him; he may have twisted a shoe or gone lame. If you push on with a tired or sore pony, you can injure him seriously.

Immediately after Strenuous Work:

- Always ease up gradually. Pulling up suddenly from a gallop can cause injury, especially in a tired pony.
- Dismount as soon as you can, run up the stirrups, loosen the girth and the noseband, and walk until he stops blowing. If he is very hot, *do not* cover him until his body temperature returns to normal (especially in hot weather).
- When his breathing comes back to normal, stop and remove the saddle. Unbridle and put on a halter. In warm weather, sponge him off with cool water and scrape him with a sweat scraper. In cold weather, scrape him and rub him with a towel, especially over his back. Get him walking again as soon as you can. Offer him a few sips of water every few minutes as he walks, and keep him walking until he is completely cooled out.
- In hot weather, be prepared to use special cooling-out procedures. (see page 239.)

Check for Injuries:

- During strenuous work, a pony may get a bump or a small injury that he does not notice at the time. Right after work, pick out his feet and check his shoes. Run your hands down each leg, feeling for swelling, cuts, overreaches (cuts on the back of the heels), or tenderness.
- After cooling him out, go over him again more thoroughly, checking his whole body, legs, feet, and the way he moves. When you groom him, notice any sore spots and treat any injuries you find.

Hacking Home:

- If you are hacking some distance back to your stable or trailer, loosen the girth one hole and ride at a walk on long reins for ten minutes or so. You can alternate walking and slow jogging to bring your pony back cool, calm, and relaxed, without taking too long. If you come to a stream, let him have a drink. When hacking home, remember to ride in good balance even if you are tired. Riding sloppily to ease your seat can give your pony a sore back and is poor thanks for his hard work.

- Back at your trailer, finish cooling out your pony, untack him, and scrape and towel him off. Offer him water. For the trip home, cover him with an anti-sweat sheet, sheet, or cooler, but be careful not to overheat him, especially in a closed trailer. Wrap his legs and tail for shipping, load him, and let him eat from a hay net on the trip home.

Care at Home after Hard Work:

- On arriving home, let your pony loose in his stall or in a sandy pen (untacked) so that he may urinate and roll if he wants to.

- Give him hay and water (lukewarm, not cold).

- If the weather is cool and his coat is still damp but *his temperature has returned to normal,* cover him with an anti-sweat sheet. In cold weather, put a wool cooler over the anti-sweat sheet to keep him from getting chilled while his coat dries. Keep him out of drafts while his coat is drying.

- Use a towel or rub rag to dry any damp places. Rub him with a handful of dry straw to dry him and remove caked mud and sweat. Sponge eyelids, nostrils, lips, and under his tail.

- If the pony is dry, brush off sweat marks with a body brush or a cactus cloth. Don't brush damp places; rub them with a towel. Check behind the ears, between the front legs, under the girth and belly, and between the hind legs.

- In cold weather, don't wash muddy legs or brush them while they are wet. This can cause "scratches," or mud fever. If you cannot dry the legs with a towel, put on dry bandages over the mud. This will let them dry overnight and will keep the legs warm.

- In cold weather, keep your pony covered and out of drafts as you work. Feel his ears to see if they are cold. If they are, gently rub and pull on the ears until they warm up.

- After work that is hard on the legs (especially galloping and jumping), it may help to apply stable bandages to all four legs to prevent the legs from swelling or filling (see page 270). These must be put on by someone experienced in bandaging correctly.
- When your pony is warm and dry and completely cooled out, put on his sheet or blanket (if he wears one). Give him a small feed of grain or a bran mash, and leave him with hay and water.
- A pasture-kept pony can be turned out after he has been cooled out and checked over carefully for injuries. If the weather is cold, he should be kept inside until his coat has dried.

About Two Hours Later:

- Go back and check your pony. Feel his ears to see whether they are cold, and check that he has not broken out in a sweat again. If he has, rub him down and dry him with a towel. He may need to be walked again to get cool and dry. If the weather is hot and humid, take him out of the stall where he will get more air circulation. However, be careful not to let him get chilled.
- Check him every two hours, with a last check late that evening.

The Next Day:

- Groom very thoroughly, paying special attention to the feet and shoes, and checking for any bumps, bruises, small cuts, thorns, or other injuries. Run your hand over the saddle and girth area to check for tenderness, saddle sores, or girth galls.
- Remove bandages, if used, and run your hands over each leg to check for heat, swelling, or tenderness.
- Jog the pony out to check for stiffness or lameness.
- Give him a rest day, but make sure he is turned out or has some gentle exercise.

CHAPTER 8

♦♦♦

SHOEING

Shoeing is necessary for many horses and ponies because of the work they do or the surfaces they are ridden on, or for correction of hoof or movement problems. Some horses or ponies can go without shoes under certain conditions. Your farrier (horseshoer) should advise you on whether or not your pony needs to be shod.

Important Reasons for Shoeing

- *Protection*: To protect the hooves from excessive wear and damage, which can cause tenderness and lameness. Shoes are especially important for horses ridden on hard or rocky ground.
- *Traction*: To prevent slipping, especially on grass. Some shoes have special traction devices (rims, calks, studs, or borium), which give the shoe more grip on slippery surfaces.
- *Improving gait*: Some horses need special shoeing to correct gait or movement problems (often related to conformation defects), or to improve their movement for competition.
- *Soundness*: Some horses need special shoeing to cope with the effects of unsoundnesses (such as navicular disease or founder).

Shoeing Schedule

Shoes protect a horse's hooves from excessive wear, but the hooves continue to grow. The shoes must be removed so that the excess growth can be trimmed, and the shoes must be reset before the hooves grow too long and get out of balance. Allowing a horse to go too long without having his shoes reset causes him to grow long toes and low heels, which stress his feet and legs and may lead to stumbling or strained tendons. As the hoof grows out, it displaces the shoe, which may cause pressure sores, or "corns."

Most horses' shoes should be reset every six weeks; some need resetting more often. (See *USPC D Manual*, page 206, for signs that resetting is needed.)

Set up a schedule with your farrier, and use your record book to record what work was done and when. Check your pony's shoes regularly; have any necessary farrier work done at least a week before a rally or competition.

You and Your Farrier

A farrier is a professional whose work is important to keep your pony sound and ridable. Sometimes finding a good farrier can be difficult, so you should be considerate and make it easy for him to do a good job for you. Here are some things to remember:

- Make appointments in plenty of time. Don't wait until the night before a rally or show to call your farrier about a lost shoe! Keep appointments, and let your farrier know well ahead of time if you must change a scheduled appointment.
- When the farrier is coming, have your pony inside, with his legs clean and dry. Don't make the farrier wait for you to catch your pony; and don't make him work on a wet, muddy pony.
- Have a clear, level area for the farrier to work in, out of the rain, wind, and sun. Your pony may be cross-tied if he is gentle, but be on hand to hold him if the farrier asks you to. Don't expect him to work on your pony if you aren't there.
- Teach your pony to have good manners when his feet are handled. Picking out his feet every day teaches him to behave well for the farrier. Don't let him nip, nibble, or lean on the farrier.
- Keep your pony's feet in good condition through good everyday foot care and attention to details. Ask your farrier what you can do to improve the condition of your pony's feet.
- Tell your farrier what kind of work your pony is doing, and about any foot, leg, or movement problems you have noticed. He may want you to lead your pony at a walk or jog so that he can see how he moves.

- Have your farrier see your pony on a regular schedule, even if you are not riding him. If you neglect his feet and let them get in bad shape, it may take a long time to get them healthy.
- If a problem comes up, like lameness or a lost shoe, call your farrier and discuss it politely. A good farrier will want to put it right.
- Finally, pay your farrier promptly!

Farrier Tools

A farrier uses special tools for various steps in removing shoes, trimming hooves, and shoeing. Some tools are used only by a farrier at the forge; others can be used by experienced horsepersons (for instance, when having to remove a shoe in an emergency.) Ask your farrier to show you how to use basic farrier tools safely.

The main farrier tools include:

- *Rasp*: A sharp, heavy file used to rasp and smooth feet and smooth clinches.

FARRIER TOOLS

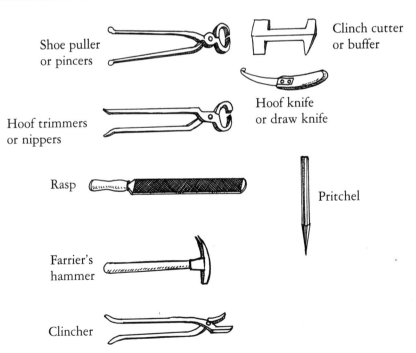

Shoe puller or pincers

Clinch cutter or buffer

Hoof knife or draw knife

Hoof trimmers or nippers

Rasp

Pritchel

Farrier's hammer

Clincher

- *Pincers, or shoe pullers*: Specially shaped pliers that grip the shoe and pry it off; also used to remove nails.
- *Hoof trimmers or nippers*: Shaped like shoe pullers, but with sharpened edges that nip off excess hoof wall.
- *Hoof knife, or drawing knife*: Sharp, hook-shaped knife used to pare away excess sole or trim the frog.
- *Clinch cutter or buffer*: Used to raise and cut the clinches when removing shoes.
- *Pritchel*: Metal spike used to hold a hot shoe.
- *Clincher*: Special tool that bends and flattens clinches into the hoof wall.
- *Farrier's hammer*: Specially shaped hammer for driving nails.
- *Farrier's apron*: Heavy leather apron that protects the farrier's legs while forging and shoeing.

Hot and Cold Shoeing

"Hot shoeing" means using a forge to heat the iron and make or modify the shoes. In "cold shoeing," ready-made shoes are shaped and nailed on without being heated. These shoes can be bent by hammering them on the anvil, but they cannot be modified as much as in hot shoeing.

Cold shoeing is a perfectly acceptable method of shoeing, if ready-made shoes fit your pony's feet without needing extensive re-shaping. Hot shoeing is preferred if the shoes your pony needs are not available ready-made, or if your pony needs special shoeing.

There are special shoes made from new materials such as plastic, which may require different methods of preparation and shaping. Special features such as borium may require welding or brazing.

Steps in Shoeing

The first thing a farrier may do, especially if he is shoeing your pony for the first time, is watch him walk and jog on a hard, level surface. He will watch the arc of each foot as it swings forward, the way it lands and breaks over, and whether or not the pony moves straight. He will also evaluate the way the pony is shod and examine the wear pattern of the old shoes. Tell the farrier about any movement problems (such as stumbling, forging, or interfering) or hoof problems you have noticed.

Next, the farrier removes the old shoe. The farrier cuts the clinches off, then uses his pincers to pry the shoe off without breaking the wall of the hoof.

The five steps in shoeing a horse are the following:

1. *Preparation*: The excess growth of the hoof is removed, and the foot is leveled, balanced, and prepared for the fitting of a new or reset shoe. The excess wall is cut away with hoof trimmers, and excess sole may be cut back with a hoof knife. Ragged parts of the frog may be trimmed away, but neither the sole nor the frog should be cut any more than necessary.

2. *Forging*: Making a new shoe, or modifying a ready-made shoe. The farrier heats the shoe in the forge and hammers it into shape on the anvil. He may draw toe clips or side clips, or modify the heels of the shoe. (In cold shoeing, the shoer measures the shoe and bends it to fit, but does not heat it.)

3. *Fitting*: Checking the fit of the shoe. The hot shoe is held against the bottom surface of the hoof for several seconds. The hot shoe leaves a mark on the hoof (which is painless), which tells the farrier how well the shoe fits and whether the hoof is level. (In cold shoeing, the fit is checked without the shoe being heated.) He makes any necessary adjustments, then checks the fit again until the shoe fits perfectly.

4. *Nailing on*: A hot shoe is cooled in water, then nailed on. The nails must be driven carefully into the white line; they curve slightly so that they come out through the wall, away from the sensitive part of the foot. The farrier can tell by the sound and feel if the nail is being driven properly.

    As each nail comes out through the wall, the farrier bends it by driving it against a nail block and cuts off the sharp end. The bent-over end of the nail forms a "clinch," which holds the shoe on tightly.

5. *Finishing*: The clinches are flattened down with a clincher and made smooth with a rasp. Any toe or quarter clips are tapped into place. The edge of the hoof is smoothed with the rasp to reduce the risk of cracking. The hoof wall should not be rasped any more than necessary, as this removes the periople (the natural covering of the hoof.)

How to Tell Good Shoeing from Bad

Some farriers do a better job of shoeing than others. It's important to know what makes a good shoeing job, and to recognize poor shoeing practices that could damage your pony's feet.

Here are some signs of good shoeing:

- The shoe is the right size for the hoof. The shoe has been fitted to the foot instead of the foot being rasped down to fit the shoe.
- The frog and sole have not been cut away too much, and the frog touches the ground (on soft ground). (On hard surfaces like concrete, the frog may not always touch the ground.)
- The type of shoe is suitable for the work the horse is used for, and the weight of the iron is suitable for the size of the horse.
- The heels of the shoe are neither too long nor too short.
- The foot is balanced so that it lands evenly, without twisting or rocking.
- The angle of the hoof is the same as the angle of the pastern. This keeps the bones of the pastern and foot correctly aligned.
- The clinches are smooth, tight, and in an even line, neither too high nor too low.
- A good farrier takes the time to watch the horse move before and after shoeing, and examines the wear pattern on the old shoes. When deciding how to shoe him, the farrier considers the horse's conformation, way of moving, and soundness or movement problems, as well as the way in which the horse is used.

SIGNS OF GOOD SHOEING:

- Angle of hoof matches angle of pastern.
- Clinches smooth and even
- Shoe made to fit the foot
- Hoof not rasped excessively
- Shoe is right size.
- Frog touches ground (on soft ground).

SIGNS OF POOR SHOEING:

- Angle of hoof and pastern do not match.
- Shoe too small
- Toe "dumped" (rasped off to fit shoe)
- Clinches rough and uneven
- Excessive rasping removes natural covering of hoof wall.
- Frog does not touch the ground.

Here are some things to watch out for:

- Cutting away too much frog. If the frog doesn't touch the ground, it cannot do its job of absorbing shock and pumping blood through the foot and lower leg.
- Cutting away too much sole. This can make a horse's feet tender.
- Shoes that are too small, especially if the toe is "dumped," or rasped down so that it looks like it has been chopped off. If the heels of the shoe are too short, they do not support the foot properly.
- Rasping too much of the outer surface of the hoof. This removes the periople (the shiny natural covering of the hoof) and can result in dry hooves that crack easily.
- Clinches that are sharp, uneven, or very low.
- A farrier who is in a hurry, who does not take time to watch the horse move, or who rasps the foot down to fit the shoe instead of fitting the shoe to the foot.

Shoeing Problems

Sometimes shoeing problems may occur as a result of an accident or mistake during shoeing, a chronic problem with the horse's feet, or something that happens to the horse after shoeing. They are *not* always the farrier's fault! A good farrier will work with you to solve any shoeing problems, but you must call him promptly and explain the problem politely.

Pricking, or Quicking   Pricking (also called "quicking") is accidentally driving a nail into the sensitive part of the foot. This may happen if a horse moves while the shoe is being nailed on; he will usually jerk his foot if it is pricked. If the horse is accidentally pricked during shoeing, the nail should be pulled, and the hole should be treated with 7 percent iodine solution. Make sure the horse's tetanus immunization is up to date.

Close Nail   If a nail is driven too close (but not into) to the sensitive part of the hoof, the horse may not show any signs of pain at the time, but the pressure may cause him to go lame later. If a horse goes lame a day or two after being shod, a close nail is a possible cause. Call the farrier; he will check the shoe and remove the offending nail.

NAILING AND CLINCHING

1. Nail is driven properly
   through white line and
   wall.

2. Close nail: Nail is driven
   too close to sensitive
   part of hoof.

3. Pricking: Nail is driven
   into sensitive part of
   hoof.

Losing Shoes   A horse may lose a shoe for many reasons—if he has
shelly hooves or soft hooves, works in mud or deep footing, or over-
reaches (grabs the heel of a front shoe with the toe of the hind hoof).
These things usually are *not* the farrier's fault; however, many farriers will replace a shoe for free (or for a small charge) if it is lost within a short time after shoeing. If your pony has a problem keeping
shoes on, you and your farrier must work together to solve the problem. This may require trying different types of shoes, keeping the
horse's feet and environment dry, working to improve the condition
of the feet, protecting the heels with bell boots during riding and
turnout, or other measures.

Types of Shoes

Shoes come in many different types. The style of shoe may change
according to the work the horse is doing, and the time of year. Some
horses need special shoes to help with a movement or soundness
problem. It's important to know the type of shoes your pony wears,
and why. Ask your farrier!

Shoes can be handmade (made by heating and bending iron "bar
stock") or machine-made (called "keg" shoes). Keg shoes come in
many different sizes and styles. Most farriers use them when

possible, because handmade shoes are more time-consuming and expensive. Keg shoes may be fitted cold or heated in a forge and fitted hot.

Shoes are named for the shape of the iron stock used to make the shoe and sometimes for the shape and any special features. Here are four common types of horseshoes:

- *Plain or flat shoe, or "plate"*: Made of flat iron
- *Fullered, or creased, shoe*: Has a groove called a "fuller" or "crease," in which the nail holes are set
- *Concave fullered shoe*: Has a fuller, or crease; and the inside edge of the shoe is concave (hollowed out). Often used on horses ridden on turf and in dirt arenas, because dirt is less likely to pack up in the hoof.
- *Rim shoe*: Has a fuller, or crease; and one edge of the shoe is higher all the way around. Often used on polo shoes, for extra traction.

TYPES OF HORSESHOES

1. Flat shoe

2. Creased, or fullered, shoe

3. Concave shoe (may also have crease or fuller)

4. Rim shoe

CHAPTER 9

TRAVEL SAFETY AND BANDAGING

As you take part in Pony Club activities or go on longer trips, you may trailer your pony more often. You should take more responsibility for travel preparations, loading and unloading your pony, and checking and preparing the trailer and tow vehicle for safe and comfortable travel.

Basic travel safety, including preparing the pony, what to take, loading, and unloading, is covered in the *USPC D Manual*; you should review this information. More travel safety checklists are included in the *USPC B/A Manual*.

PREPARING FOR LONGER TRIPS

Longer trips require good preparation and planning, especially if you will be on the road for more than a few hours or will be stabling your pony away from home overnight.

The driver must be experienced in hauling horses and should stop or let another person drive if he or she is not feeling alert. It is safer never to haul horses alone, especially on a long trip, no matter how experienced one may be.

If you are going to a rally, show, or competition, find out what health certificates and inoculations may be required. Get complete information on the location, directions, and length of time required to get there. Ask about stabling arrangements and what you should bring (you may need to bring stall guards or stall screens for temporary stalls). If you are traveling with someone else, get together and plan who will bring what.

Take along the appropriate rule book, prize list, or information on the event; your membership number; and any health and registration papers required for your pony. You will need a road atlas or map, and you may need to make motel reservations. Have your veterinarian's phone number and a phone number for someone at your destination you could call in an emergency. Leave a number where you can be reached.

You can usually haul horses for eight to twelve hours in one day. If a trip will take several days, you should plan overnight stops, or consider shipping your horse with a commercial shipper.

Before leaving for a trip, let the people at your destination know when you expect to arrive. If you are delayed, call ahead; it is inconsiderate to keep people waiting, worrying, and wondering where you are.

Care of Your Pony during Travel

Traveling for long distances is stressful for horses, but consideration and good care can make it easier for them. Here are some things to remember:

- A few inches of shavings in the trailer will provide a comfortable surface and encourage the horse to urinate when he needs to. Many horses will not urinate on rubber mats or hard surfaces because they dislike splashing their legs.
- A horse must be able to put his head down in order to keep his balance, clear his nose and throat, and reach his hay net. If you tie his head too high, he may have trouble keeping his balance and may be congested when he arrives.
- Be aware of temperature and ventilation (or draft) inside the trailer. Horses generate heat inside a closed trailer, and your pony may sweat. In hot weather, he can suffer heat exhaustion if left in a closed trailer parked in the sun. A well-ventilated or drafty trailer will keep horses cool when moving even on a warm day; on a cool day they may need sheets or blankets.
- Stop every two to three hours to check on the horse. Make sure he has hay, and offer him water. It's important to keep offering water, as horses easily get dehydrated during travel, which may lead to colic. Check his bandages, and remove or put on clothing as necessary for his comfort.
- When you stop and check the horse, notice whether he has urinated. Some horses will not urinate in a trailer; they should

be unloaded every few hours and walked around until they urinate.

- It is usually safer to leave a horse in the trailer for the whole trip, up to a limit of eight to twelve hours, unless he is easy to load, unload, and handle, and you can find a safe place to stop and unload him. Ask your veterinarian how long your pony can be in the trailer.
- Smooth, careful driving is very important for the safety and comfort of horses and people. The driver should keep to a slightly lower speed than usual, and plan well ahead to avoid sudden acceleration, stops, or swerves. Go very slowly around all turns.
- On arrival, or at rest stops, walk the horse for ten to fifteen minutes to relieve stiffness. If a paddock is available, he may be turned loose to roll. Don't let him graze at roadside stops; the grass may be treated with harmful chemicals.

Checklist: Equipment for Care and Safety of Pony During Travel

- Hay net (filled with fresh hay for each trip)
- Water bucket
- At least 5 gallons of water (in jerrycan or bucket with snap-on lid)
- Horse first-aid kit (see page 228)
- Extra tie rope and chain-end lead shank
- Muck basket, shovel, rake, broom, manure disposal bags

Loading

Before a trip, make sure that your pony (and any other horses you are hauling) is used to loading, traveling, and unloading quietly. Pack the tow vehicle, and check off all items before loading the horses.

Review safe loading and unloading procedures (see *USPC D Manual*, page 224). More information on loading is found in the *USPC B/A Manual*.

BANDAGING

At C Level, you should learn to apply two kinds of bandages: shipping bandages for protection against bumps and scrapes during travel, and stable bandages for warmth and protection in the stall and to prevent swelling of the legs after hard work.

Other kinds of bandages, including treatment bandages, tail wraps, and exercise bandages, will be covered in the *USPC B/A Manual*. If you need to use these on your pony, a more experienced person should put them on for you.

Caution: *All* bandages must be applied correctly, or they may do more harm than good. Uneven pressure from a poorly applied bandage or a tight ring of pressure around a leg can cause lameness or damage the tendons. This is called "cording" a leg. Bandages and bandage fastenings must be put on evenly and with the right amount of pressure.

Do not try to put on a bandage until you have hands-on instruction from someone who has experience in bandaging correctly.

Bandage Materials

Bandages are made up of leg wraps, leg pads, and fasteners. Many kinds of bandage materials are available, but Pony Club uses only certain kinds. These are the safest and most suitable for the kind of bandaging you do and are less likely to cause damage to your pony's legs.

Bandages, or Wraps   Leg wraps, or bandages, are usually 4 to 5 inches wide and from 10 to 15 feet long, and made of washable material. If made from a material with some stretch, they conform to the shape of the leg more easily.

Types of leg wraps include the following:

- *Flannel Bandages*: Made of heavy flannel, which can be bought by the yard and torn into bandage strips. They should be 4 to 5 inches wide and about 15 feet long (large horses may need shipping bandages 5 inches wide and 16 feet long).
  Flannel bandages are easy to launder and mend, but they do not stretch and may be bulky.
- *Knit Bandages (Track Bandages)*: Made of cotton knit (stockinette) or polyester double-knit, 4 to 6 inches wide and 7 to 10 feet long. Most come with Velcro fasteners. The type with narrow tie tapes should have the tapes cut off. Most cotton knit bandages are too short and narrow for shipping bandages; two bandages sewn together end to end make one bandage the right length for shipping.

• *Other bandages*: There are other types of bandage materials, including elastic, crepe, conforming gauze, and others. These are often designed for special purposes, such as treatment or exercise bandages. Don't use them without assistance from your instructor or veterinarian, as certain bandage materials make it easy to damage a horse's tendons.

Note: Pony Club discourages the use of polo bandages (synthetic fleece bandages) because they are designed to be used without padding underneath, which can cause tendon damage. They also tend to stretch and slip when wet, which makes them unsafe for use when riding cross-country. If your pony needs leg protection when ridden, use properly fitted boots or have an experienced person apply exercise bandages, instead of using polo wraps.

Leg Pads   A bandage must *always* be applied over a leg pad. The padding distributes the pressure evenly and is compressed so that it fits snugly against the structures of the leg. Padding must be soft, smooth, and thick enough to distribute pressure evenly, without binding or causing too much pressure on a tendon, joint, or bony prominence. The size and thickness of the padding depends on the type of bandage and the size of the horse's leg.

Leg pads are usually from 14 to 18 inches high (depending on the length of the horse's leg, and whether used for stable or shipping bandages) and about 18 to 24 inches long.

Sheet cottons are preferred for use in Pony Club. A single leg pad is made by putting together 6 to 10 sheets of cotton, folded lengthwise. (For hind leg pads for large horses, use 7 or 8 sheets and re-fold them width-wise, to make them taller.) For shipping bandages, the cotton should reach from the ground to 1 inch above the bottom of the hock or knee joint. For standing bandages, they should be slightly shorter (from hock or knee joint to the coronary band).

Sheet cottons can be covered with cheesecloth to make them last longer. They are not washable and should be discarded when they become soiled or lumpy.

There are other kinds of leg pads, including polyester batting and cotton quilts. Check with your instructor before using these, especially for Pony Club rating tests.

Fasteners   The end of a bandage must be securely fastened so that it cannot come loose and trip the horse. Fasteners must be placed on the outside of the leg so that they cannot be pulled loose if struck by the opposite foot. They should be placed in the cannon area, never over a joint or the back of a tendon.

To fasten a bandage, use two bandage pins (large safety pins) per leg. The pins are fastened through several layers of bandage and may be crossed. Do not use the narrow tape ties that come attached to some bandages. These can cause a tight ring of pressure around the horse's leg, which may interfere with circulation or damage the tendons. Velcro fasteners may be used if they do not cause a continuous ring of pressure around the leg.

Fasteners such as safety pins or Velcro fasteners may be reinforced with masking tape. This should be applied in a spiral, not in a continuous band. *Never apply any kind of fastener in a way that makes a continuous band around a pony's leg or indents the bandage.* This can put harmful pressure on the tendons and can interfere with circulation in the leg.

Removing Bandages

When you remove bandages, undo them gently but quickly by passing them from one hand to the other; don't try to roll them up as you take them off. Rub the legs (especially the back tendons and fetlock joint) after removing the bandages. Re-roll the leg pads, and either re-roll the bandages for use again or set them aside to be laundered.

Shipping Bandages

A shipping bandage protects the lower leg, coronary band, and the heels during travel, in case a horse steps on his own feet or strikes his legs against the trailer.

A shipping bandage must cover the heels and coronary band, pastern, fetlock joint, and tendons, to the base of the knee or hock. It must be well padded, firm, and snug, but never excessively tight (you should be able to slip two fingers under the bandage).

Shipping bandages must be fastened securely, as they can trip a horse if they are applied too loosely and slip down. They must be fastened on the outside of the leg so that the horse cannot pull the fastening loose if he should strike the inside of the leg with his opposite hoof.

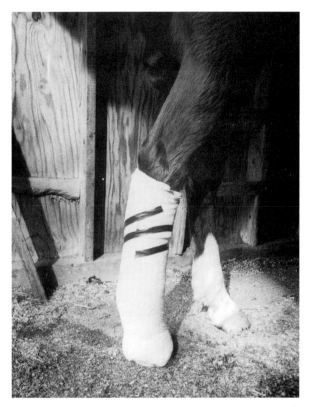

A shipping bandage, correctly applied. *Photo: Ruth Harvie*

How to Apply a Shipping Bandage

You will need the following items:

- Four bandages: knitted stockinette "track," polyester, or flannel bandages, 12 to 16 feet long
- Four leg pads (sheet cottons preferred) long enough to cover the leg from knee or hock to the ground. NEVER put on bandages without leg pads!
- Fasteners (two bandage pins for each leg; masking tape)

Here are the steps in applying a shipping bandage:

1. With padding touching the ground, wrap it smoothly around the leg. Start the edge of the leg pad next to the cannon bone on the outside of the leg. Wrap from front to back and outside to inside.

2. Start the bandage on the outside, near the middle of the cannon bone. Tuck the end under the edge of the pad, and wrap once around the leg to anchor the bandage. Always wrap the bandage in the same direction as the leg pad. This makes the inside of the bandage smoother and avoids creating a ridge that can press against the tendon.

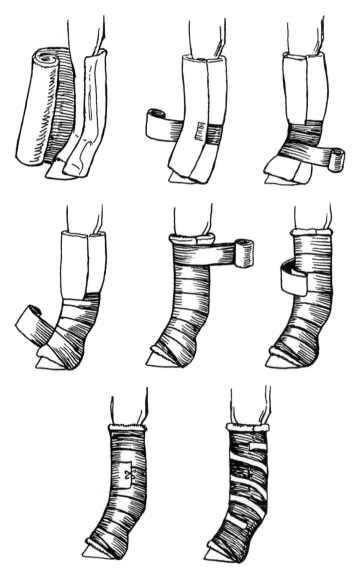

Steps in Applying a Shipping Bandage

3. Wrap downward, overlapping each wrap about one-third to one-half the width of the bandage, keeping the wraps parallel to the ground. Pull the bandage snug by pulling backward against the cannon bone rather than pulling forward against the tendons. Make the bandage firm enough to compress the padding evenly, but not so tight that you cannot get a finger underneath.

4. Make several turns around the bulbs of the heel and coronary band. At least half the width of the bandage must go under the heel to keep the bandage from sliding up. At least 1/2 inch of padding should extend below the bottom edge of the bandage, to keep it from binding.

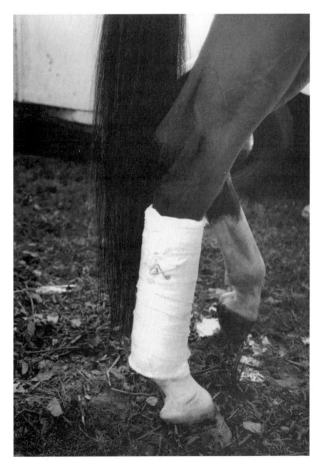

A stable bandage, correctly applied. *Photo: Ruth Harvie*

5. Bandage back up the leg to just below the knee or hock. Leave at least 1/2 inch of padding above the bandage, and be sure that it does not bind at the knee or hock. Continue bandaging back down the leg.

6. Finish the bandage on the outside of the leg in the cannon area, not over a tendon or a joint. (You can fold the end of the bandage underneath itself for a few inches if necessary.) Fasten with crossed bandage pins on the outside of the leg. Apply strips of masking tape in a spiral, not in a circle, around the leg.

Stable Bandages

Stable bandages are used for protection in the stable, to prevent "filling," or swelling, of the legs after hard work, for warmth, and sometimes to treat injuries or cover a wound dressing. When applying stable bandages, always bandage the legs in pairs—that is, both front legs, both hind legs, or all four. If one leg is bandaged and the other is not, the unbandaged leg may be stressed and may swell. Stable bandages must be removed and reset at least every twelve hours (morning and night).

A stable bandage is put on like a shipping bandage, but it ends just below the fetlock joint. It must be snug enough to compress the padding around the tendons and other structures of the leg. The pressure must be evenly distributed over the entire bandage, and not too tight (you should be able to slip two fingers inside the finished bandage). The bandage must be run in the same direction as the leg pad.

How to Apply a Stable Bandage

You will need:

- Two or four flannel, polyester knit, or cotton stockinette bandages approximately 10 to 12 feet long
- Two or four leg pads (sheet cottons preferred). They should reach from just below the knee or hock to just below the fetlock joint (usually 14 to 16 inches long, depending on the size of the horse).
- Fasteners (two bandage pins per leg; masking tape)

Here are the steps in applying a stable bandage:

1. Apply the leg pad as in a shipping bandage, but the padding only comes to below the fetlock joint, not to the ground. Apply the pad starting on the outside of the leg behind the cannon bone, wrapping from outside to inside.

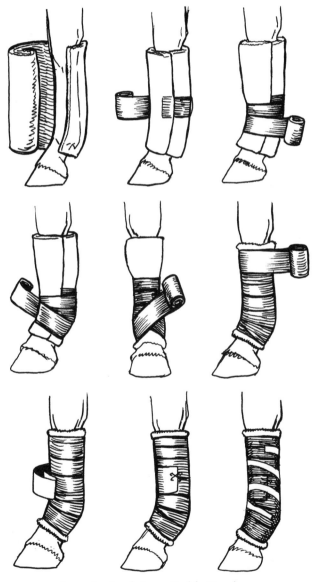

Steps in Applying a Stable Bandage

2. Start the bandage as for a shipping bandage, and wrap down to the fetlock joint. Always wrap in the same direction as the leg pad. Keep the wraps parallel to the ground, with pressure snug and even but not too tight. Overlap each wrap one-third to one-half the width of the bandage. Adjust the tension by pulling backward against the cannon bone, not by pulling forward against the tendons.

3. At the fetlock joint, drop the wrap under the back of the joint and bring it higher in front, to make an upside-down V at the front of the joint. This supports the fetlock joint and allows the leg to bend.

4. Leave 1/2 inch to 1 inch of padding showing below the lower edge of the wrap, to keep the edge of the bandage from binding.

5. Wrap back up the leg. Leave at least 1/2 inch of cotton above the top wrap to keep the edge of the bandage from binding the knee or tendons.

6. End the bandage on the outside of the leg, in the cannon area, never over a tendon or joint. Fold the end back under for a few inches if necessary. Fasten with crossed bandage pins and reinforce with masking tape, applied in a spiral. Don't put a continuous band of material around the leg or pull the fastener tight enough to indent the bandage.

When applying a stable bandage to protect a wound, first attend to the wound and cover it with a sterile gauze pad. Hold the gauze pad in place with several loose turns of conforming gauze. You apply the stable bandage over this. (For more information on treating and dressing wounds, see Chapter 6, page 230.) If you need to apply a treatment bandage, you should have assistance from a veterinarian or someone experienced in applying this kind of bandage according to Pony Club Standards.

Important Points for Safe Bandaging

- Don't sit or kneel when bandaging. Bend or squat so that you can keep your balance and get out of the way if the horse should move.
- Clean the legs before bandaging, and make sure there is nothing underneath the padding that could irritate the leg or cause pressure. It is okay to bandage over a leg that is wet but clean; bandaging with an absorbent padding like sheet cotton is a good way to dry the leg.

- Make sure there is sufficient padding under the whole bandage, and that the padding is smooth and distributed evenly. Don't bandage over lumps, folds, or wrinkles.
- Wrap snugly but not too tightly. You should be able to slip two fingers under the finished bandage.
- A bandage must not bind at the knee, hock, or fetlock joint. Don't bandage the back surface of the knee, as this can cause excessive pressure when the horse bends his knee. The padding must extend at least 1/2 inch beyond the top and bottom edges of the bandage, to keep the edge of the bandage from binding.
- A finished bandage should feel firm and even over its whole length. No part of the bandage should be looser or tighter, and no wrap or fastener should make an indentation in the bandage.

BANDAGING MISTAKES

1. Uneven padding; does not cover heels; too short; lumpy and uneven

2. Uneven padding; too short; no padding showing above and below edges of bandage; fastened with strings over a joint

3. Continuous band of tape indents bandage; padding uneven and sloppy.

4. Uneven wrapping; pulling against tendon instead of cannon bone; indents bandage

- Liniments must be used with caution, if at all. Some liniments may blister the skin if used under a bandage, especially if the leg is bandaged when wet. Use liniments only on the advice of your veterinarian or your instructor, and make sure the liniment is safe to use under bandages. Hand rubbing each leg (in an upward direction) for at least five minutes is safer and often more effective than using liniment.
- A bandage must be wrapped in the same direction as the leg pad. This makes it smooth instead of creating a lump or ridge that could press against the tendons and cause cording, or damage.

CHAPTER 10

GROUND TRAINING: HANDLING, LEADING, AND LONGEING

Horses and ponies do not think the same way people do. They learn by association: they associate (connect) a signal (something they hear, see, or feel) with whatever happens immediately afterward. In training, we teach a pony to connect signals, or cues, with specific behaviors (what he does). This is the basis for all training.

How Horses Learn

To train a pony, you use "reinforcement," or rewards and corrections. Rewards encourage the pony to repeat the behavior. Rewards can be food, patting, kind words, release of pressure, or best of all, a break from work. Correction means anything that discourages specific behavior. Correction *does not* always mean punishment. It can be a word such as "No" or "Quit"; a sharp, disapproving tone of voice; making the pony stop and wait; or making him do something over again. Think of correcting a pony's mistake rather than punishing him.

In order to learn, a pony must connect the signal, the behavior (what he does), and the reward or correction within a very short time: one to three seconds. If you are even a few seconds late in rewarding or correcting him, the pony becomes confused. You must always give the signal in the same way, and you must be consistent about which behaviors you reward or correct. It's unfair to let your pony get away with an undesirable behavior sometimes, and correct him for it at other times.

Ground Manners

Good ground manners are a matter of attitude between pony and handler. Each must pay attention and be aware of the other; the handler must communicate clearly, and the pony must be obedient and responsive. Good ground manners make a pony safer and easier to handle, but they also are important for all training because they teach a pony how to pay attention and to learn from his handler.

A well-mannered pony should do the following:

- Turn to face you when you come into his stall, and be easy to halter.
- Wait for you to lead him through a stall door or gate.
- Stand still, on a loose lead line, when you say "Whoa" or "Stand."
- When being led, stay beside you (even with your shoulder) without crowding, pulling ahead, or hanging back. He should move off promptly in a walk or trot, and stop when you do, on a loose lead line.
- Obey simple voice commands such as "Walk on," "Trot," "Whoa," "Stand," and "Over."
- Lift each foot easily when you ask him to.
- Accept gentle touching with a whip, without fear or resentment.

Teaching ground manners requires awareness, patience, and attention to details. Letting a pony make mistakes and then punishing him for them is bad training. If you are paying attention to your pony, you can stop him *before* he makes a mistake and reward him for doing well.

Above all, you must handle your pony correctly and consistently *all the time.* Careless and inconsistent handling is unfair to your pony and potentially dangerous. It lets him develop bad habits that will have to be corrected. This is the fault of the careless handler, but the pony gets blamed for it.

Standing Still   One of the most important things your pony can learn is to stop and stand still when you ask him to. This is important for his safety and for yours, and makes him easier to work around.

Teaching your pony to stand still is like teaching a dog to "stay." Your pony must learn to stop when he hears "Whoa," and to stand

Teaching Pony to Stand Still at a Distance from the Handler

still without moving his feet (on a loose lead line) when he hears "Stand." At first, ask him to stand for only a second or two; gradually work up to asking him to stand for several seconds at a time, then longer. When you are practicing "Stand," keep the lead line loose and stand facing the pony; if you tug on the lead line or turn away from him, he may think you are signaling him to move. He should be allowed to turn his head, but if he moves his feet, correct him by saying "No, stand!" and moving him back into exactly the same position he was in before he moved.

As your pony gets better at standing still, you can teach him to stand while you move farther away (5 or 6 feet, then 10 feet away), and move around to his other side.

Accepting the Whip   In order to train a pony, you must teach him to accept seeing a whip and being touched gently with it. Some ponies need special help to teach them that the whip will not hurt them.

Use a stiff dressage whip or a driving whip about 4 feet long. Stand next to the pony's shoulder. At first, just show him the handle of the whip; let him sniff it, speak to him kindly, and stroke him gently with it. Gradually stroke him all over his body and legs with the handle and then with the tip of the whip. Be gentle and patient, especially if he is uneasy about it. When he stays relaxed while you touch him all over his body with the whip, repeat the process using a longe whip, with the lash wrapped up. Finally, unwrap the lash and gently get him used to the lash touching him. You must do all this work on both sides of his body.

Work in Hand

"Work in hand" means training while leading your pony. Review the section on leading and voice commands in the *USPC D Manual* (pages 138–140). Now you must refine his work in hand, which lays the foundation for proper longeing.

Parallel Leading and Parallel Longeing   Parallel leading is an important step in teaching a pony to longe. *Before* he can learn to work at the end of a 30-foot longe line, he must learn to move forward, stop, and obey voice commands when he is several feet away from you. This procedure develops into parallel longeing (when you are 6 to 10 feet away from him), which prepares the pony for actual longeing.

To begin parallel leading, start by leading your pony with the lead line in the hand next to the pony (as usual). Carry the longe whip (with the lash wrapped up) in the other hand, pointing down and backward. Gradually move out until you are 3 to 4 feet from the pony's shoulder; at this distance, practice leading, transitions, and voice commands on both sides.

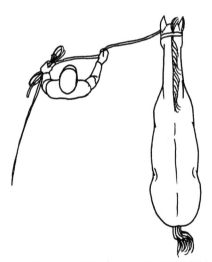

Leading at a Distance of 3 to 4 Feet

To slow down or stop, use the same hand and rein aids you use while longeing. Repeated short squeezes (backward, toward his chest) act as half-halts and ask him to slow down or stop. If he does not stop promptly after a light touch, don't pull backward or sideways. Instead, stop walking, hold your arm and elbow in one place, and give small "vibrations" with your hand, making your fist "shiver." This teaches your pony to pay attention to a light signal instead of a pull.

Next, move out so that you are 4 to 5 feet from the pony's shoulder, and turn toward him. Hold the line in the hand closest to the pony's head, and the whip (still pointing backward and down) in the hand that is closer to his hindquarters, as when longeing. Practice walking, transitions, and voice commands in this position, while you and your pony move in a large circle. You walk a circle about 5 feet smaller than your pony's circle. As your pony gets better at working this way, you can gradually move farther away—first 6 feet away, then 10 feet, and so on. Be sure to practice in both directions.

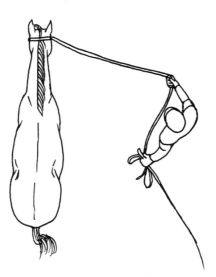

Parallel Leading: Handler Has
Changed to Longeing Position.

Longeing

Longeing (also spelled lungeing) is a way of giving a horse controlled exercise without riding him. The horse works in a 60-foot circle around the trainer, on a longe line about 30 feet long.

Longeing is useful for several reasons:

- To exercise a horse when he cannot be ridden
- To settle down a horse that is full of energy, before riding him

- To train the horse to pay attention to voice commands and the trainer's body language
- To develop the horse's rhythm, balance, suppleness, and way of moving
- Longeing a rider on a trained horse is a way to improve the rider's seat and position.

PARALLEL LONGEING AND REGULAR LONGEING

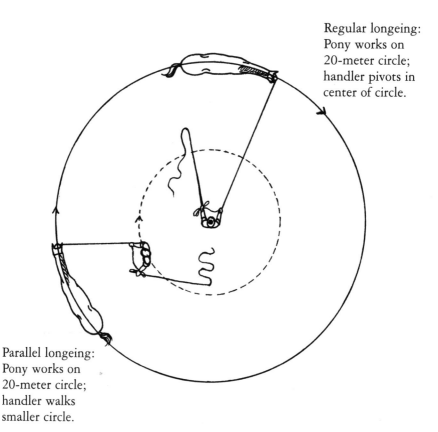

Regular longeing: Pony works on 20-meter circle; handler pivots in center of circle.

Parallel longeing: Pony works on 20-meter circle; handler walks smaller circle.

Before You Start

Caution: Don't try to longe your pony without hands-on instruction from your Pony Club instructor. You *must* learn to longe a pony that is experienced and easy to longe *before* you try to longe one that does not know how to longe. You will need a safe place to longe and special equipment.

Where to Longe   The best place to longe is in a round longeing ring about 60 feet in diameter. You can also longe in a regular riding ring, in one end or near a corner. It is easier to control the horse if the longeing circle is enclosed with barrels, hay bales, or jump poles on buckets. Don't use jump standards or cavaletti because they can get caught on the longe line or hurt the pony if he bumps into them. Many horses are hard to control in an open field or in the middle of a large arena. The place where you longe must have good footing that is not hard or slippery. For safety, no one should be riding in an area where a horse is being longed.

Safe Dress When Longeing   Gloves are essential when longeing, to keep your hands from getting cut or burned by the longe line. Don't wear rings; these can get caught on the longe line and cause injury. Safe footwear is essential (hard-soled boots that cover the foot and ankle), and you must wear your safety helmet, properly fastened, when longeing, especially when working with a young horse. Spurs should be removed when longeing because they could get caught in the longe line and trip you. You will need a watch or a kitchen timer to time the longeing session.

Equipment for Longeing

The equipment used for longeing includes:

- *Longe line (also called the "longe")*: Made of flat cotton webbing 1 to 1 1/2 inches wide, or 1/2-inch-round spun nylon or Dacron line, with a swivel snap or buckle on one end, *not* a chain. Don't use narrow, lightweight nylon lines because they slip and can burn your hands. If the longe line has a loop sewn in the end, cut off the loop so that you cannot catch your hand in it. A longe line must be at least 30 feet long so that the longeing circle can be close to 60 feet in diameter. Never longe with too short a line, because working on too small a circle puts great strain on a horse's legs and muscles, and can cause serious injury.

  Do *not* use the type of longe line with a chain on one end. The chain is too severe, and the weight of the chain spoils your contact with the pony.

- *Longe whip*: Has a long handle (about 5 feet long) and a long, light lash used to signal the pony. The whip should be light and well-balanced so that you can handle it easily. Don't try to longe a horse with a short whip (dressage whip or driving whip), or use the end of the longe line as a whip.

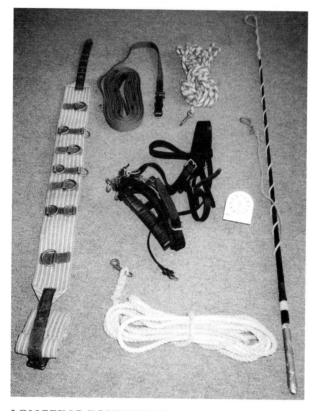

LONGEING EQUIPMENT:

Top (left to right): Surcingle; cotton web longe line; round, spun Dacron longe line; longe whip.

Center: Longe cavesson, timer

Bottom: Cotton rope longe line. *Photo: Ruth Harvie*

• *Longe cavesson*: Special headstall made of leather or nylon, with a padded metal noseband and rings to attach the longe line. This is the best headgear for longeing, because it gives you good control without danger of hurting the horse's mouth. You may use a longe cavesson alone or with a snaffle bridle.

A longe cavesson must be adjusted properly so that it will not be pulled out of position. The noseband should rest about 4 fingers above the horse's nostrils and be fastened snugly, but not be uncomfortably tight. It must be on the nasal bone, not the cartilage. If the noseband is too loose or too low, it is very uncomfortable, and may interfere with control. The jowl strap must be fastened snugly so that the cavesson cannot slip up into the horse's eye.

When used with a snaffle bridle, the longe cavesson is put on over the bridle. The noseband of the longe cavesson goes *inside* the bridle cheekpieces, to prevent pinching and to allow the bit to fit properly. The bridle cheekpieces should be lengthened to allow for the longe cavesson underneath. The noseband of the bridle must not be caught under the longe cavesson; it is best to remove it.

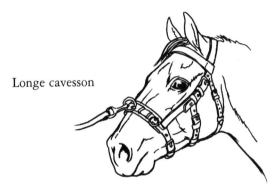

Longe cavesson

- *Snaffle bridle*: A pony may be longed in a snaffle bridle, without a longe cavesson. To avoid injury to the pony's mouth, this must be done only by persons experienced in longeing, and only with ponies that are well-trained to longe. The reins can be removed from the bridle or twisted several times under the throat and the throatlash buckled through them, to keep them from hanging down too low.

LONGE CAVESSON WORN OVER SNAFFLE BRIDLE

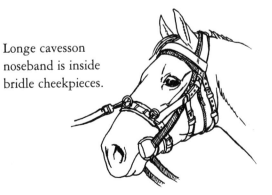

Longe cavesson
noseband is inside
bridle cheekpieces.

LONGE LINE ATTACHED TO SNAFFLE BRIDLE (OVER HEAD)

Longe line runs
through inside bit
ring, over poll, and
snaps to outside bit
ring. (Must be
changed when
changing directions.)

Snaffle reins are secured by twisting
several times, then buckling throatlash through reins.

Caution: This method acts like a gag
bit and can be severe.

Run the longe line through the inside snaffle bit ring,
over the pony's poll, and fasten it to the bit ring on the other
side. This arrangement is quite severe, so handle the longe
carefully. It has the same effect as a gag snaffle because pressure on the longe line pulls the bit up into the corners of the
pony's mouth and presses down on his poll. When changing
direction, you must change the longe line over to the other
side.

Never attach a longe line to one side of the bit or run it
under the pony's chin, as this can hurt his mouth. Never
attach a chain-end longe line to the bit.

• *Protective boots or bandages*: Should be used on all four legs when
longeing, as a horse is more likely to interfere when working
on a circle, especially if he is green or excitable. Bell boots can
be used to protect the heels of the front feet, and splint boots
or tendon boots can be used on the front and hind legs.
Exercise bandages may be used to protect the legs, but these
must be put on by an expert.

• *Saddle*: A horse may be longed while wearing his saddle, but
the stirrups must be fastened up so that they will not come
down and bang against him. (See diagram.)

STIRRUPS FASTENED UP FOR LONGEING

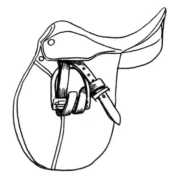

1. Run up stirrups as usual.

2. Wrap end of leather around iron, then upward under branch of iron.

3. Put end of leather through loop; then secure in keeper.

- *Surcingle*: A band with rings attached, which is buckled around the pony and used instead of a saddle, to attach side reins.

- *Side reins*: Used on more advanced horses, to encourage correct head carriage and balance. These reins are attached either to the girth or billet straps of the saddle or to a surcingle, and snapped to the rings of a snaffle bit. Side reins *must* be adjusted correctly, or they can cause great harm.

  Side reins are for work in the trot and canter, and should not be used in the walk because they can cause a horse to shorten his stride and spoil his walk. Side reins must be used only after the horse has warmed up without them. They should be adjusted a bit long at first and gradually shortened to the correct working length (so that there is a little slack when the horse is standing at ease, with his face in front of the vertical). As soon as the trot and canter work is finished, the side reins must be unsnapped. A horse must not be asked to stand still or walk around with side reins fastened.

  Caution: Side reins are advanced training equipment, to be used only by experienced persons who know how to use them correctly. If used incorrectly, they can hurt your pony and spoil his training, and can cause accidents. *Do not use side reins except under the supervision of your Pony Club instructor.*

SIDE REINS

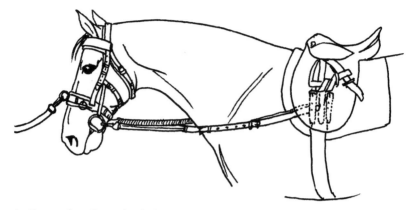

1. Correctly adjusted: Slight slack when pony's face is slightly in front of vertical.

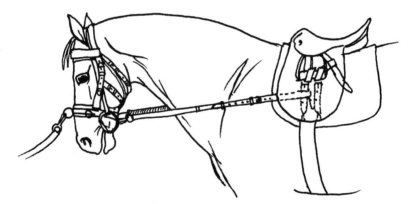

2. Wrong: Side reins too short; pony's face behind vertical.

Time Limits and Changing Directions

Longeing is harder work than ordinary riding, because working on a circle puts more stress on the pony's legs, muscles, joints, and tendons. It also is boring, because horses have a short attention span. You must consider the horse's age, experience, and fitness when deciding how much longeing he can do. Longeing in hard, deep, or muddy footing; on small circles; or at fast gaits is extremely hard on horses and must be avoided.

When longeing, change directions every five minutes to avoid overworking the muscles on one side. Changing gaits frequently also helps.

A horse that is out of condition or not accustomed to longeing should be longed for only five to ten minutes (half the time in one direction, half in the other), with frequent breaks at a walk. The extra bending that longeing requires can make him sore if you longe him too long or too hard when he is not fit.

Horses that are fit and accustomed to working on the longe can be longed for a total of fifteen to twenty minutes, changing gaits frequently and working half of the time in each direction.

Safety when Longeing

To be safe for you and your pony, longeing must be done correctly. Here are some important safety procedures:

- Longe in a safe, level area (preferably an enclosed ring) with good footing.
- Use the right equipment (see above), including proper dress for the handler and protective boots for the horse. Make sure everything is adjusted correctly before you start.
- Learn to longe correctly, using a trained, quiet horse. Before trying to longe on your own or longeing an inexperienced horse, get help from your instructor. Practice handling the longe line and longe whip before trying to longe any horse.
- Hold the end of the longe line in folds, not loops. *Never* coil the end of the line or wrap it around your hand. Keep the longe line and any extra folds from dragging on the ground.
- Be careful when starting a horse out on the longeing circle, especially if he is fresh. Stay out of kicking range.
- Do not longe a horse in small circles. This puts great strain on his legs and muscles and can cause injury.
- Handle the whip quietly, and use the lash in an upward direction, toward the horse's shoulder, belly, or hocks. Don't wave the whip around.

Communication

The aids used to communicate with the horse while longeing are the voice, the handler's body placement, the whip, and the longe line.

The Voice   To keep your pony responsive and paying attention, you should keep quiet except when giving him a command. If you talk all the time, the pony will get confused and will not pay attention to your voice.

Your tone of voice and the way you say the words are more important than the actual words used. Give commands in a confident, cheerful tone as if you expect him to obey you, not as if asking a question. Each command must have a different sound so that your pony can tell them apart. To encourage your pony to go forward or pick up a faster gait, your voice should sound brisk and should "lift" at the end of the command. To ask him to slow down, lower your voice and draw the word out.

The voice aid should be used first, repeated once or twice if needed, then reinforced with the whip or longe line as appropriate.

Voice Commands   The following words are commonly used to communicate with the horse while longeing. You may substitute other words, but always use the commands to which your pony is accustomed.

- To walk on: "Walk ON" or "Wa-a-LK," spoken firmly, raising the tone of voice on the last syllable.
- To walk from trot: "WA-a-a-lk" or "A-a-a-nd WALK," spoken slowly and quietly, but firmly, dropping the tone of voice at the end. The word "and" is used like a half-halt to prepare the horse when asking for a downward transition.
- To halt: "WHo-o-a-a" or "A-a-a-nd Whoa," spoken slowly and quietly, but firmly, dropping the tone of voice at the end. "Whoa" means "Stop and stand still," so to avoid confusion it is best to use another word (such as "Slowly" or "Easy") to slow down without stopping.
- To trot from a walk: "Trot ON" or "T-rr-ROt," spoken briskly, raising the tone of voice and stressing the last part of the command.
- To canter from a trot: "Ca-a-a-n-TER," spoken briskly, raising the voice on the end of the word.
- To trot from a canter: "Tr-o-o-t" or "A-a-a-nd Trot," spoken slowly and quietly, as in other downward transitions.
- "Easy" or "Steady" (spoken slowly and quietly) may be used to calm an excited horse.
- Clucking with the tongue (single, short, sharp clucks, not continuous clucking) can encourage a lazy horse to move with more effort. To be most effective, a cluck should be used in rhythm with the inside hind leg. If you cluck too much, the horse will stop paying attention.
- "OU-u-ut," spoken firmly, may be used to ask the horse to move out onto the circle, away from the handler.

- "Good Boy" (or any other appropriate term) can be used as a verbal reward. It should be spoken immediately when the horse does something well. (Don't use this word only when stopping, or your pony may learn to stop working whenever you praise him!)
- "NO!" This is a verbal correction, to be used *instantly* when required. It should be spoken in a sharp, displeased tone of voice.

Hand and Rein Aids on the Longe Line   When you are longeing, your hand on the longe line acts as your hands and rein aids do when you are riding. Neither you nor your pony should pull on the longe line; you should keep a light contact with each other and communicate with light rein aids.

HOLDING THE LONGE LINE

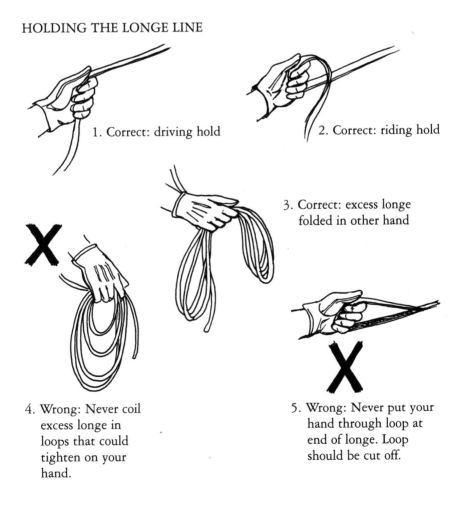

1. Correct: driving hold

2. Correct: riding hold

3. Correct: excess longe folded in other hand

4. Wrong: Never coil excess longe in loops that could tighten on your hand.

5. Wrong: Never put your hand through loop at end of longe. Loop should be cut off.

To give correct rein aids, you must hold the longe line correctly. If your horse is going to the left, your left hand is your longe hand, or "leading hand," used to give rein aids; the other hand holds the longe whip. The folded loops of the longe line can be held in either hand.

You can hold the longe line in either of two ways: as you would hold a snaffle rein for riding (the longe comes out toward the horse under your little finger, or between your little finger and ring finger), or as you would hold a driving rein (the longe comes out between your first finger and thumb). Hold the longe hand fairly close to your body, with a softly bent elbow, and a straight line through your hand to the horse's nose. Your hand should be closed in a soft fist. Just as in riding, you give rein aids by squeezing or turning your hand, *not* by pulling.

For safety's sake, any extra line at the end of the longe must be folded into flat loops. These loops must not be large or sloppy, or drag on the ground where you could get tangled in them, and they must never be coiled around your hand. You must be able to take up or let out the longe as necessary.

Rein aids given with the longe line must be coordinated with voice, body placement, and whip, just as rein aids must be coordinated with leg, seat, and voice aids when riding. As in riding, rein aids are always given with a short "squeeze and relax," never a long, continuous pull.

Here are the rein aids used when longeing:

+ *Opening or Leading Rein*: The longe hand moves outward and sideways, away from your body. This leads the horse forward and asks him stretch his neck out.
+ *Direct Rein*: The longe hand gives short squeezes on the rein, toward your elbow. This asks the horse to make the circle smaller, to bend toward you, or to stop pulling out away from you.
+ *Indirect Rein*: The longe hand moves inward and sideways, toward your opposite hip, giving short squeezes. This puts pressure backward on the longe and asks your horse to slow down or stop.
+ *Giving the Longe*: The longe hand moves briefly forward and out toward the horse's head, then smoothly takes up the contact again. This releases pressure on the longe for an instant. It is used to reward the horse, to ask the horse to lower his head, or to allow him to move out onto a larger circle. Don't

REIN AIDS IN LONGEING

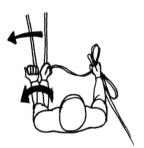

1. Opening or leading rein: Hand rotates to side.

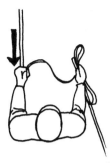

2. Direct rein: Hand squeezes straight back, toward body.

3. Indirect rein: Hand moves inward, toward handler's opposite hip.

4. Vibrating the longe: Hand "shivers" in place.

5. Giving the longe: Hand moves slightly forward, toward horse.

lose all contact or let the longe line become dangerously slack; the horse could step over it if he turns in.

• *Vibrating the Longe*: The longe hand gives tiny "shivers." This calls the horse's attention to a light signal without pulling against him. It is very useful for halting and slowing down without pulling.

• *Half-Halts on the Longe*: A half-halt is a brief call for attention; it asks your pony to listen to you, to rebalance himself, and to prepare to do something. To give a half-halt on the longe line, you coordinate all your aids just as you do when riding. Lift the tip of the whip or point it toward the pony's hocks to ask him to engage his hind legs. As you stand taller, give a short lift and squeeze of your hand on the longe line, and give a voice command. A warning word such as "A-a-a-and" before a command has the effect of a half-halt because it tells the pony that another command is coming.

Communicating with the Longe Whip   In longeing, the longe whip takes the place of your leg when riding. The longe whip asks the horse to go forward or move away from the handler, and can help maintain liveliness or impulsion.

You hold the longe whip with the tip low and the lash dragging on the ground. Usually the longe whip is pointed toward the horse's hocks or slightly farther back. If a horse is fresh or reacts too much to the whip, it may be held pointing backward (behind the handler). When you go out to the horse (to adjust equipment or when changing directions), you should catch up the lash, turn the whip backward, and hold it under your arm.

The longe whip must be used quietly and tactfully. If you crack it or wave it around, a horse may become frightened and hard to control, or he may learn to ignore your whip signals.

The whip can be used in several ways:

• Close to the ground, with a forward rotating motion: This asks the horse to move forward.
• Flicked at the hocks (from back to front): This asks more strongly for forward movement.
• Flicked forward and upward toward the belly so that it lands on the area where the rider's leg is normally used (it takes considerable skill and practice!): This asks for forward and outward movement.

HANDLING THE LONGE WHIP

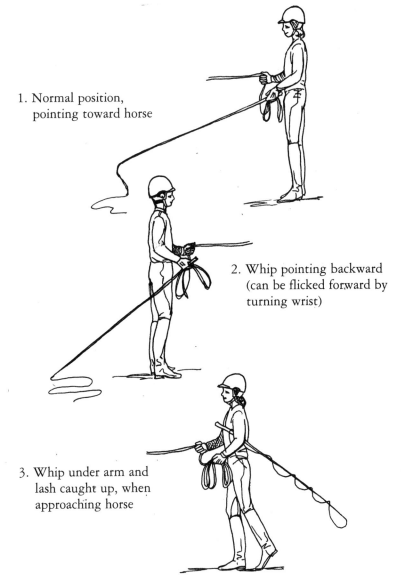

1. Normal position, pointing toward horse

2. Whip pointing backward (can be flicked forward by turning wrist)

3. Whip under arm and lash caught up, when approaching horse

- Cracking the whip: A sharp call for immediate forward movement. Use this only when all other signals fail, because it may upset the horse. If you crack the whip too often, your horse may learn to ignore all whip signals.
- Pointing the whip toward the horse's shoulder: This asks the horse to move out on a larger circle, or stops him from cutting in toward the handler.

♦ Moving the whip under the longe line and in front of the horse's head: This asks the horse to slow down and stop. (It requires considerable skill, tact, and practice. Poking the horse or waving a whip around his head will surely upset him!)

Communicating with Body Language   In longeing, the way the handler uses his body is one of the most important aids. Horses often pay more attention to body language than to other aids because it is more like the way they communicate with other horses. Even if you give other aids properly, if you don't use your body the right way, your pony will have a hard time understanding you and will be harder to control.

When longeing, you and the horse form a triangle (like a piece of pie); you stand at the point of the triangle. The horse is one side of the triangle; your longe hand and longe line are one side, and your whip is the other. The point of the triangle (you) should be opposite the pony's girth area, just behind his shoulder.

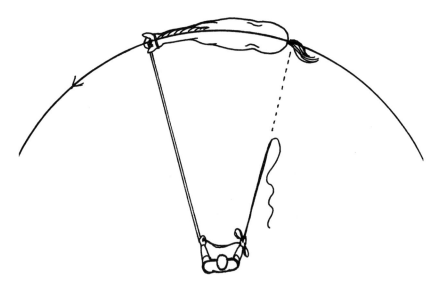

Longeing Position: The Control Triangle

If you move too far toward the *back* of the triangle (toward the horse's hip), the horse acts as if you were chasing him from behind, and he might rush forward, kick, or bolt. When you move toward the front of the triangle (toward his head), he acts as if you were getting in front of him and cutting him off; and he will slow down or stop. Normally, your body position should keep the triangle "balanced": that is, you should be far enough back to keep your pony moving freely forward, but close enough to the front to control him easily. A small shift of your body in either direction will either send your pony forward or slow him down.

Horses react to the way you use your body. If you move toward him suddenly and strongly, you appear threatening, and the pony may try to escape by rushing forward (if you move toward the rear) or by stopping suddenly and turning around (if you move toward the front). If you move timidly, stiffly, too little, or too late, he may decide you are not worth bothering about and ignore you.

Good body communication makes longeing easier and helps a pony understand what you want. When you do it well, you will notice and react to small changes in your pony's attitude and movement, and he will react to subtle movements of your body. It's like dancing with your pony!

Practice without a Pony First!   To be safe, you must learn to use the longe equipment safely and effectively *before* you try to longe a pony. If you try to longe a pony before you can do it properly, you both could get into a dangerous situation. Here are some safe procedures to practice:

- Hold the longe line with the extra loops of line folded correctly. Practice letting the line out and shortening it, without big loops that could trip you. Do this in both directions, and practice especially with the hand that is more difficult for you.
- Practice signaling with the longe whip, using a sawhorse or section of fence. Try to flick the lash so that it lands on the "horse's" hind leg below the hock; and on the barrel, just where a rider's leg would touch him; and on the shoulder. Do this in both directions, until you can use the whip easily with either hand.
- Practice longeing with another person acting as a pony. (For safety, wrap up the lash of the longe whip, and signal only with the tip of the whip.) Your human "pony" should tell you whether your longe line and whip signals, voice commands, and body language are clear. Trade places so that you get to experience longeing from the pony's point of view, too.

Longeing a Trained Horse

You should learn to longe on a horse or pony that is well-trained and easy to longe, with help from your instructor. Your instructor will check the adjustment of the longeing equipment and should longe the pony first, to be sure he is behaving well. The instructor should stand behind you in the middle of the longeing circle and help you at first.

Starting Out: Basic Control at the Walk   To start a pony longeing to the left, stand by his left shoulder, facing forward and toward the pony. Hold the longe in your left hand about 3 feet from the cavesson, with the end of the longe folded correctly in your right hand. Your right hand holds the longe whip, pointing backward toward the pony's hind hoof, with the tip on the ground. Give a voice command, "Tony, Walk on," and lead him forward with your left hand as you move with him, staying opposite his girth. (If he doesn't move forward, point the whip toward his hocks and give the command again.)

Say "Out," and let the longe line slip through your left hand until he is a little farther away—about 6 to 10 feet. Stay opposite his girth, and walk with him so that he moves on a large circle about 30 feet in diameter, while you make a slightly smaller circle. Be careful when starting out, especially with a pony that is feeling fresh; never get into a position where you could be kicked.

To stop, give a quiet voice command such as "Tony, Whoa," and step toward his shoulder. Quietly bring the longe whip forward so that it points in front of his chest (don't bring it up too high or fast, or you may scare him). When the pony stops, he must stay out on the circle. Do not let him turn in and come toward you. Practice walking and stopping until he understands your commands and is going forward and stopping well on the circle.

Next, ask your pony to go out on a larger circle. Let out more longe line as you say, "Out" and point your whip toward his shoulder. Now you will stand on one spot in the center of the longeing circle and turn on your heel, making a center point for a perfectly round circle. Don't let out so much line that it sags or touches the ground; the pony should keep the longe line slightly taut with light contact. If it becomes slack, control is lost.

Keep your pony "in the triangle" between your longe whip and the longe line. Stay opposite his girth area. If you get too far forward, he may stop or even duck back and turn around. If you get too far back, he may go forward too fast, and control will be lost.

If a pony tries to cut into the center of the circle, point the whip at his shoulder and say, "Out." If he pulls against you, give a short tug and release on the longe line, like a half-halt. As soon as he responds, return to a light contact.

Trotting on the Longe   When your pony walks and halts well from a walk, you may ask for a trot. Give a voice command, "Tony, Trot" or "Trot on," and point the whip toward his hindquarters. If he doesn't respond, repeat the command and tap the whip on the ground behind him, or flick it toward his hocks. When he trots, keep him moving at a steady pace on a large circle. After a few minutes, ask him to come back to a walk by saying "Tony, Wa-a-alk" or "A-a-and Walk" as you step toward his shoulder. After practicing walking and trotting, bring him back to a halt from the walk.

Changing Directions   It's important to work both directions equally, to keep the pony from getting sore or becoming one-sided. To change directions, you stop the pony, tuck the whip under your arm (with the end pointing out behind you), and go out to him. Lead him around in a reverse (you may have to change the longe line from one side to the other if you are using a bridle or halter). Change the longe line and whip from one hand to the other.

Start off in the new direction just as you did in the beginning. Some ponies do not like to change directions and might try to turn around. You may have to start with a shortened longe line and walk a large circle with the pony until he gets used to going forward in the new direction. Stay behind his shoulder point, where you can control him most easily. When he is moving forward well, move out to the center of the circle as you did in the other direction.

Cantering on the Longe   Cantering on the longe line is more difficult than trotting, because it is harder for a pony to keep his balance cantering in a fairly small circle. Don't expect a pony to canter on the longe until he longes quite well at the trot and has excellent balance in both directions.

To ask for a canter, use a voice command ("Tony, Can-TER"), and reinforce it with the longe whip if necessary. Some ponies may have trouble keeping their balance at a canter on the longe line, or may get excited and pull. You can help with short half-halts on the longe line and a calm, quiet voice command such as "Easy," but don't do too much cantering, especially if your pony finds it difficult.

When longeing, a pony should canter on the correct lead. If he picks up the wrong lead, bring him back to the trot and let him get balanced before you ask him to canter again. Never canter on the longe line when the ground is slippery; he could slip or fall down.

Rhythm and Relaxation   The main goals for longeing at this level are simple obedience, rhythm, and relaxation. When a pony is calm, relaxed, and under control at a steady, even gait, he will eventually find his best working rhythm and tempo. This is the rhythm and tempo (speed of rhythm) at which his muscles work most easily and he moves with his best balance and stride.

Pony is moving well on the longe, with round back, extended neck, and good rhythm and relaxation.

Following are some signs that your pony is moving with good rhythm and relaxation:

- His strides become even and steady, and his speed stays the same, without rushing or slowing down. You can count in a steady rhythm with his hoofbeats.
- His hind legs reach well forward under his body. (However, at this level, he does not have to "track up.")
- He stretches his neck and his back, and his back looks "round" instead of flat or hollow.
- He breathes evenly and may snort gently while stretching his neck and back.

Remember that longeing is hard work for a pony—much harder than riding for the same amount of time. Don't longe him too long or too hard, and be sure to walk for at least ten minutes to warm his muscles up before work and cool them down afterward. Always end a longeing session on a good note: Ask your pony to do something he usually does easily and well; then halt him, go out to him, and reward him with praise, a pat, and perhaps a tidbit.

CHAPTER 11

TEACHING AND ASSISTING WITH PONY CLUB ACTIVITIES

We are all teachers, even when we are not teaching formal lessons. Whenever you ride or work with horses, other people (especially younger or less experienced people) learn from what you do. This is a big responsibility because it means that what you do with your pony affects other people and their horses and ponies. If you are safe and thorough, and keep a high standard of horsemanship, they learn safety and good horsemanship habits from your example. However, if you cut corners, let down your standards, or fail to follow safety rules, they will feel free to do as you do, no matter what you say. This could lead to someone having an accident, for which you would be at least partly responsible. The only way to teach safety and good horsemanship is to follow the standards yourself, all the time. Then you can insist that others follow them, too.

Teaching and helping younger Pony Clubbers is an important part of Pony Club. Without instructors, volunteers of all ages, and Pony Clubbers to help teach, there would be no Pony Club. As you pass your knowledge on to newer members, you are helping Pony Club to continue.

Teaching can be rewarding in many ways. Besides helping Pony Club, you help your students and their ponies. Teaching can also help you learn to work well with people, to plan and organize your material, and to present it well to a single student and to a group. You have an important effect on your students—you help them to be safer, to take care of their ponies better, and to get a good start in horsemanship and Pony Club.

What Makes a Good Teacher?

What makes a good teacher? It isn't just knowledge, riding ability, winning in competition, or becoming an adult. To be a teacher, you must understand and care about other people and horses. You must have knowledge and experience, but you must be able to communicate it to others. No matter how much you know, it is no good to your students if it stays locked in your head.

If you think about the best teachers you have known, you'll probably find that they had the qualities listed below. Can you think of any other things that you feel are important in a teacher of horsemanship?

Here are some qualities of a good teacher:

- Has a real liking for people and horses, and the desire to help them understand each other.
- Always puts safety first, followed by kindness and consideration for the horse.
- Has energy, enthusiasm, imagination, and a sense of humor, which make learning fun.
- Knows the subject well and doesn't try to teach what he or she has not experienced and learned thoroughly.
- Is well prepared and organized, and plans each lesson beforehand. He or she teaches one step at a time, with basics first.
- Has good communication skills, including the ability to show and tell, and a good teaching voice. A good teacher takes time to answer students' questions and pays attention to what students communicate to him or her.
- Has self-control, calmness, patience, and common sense
- Can see things from the student's point of view and adapts the way he or she teaches to the age and level of the students, without ever "talking down" to them.
- Has "positive authority," which is the ability to keep control or enforce the rules in a positive way, being firm when necessary, but always fair and pleasant.

Helping Younger Pony Clubbers

The first teaching you do in Pony Club will be helping younger and less experienced Pony Clubbers, especially in safety inspections and in preparing themselves and their ponies for turnout. When you help younger Pony Clubbers, a qualified adult must be in charge because USPC Standards do not allow any child to be responsible for another child.

To help another Pony Clubber, you must know what you are teaching, why it's important, the right way to do it, and the reasons for doing it that way. Review the *USPC D Manual*, especially the Standards and test requirements for your D-1 or D-2 student. It helps to have the *USPC D Manual* handy.

How to Perform a Safety and Tack Inspection Safety and tack inspections are for teaching as much as for inspection. You should show the Pony Clubber how to hold his pony safely for inspection, and explain what you are checking and why it's important. Be friendly, positive, and helpful; praise anything he or she has done right. If you find something wrong, show him what it is, why it must be corrected, and how to improve or correct it. Remember that Pony Clubbers want to get on with their riding, so be efficient and thorough, not "picky."

Here is a checklist for safety and tack inspections. (Also review the requirements for D-1 and D-2 Levels in the *USPC D Manual*.)

Rider:
- ASTM/SEI helmet, properly fitted, with chin strap fastened
- Safe footwear (see *USPC D Manual*).
- No gum or candy in mouth
- No rings, earrings, or jewelry that could catch on reins or cause injury. No hairpins, combs, or barrettes that could cause injury in a fall.
- No waist packs, long scarves, or loose clothing
- Clothing that is safe for weather conditions, including gloves and warm clothes in cold weather. No sleeveless shirts or tank tops. Use sunscreen when necessary.

Saddle (check both sides), including:
- Saddle pad: Pulled up into gullet of saddle; no wrinkles; correctly attached to billets (above buckle guards)
- Proper fit: Fits pony and rider; properly balanced, with dip in center; no weight on any part of spine; two to three fingers' clearance at withers
- Condition of leather and stitching, tree not broken
- Safety bars in open position
- Stirrup leathers: All stitching sound, no cracks or torn holes, enough holes to adjust leathers to proper length for rider
- Stirrups: Proper size for rider (1 inch wider than boot; shows 1/2 inch on each side of foot when mounted)

A C Pony Clubber performs a tack and safety inspection for a younger member. *Photo: Micki Dobson*

- Billet straps: Three on each side, stitching and leather sound, no cracks or torn holes
- Girth: Proper size (at least two holes above and at least one hole below buckles on each side when tightened); leather, elastic, stitching, and buckles sound; no cracks, dirt, or roughness which could cause girth sores

Bridle (check both sides and overall fit), including:
- Condition and soundness of all leather and stitching, especially at stress points such as bit and rein fastenings
- Bit: Right way up, correct size and adjustment, curb chain (if used) flat and correctly fitted. Does not pinch or rub pony's lips.

- Cheekpieces: Buckles 1 to 1 1/2 inches above eye, with at least 1 extra hole above the buckle when bit is correctly adjusted.
- You should be able to slip a finger under the bridle at any point. Crownpiece and browband must not pinch or rub ears. Noseband 1/2 to 1 inch below cheekbones and adjusted snugly but not uncomfortably tight. A fist should fit between throatlash and pony's cheek. All strap ends properly buckled, in keepers and runners.
- Reins: Check bit fastenings for wear. Reins must be proper length (often too long on small ponies, leaving a loop that could catch the rider's foot). Shorten reins by tying a knot in the end (but without creating a dangerous loop in the end), or replace them with a shorter pair if available.

Pony:

- Feet and shoes: Cleaned out, shoes tight, no long toes, loose shoes, or risen clinches. Notice any cuts, overreaches, or interference marks.
- Head: Brushed clean, eyes and lips sponged. Check for rubs or sores on lips and chin. Mane and forelock smooth under crownpiece.
- Saddle area, girth, elbows, and between front legs: Brushed clean and smooth; no sores, rubs, or dirt
- Legs: swelling or obvious injuries (check further if you notice any).
- Pony must be sound enough and in condition for activity. (If a pony is obviously overweight, thin, or out of condition, ask the Examiner or instructor to check him.)

Other Equipment:

- Martingale: Correctly adjusted, fitted with rubber ring at chest. Rein stops *must* be used with running martingales.
- Breastplate, or breast collar: Correctly adjusted (a fist should fit between breastplate and chest). Strap ends in keepers.
- Any other equipment: In safe condition and properly adjusted.

What to do if something is not safe:

- Fix it if possible.

- Don't leave the student with a problem. You may have to change tack, punch more holes, or borrow an item.
- A student cannot be allowed to ride without a properly fitted ASTM/SEI helmet, with unsafe footwear, or if the condition of tack or pony is unsafe.
- If you find tack that needs repairs or a problem that needs to be corrected at home (for example, a pony that is seriously out of condition or badly needs shoeing or hoof trimming), ask your adult adviser (Examiner, District Commissioner, or instructor) to speak to the Pony Clubber's parents about the problem and what should be done to correct it. This must be done in a clear, helpful, and tactful way, and should be done by an adult.

Helping Younger Pony Clubbers Prepare for Turnout Inspection   Younger Pony Clubbers need help and instruction in preparing for Turnout Inspections. Your job is to teach and help so that your students learn to do it for themselves, not to do it for them. Small children, however, need extra help—for example, when carrying things that are too heavy for them, grooming areas they can't reach, and doing anything else they cannot handle by themselves.

Safety must always come first, especially with younger children and less experienced Pony Clubbers. Always be aware of how the pony is being handled, and step in if you must to prevent a problem. Be sure you set a good example: Don't kneel or sit on the ground near a pony, or lead a pony without a lead rope, even for a few seconds.

It's important to be tactful when helping. Be pleasant and friendly, and praise anything your students do that is right or that shows improvement. If you sound critical, bossy, or impatient, they won't want to accept your help. Give reasons for anything that must be improved or done differently. Remember that Pony Club expects good work and improvement, not perfection, so don't discourage students if they don't get it 100 percent right the first time.

Work in a safe place, and have all the equipment you will need (such as grooming kit or tack cleaning supplies) assembled beforehand. Show your students a procedure (for instance, how to use a currycomb or how to clean tack), and let them get started. You can work along with them (especially if you are cleaning your own tack, too), and help them if they run into difficulties.

As you work, talk with your students about what is required for inspection and why. Make sure they understand why they must take good daily care of their ponies and tack instead of trying to do a big cleanup just before a rally. (If possible, show them the difference between tack that has been well cared for and tack that has been neglected.) Show them the most important places to check, and let them check your work so that they can see how it should be done. Encourage them to talk with you about what you are doing, and to ask questions. If your students learn to take pride in taking good care of their tack and their ponies, you have taught them well.

Assisting in Dismounted Instruction   Dismounted instruction is as important as riding lessons for Pony Clubbers. Safety, horse handling, horse care and management, horse knowledge, and practical subjects such as bandaging and grooming are all covered in dismounted instruction. There are several ways of teaching a dismounted lesson, but a practical lesson is usually best. This type of lesson lets the students see and do as well as hear about the subject. It often involves using a horse or pony, or demonstrating something such as bedding a stall or cleaning tack. If possible, every student should get a chance to practice whatever is taught.

Assisting in dismounted instruction is a privilege for Pony Clubbers who are becoming more proficient in their own horsemanship skills and knowledge. It's a good way to learn to teach, because you work with an experienced instructor, helping where needed and giving short demonstrations. You aren't left on your own to teach, because the Pony Club Standards do not allow children to be responsible for other children.

When you help with a lesson, you are an assistant to the instructor. A good assistant helps the lesson run smoothly, without distracting the students' attention from the teacher. The instructor will go over his or her lesson plan with you and explain what he wants you to do. Some things you might be asked to do are:

- Help set up an area for a lesson and collect the equipment needed.
- Hold a pony during a lesson or demonstration.
- Demonstrate a skill you know and can perform correctly (such as grooming, cleaning tack, or tying a quick-release knot) or help the instructor with a demonstration. It's important to demonstrate good safety practices as well as the skill that is being taught.

- Help students practice the skill they have been taught and check their work.
- Give special help or extra practice to any student who needs it (for instance, a student who is younger or less experienced than the rest of the class).
- Take part in a discussion of the subject.
- As you become more experienced at teaching, the instructor may ask you to teach part of the lesson (with supervision), or answer students' questions.

Before assisting with a lesson, review that section in the *Pony Club Manual* and the D Standards. If you will be giving a demonstration, practice to be sure you can do it smoothly and correctly.

When demonstrating, always set a good example in safety and horse handling. (Demonstrators sometimes get so wrapped up in their subject that they forget safety rules such as not sitting down close to a pony, or keeping a hand on the rump when passing behind a pony.) Have all your tools neatly lined up where you can reach

TEACHING A DISMOUNTED LESSON

- Pony tied safely
- Instructor dressed neatly and properly
- Instructor demonstrating clearly
- Students placed where they are safe and so that all can see and hear

them, but out of the pony's way. Show each step clearly, and make sure everyone can see.

When you explain something to a group, speak slowly and clearly, and look at your students. If you look down or mumble, they can't hear or understand you. If you are asked a question and you don't know the answer, don't pretend. A good teacher will say, "I don't know, but I'll find out." You may be able to look it up in the *Pony Club Manual*.

Help the instructor by avoiding interruptions or distractions while he or she is teaching. Don't encourage students to talk to you when they should be listening to the instructor. If you see that a student has a question or has not understood what the instructor said, you can quietly point it out to the instructor when he or she is finished.

Some Topics for Short Dismounted Lessons   As a C-3 Pony Clubber, you will be asked to plan and present short dismounted lessons (no longer than ten minutes) for D-1 or D-2 Pony Clubbers. Remember to choose a small part of a larger subject and teach it thoroughly; you can't teach everything about any subject in ten minutes!

Here are some sample topics (you may think of others):

Grooming
Basic Grooming Tools
How to Pick Out a Foot
How to Care for a Pony after
   Riding
How to Get a Muddy Pony
   Clean

Pony Care and Management
Cooling a Pony Out after
   Work
How to Tie a Quick-Release
   Knot
Stable Vices

Hoof Care
How to Pick up Feet Safely
Daily Hoof Care

**How to Help Your Pony Be
Safe in the Trailer**

Pony Knowledge
Parts of a Pony
Pony Colors
Leg and Face Markings

Feeding and Watering
Rules for Safe Feeding
Kinds of Feed
Watering Your Pony

Tack
Saddling and/or Bridling
Cleaning Tack
Oiling and Conditioning Tack
Parts of Tack
Checking Tack for Safety

There are many other possible topics. Check the D-1 and D-2 Standards and the USPC Flow Chart for more ideas. Lesson plans and lesson format are discussed in the *USPC B/A Manual*.

CHAPTER 12

CONFORMATION, MOVEMENT, AND SOUNDNESS

To understand how your pony is built, how he moves, and what can go wrong with him, it helps to know some horse anatomy. Horses have basically the same bones and muscles as people do, although some of their bones and muscles have different shapes for different purposes. It is easier to understand horse anatomy if you compare each part of the horse with the same part of your own body. (It helps to remember that if you were a horse, you would be walking on all fours, on your middle toes and fingers.)

BASIC HORSE ANATOMY

- *Bones and Joints*: Bones are the framework of the body. They support the horse, protect his organs, and act as levers to move him. Bones are held together by ligaments, which are strong, slightly elastic fibers.

    A joint is a place where bones meet. Flexion (bending) can take place only at a joint. Joints also absorb shock.
    The ligaments around a joint form a closed "joint capsule." Inside the joint capsule is a slippery oil called synovial fluid, which lubricates the joint. The ends of the bone are covered with smooth cartilage, which cushions the joint, absorbs shock, and helps it move freely.
- *Muscles and Tendons*: Muscles move the body. Tendons, which are like strong cables or straps, attach muscles to bones.

HORSE AND HUMAN SKELETONS

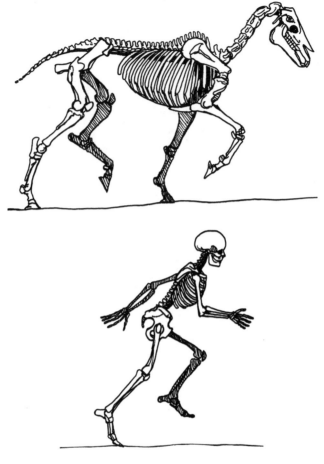

Muscles are made up of fibers that can contract (or shorten), and pull on the tendons to move the bones.

Because muscles can only pull, not push, they usually work in pairs. One muscle flexes (bends) a joint; the other extends (straightens) it. Muscles and tendons that bend or flex a joint are called "flexors"; those that extend or straighten a joint are called "extensors."

• *Lower Leg Anatomy*: There are no muscles in the lower legs, only bones, tendons, ligaments and other structures. To know what a sound leg looks like, and to understand what can go wrong, it helps to know the basic anatomy of the lower leg.

MUSCLES AND JOINTS

Muscle:

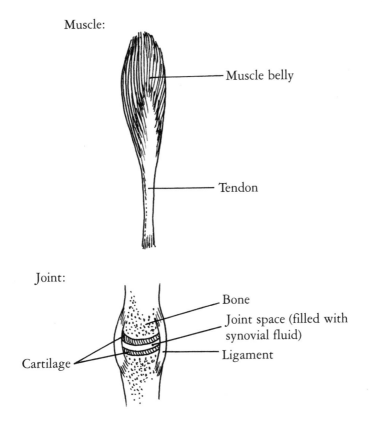

Muscle belly

Tendon

Joint:

Bone

Joint space (filled with synovial fluid)

Ligament

Cartilage

Conformation

"Conformation" refers to the way a horse is built. Good conformation is attractive, but, more important, good conformation is functional, or built to work better. This makes a stronger, sounder horse that can move well. Different types of conformation make some horses more suitable for certain jobs such as cross-country riding and jumping, working cattle, or pulling heavy loads. The type of conformation that would make a good cow pony would not be suitable for an Olympic-level dressage horse. However, both horses may have good conformation for their own type.

Regardless of breed or type, some basic principles of conformation are always the same. These make a horse sound, strong, and well-balanced.

STRUCTURES OF THE LOWER LEG

1. Foreleg:

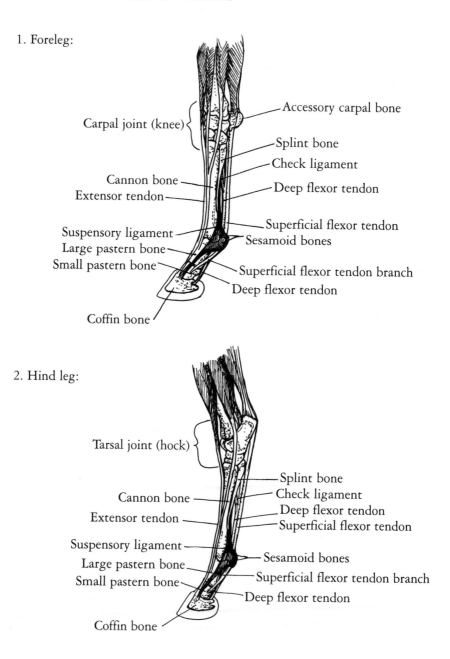

Accessory carpal bone

Carpal joint (knee)

Splint bone

Check ligament

Cannon bone

Deep flexor tendon

Extensor tendon

Suspensory ligament

Superficial flexor tendon

Sesamoid bones

Large pastern bone

Small pastern bone

Superficial flexor tendon branch

Deep flexor tendon

Coffin bone

2. Hind leg:

Tarsal joint (hock)

Splint bone

Cannon bone

Check ligament

Deep flexor tendon

Extensor tendon

Superficial flexor tendon

Suspensory ligament

Large pastern bone

Sesamoid bones

Small pastern bone

Superficial flexor tendon branch

Deep flexor tendon

Coffin bone

The Horse's Balance and Movement When standing still, about 55 percent of a horse's weight is carried on his front legs and about 45 percent on his hind legs. His "center of gravity" is an imaginary balance point located close to his heart girth line. As a horse moves, his balance changes. When he carries more weight on his forehand, his center of gravity shifts forward. When he tucks his hindquarters under himself, he shifts his balance and center of gravity backward.

The horse's head and neck are especially important in changing his balance. When he carries his head forward and down, it moves his balance forward. Raising his head and neck shifts his balance backward.

LOCATION OF HORSE'S CENTER
OF GRAVITY (AT A STANDSTILL)

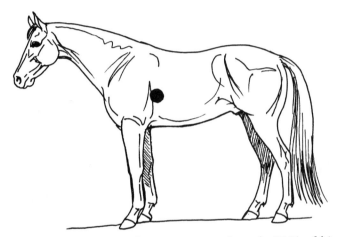

A horse (at a standstill) carries approximately 55% of his weight on the forelegs and approximately 45% on the hind legs.

A horse is a "rear-engined" animal; that is, his power comes from his hindquarters. At each stride, his hind legs reach forward (engage), push against the ground, and move him forward; and his front legs reach out and carry his weight.

Good movement is more efficient, safer, and easier for horse and rider. When a horse moves well, his legs move straight, without swinging sideways or striking each other. He moves with good engagement (reaching well forward with his hind legs), for power and good balance. His legs (especially his front legs) absorb shock, or concussion, so he moves smoothly.

Good conformation enables a horse to move well, whereas poor conformation handicaps him in the way he moves.

HIND LEG ENGAGEMENT

Good engagement: Hind legs reach far under body.

Poor engagement: Short, lazy stride

Balance and Proportion in Conformation   Good conformation makes it easier for a horse to move and carry a rider in good balance.

A horse should have a well-balanced appearance: No part should look too large or too small, and all parts should blend smoothly into each other. His legs should be in proportion to his body, not extremely long or short. His neck should be long enough for good balance, and his head should not be too large.

A horse's body should appear fairly level from the neck back so that his rump is not higher than his withers. Horses built low in front and high behind tend to carry too much weight on their forehands, which makes them hard to balance and can put extra stress on their front legs.

Good Foreleg Conformation (Side)   A horse's front legs reach out and carry his weight, and absorb concussion (shock) at every stride. To do this well, they must be strong and well developed and set under him properly.

A vertical line (called a "plumb line") should run from the center of the shoulder blade, down the middle of the leg, to the fetlock joint. Half of the leg should be in front of the plumb line and half behind it.

Foreleg Conformation Faults (Side):

• *Standing Under:* Leg set too far back; most of the leg is behind the plumb line. This puts the horse's balance too far forward.

- *Camped Out in Front:* Leg set out in front; most of the leg is behind the plumb line. This puts more strain on the legs.
- *Over at the Knee:* Knee is slightly bent, putting the lower leg too far back.
- *Back at the Knee (Calf Knee):* Knee has a slight backward bend, with cannon bone slanting forward. This puts extra stress on tendons and fetlock joints, and especially on the bones of the knee (carpal bones). It may lead to bone chips or fractures of the carpal bones when the horse is worked at speed, over fences, or when he is fatigued.

FORELEGS (SIDE VIEW)

1. Well-set foreleg   2. Standing under   3. Camped out in front

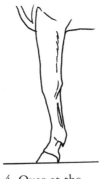 

4. Over at the knee   5. Back at the knee

Good Foreleg Conformation (Front)   The front legs should be straight and parallel, not too close together or too wide apart. This lines the bones up properly so that each leg moves straight, and helps distribute concussion (shock) evenly.

A vertical line (plumb line) straight down from the point of the shoulder should pass through the middle of the forearm, knee, cannon bone, fetlock joint, pastern, and foot.

Foreleg Conformation Faults (Front):

- *Base Narrow:* The legs are closer at the feet than at the chest. This places the feet too close together, and puts more weight and concussion on one side of the foot. Base-narrow horses may interfere (strike one leg against the other) or may place one leg in front of the other, as if they were walking on a tightrope. This is called "plaiting," and can cause interfering or stumbling.
- *Base Wide:* The legs are wider apart at the feet than at the chest. This conformation often goes with a narrow chest. It puts more weight and concussion on one side of the foot and may lead to ringbone.
- *Knock-Knees:* Knees that bend inward, inside the plumb line. This puts extra stress on the knees and the inside of the legs. Knock-kneed horses are prone to develop splints.
- *Bowed Knees:* Knees that bend outward, outside the plumb line. This puts extra stress on the knees and the outside of the legs.
- *Bench Knees (Offset Knees):* The cannon bones do not line up exactly with the center of the knees, but are set slightly to the outside. This puts extra weight and stress on the inside of the lower leg and often leads to splints on the inside of the cannon bone.
- *Toeing out (Splay-Footed):* The toes point out, so the foot swings in toward the opposite leg, which is called "winging in." This may lead to interfering and may cause lameness. It also causes uneven weight and concussion on the insides of the feet and legs, and may lead to ringbone.
- *Toeing in (Pigeon-Toes):* The toes point in, which makes the foot swing outward; this is called "paddling." It is less likely to cause lameness than winging in, but it puts uneven weight and strain on the outsides of the feet and legs, which may lead to ringbone.

FORELEGS (FRONT VIEW)

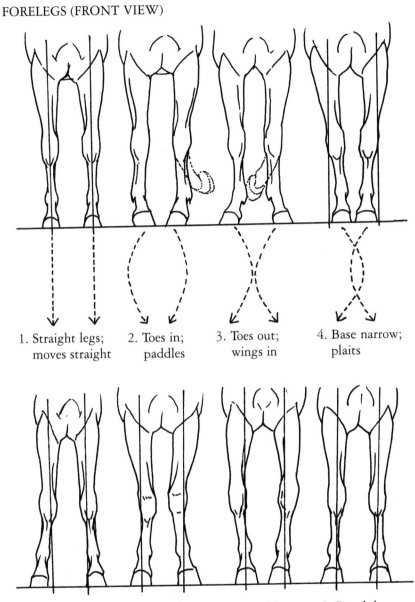

1. Straight legs;   2. Toes in;   3. Toes out;   4. Base narrow;
   moves straight   paddles   wings in   plaits

5. Base wide   6. Knock-knees   7. Bowed knees   8. Bench knees

Good Hind Leg Conformation (Side) A horse gets his pushing power from his hind legs. The hind legs must reach forward under his body (engage) at every stride, which provides the ground-covering pushing power. He also uses his hindquarters to balance himself in stops, turns, transitions, and collected gaits. Good hind leg conformation gives a horse strength, power, and better balance.

When you look at the hind legs from the side, the cannon bones should be vertical, and a vertical line (plumb line) from the point of the buttock should run down the back of the hock and leg down to the fetlock joint. This gives the bones of his hind legs the best angles for strength and good movement.

HIND LEGS (SIDE VIEW)

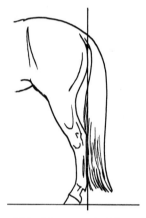

1. Good hind leg; vertical line from point of buttock runs down back of hock, tendon, and fetlock joint.

2. Stands under; sickle hocks

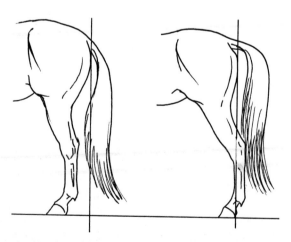

3. Post leg; too straight; in front of vertical line from buttock

4. Camped out behind; behind vertical line from buttock

Hind Leg Faults (Side):

- *Camped Out Behind:* Hind leg set too far back, behind the plumb line. This makes it harder to engage the hind legs (reach forward) and is weaker than a correctly set leg.
- *Standing Under (Sickle Hock):* Hock is slightly bent, with the lower leg angled forward. This puts extra stress on the hocks, which may lead to problems such as curbs, thoroughpins, bog spavins, or bone spavins.
- *Too Straight (Post Leg):* Too straight in the hock and stifle joints. It is easy to swing the leg forward without bending it much, but puts more stress on the hind leg, especially the hock and pastern.

Good Hind Leg Conformation (Rear) The hind legs must be lined up properly so that the horse can move straight. However, correct hind legs are not straight in quite the same way as front legs. The stifles must point out a little so that the horse can swing his hind legs forward without hitting his belly. The hocks and lower legs should be parallel and straight up and down, and the hind legs must not be too close or too wide apart.

HIND LEGS (REAR VIEW)

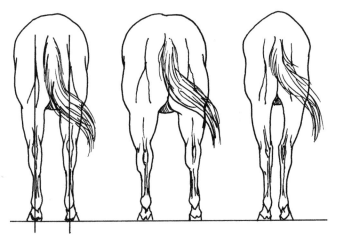

1. Good hind legs; straight; parallel; well-set

2. Hind legs set too wide

3. Hind legs set too narrow

(continued)

HIND LEGS (REAR VIEW)

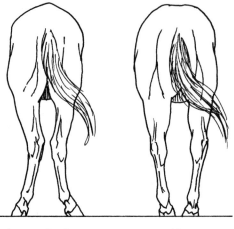

4. Cow hocks   5. Bowed hocks

Hind Leg Conformation Faults (Rear):

- *Cow Hocks:* Hocks that point in toward each other, with cannon bones slanting outward. This puts extra stress on the inside of the hocks, which may lead to bone spavins, bog spavins, or thoroughpins.
- *Bowed Hocks:* Hocks that point outward, with cannon bones slanting inward, putting extra stress on the hocks and the outside of the leg. This may lead to bog spavins or thoroughpins.
- *Too Wide:* Hind legs placed too far apart make it hard for the horse to reach well forward with his hind legs, which causes short strides.
- *Too Narrow:* Hind legs too close together often lack good muscle development. They make it easy for a horse to interfere, which may cause injuries and lameness.

Good Lower Leg and Joint Conformation   The lower legs and joints should be "clean" (free from thickness or swelling), and the bones, tendons, and other structures should stand out clearly.

The cannon bones should be fairly short, with clean, strong, and well-developed tendons. Short cannon bones usually mean stronger legs and better movement.

Knees and hocks should be wide, flat, and clean, with clearly defined bones. Small, round joints are weaker and more easily injured.

LOWER LEG CONFORMATION

1. Good foreleg: clean, wide, well-defined joints and tendons; short cannon bone; medium length and slope of pastern

2. Poor foreleg: small, puffy joints; tied in below knee; long cannon bone; short, steep pastern

3. Good hind leg: clean, wide, well-defined joints and tendons; short cannon bone; strong pastern with medium length and slope

4. Poor hind leg: small, puffy joints; long cannon bone; long, flat pastern

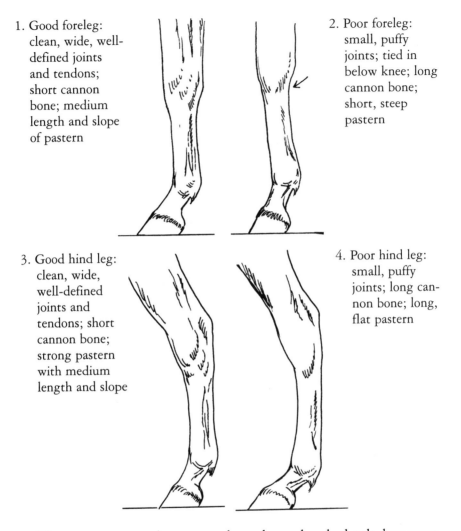

The pasterns must have enough angle to absorb shock, but must not be so long or sloping that they are weak and can easily be injured. The front pasterns usually have a little more slope than the hind pasterns.

Lower Leg and Joint Conformation Faults:

- *Tendons "tied in" below the knee:* Small, narrow tendons look as if they are squeezed in just below the knee. They are weak and poorly developed.
- *Pasterns too long and sloping:* Weak and easily injured. They also put more stress on the tendons, which can contribute to bowed tendons.

- *Pasterns too short and steep:* Do not absorb shock well, make the gait rough, and transmit more concussion (shock) to the foot and leg. This may contribute to problems such as ringbone, sidebone, and navicular disease.

Good Foot Conformation   The feet are especially important because they must carry the horse's weight and absorb shock with each step. The hoof expands (grows wider) with each step, which helps absorb shock; it contracts as the weight comes off the hoof. This pressure on the frog (and the cushion above it) helps pump blood through the hoof and back up the leg with every step. Good hoof conformation promotes strong, sound, and healthy feet.

The feet should be large and strong, with wide, well-developed heels and prominent bars. The frog should be large and should touch the ground, to promote good circulation and help the heels expand with each step. The sole should be arched or concave (like a saucer turned upside down), not flat, and the horse's weight should be carried on the wall, not the sole. The walls should be strong and smooth, without cracks or rings.

Hoof Conformation Faults:

- *Too-small feet:* Receive more concussion, especially to the navicular bone and coffin bone, because there is less area to absorb shock. They are more prone to develop navicular disease.
- *Contracted heels:* The heel is very narrow; the frog is pinched in and small, and does not touch the ground. Contracted heels can be caused by foot problems such as navicular disease or by poor trimming and shoeing. They also can be a conformation fault.
- *Flat soles:* Cause weight to be carried on the sole instead of on the wall, which makes the feet tender. A "dropped sole" can be the result of laminitis or founder, which causes the coffin bone to rotate and drop down.
- *Shelly hooves:* Thin, brittle walls that crack and break off easily. This makes the feet tender and can make it hard to keep shoes on.

Blemishes and Unsoundnesses

An "unsoundness" is a physical problem than makes a horse lame or unable to work. A "blemish" (such as a lump or a scar) may be unsightly but doesn't keep him from being able to work. Poor conformation contributes to unsoundnesses by making a part weaker or by putting it under more stress. Some unsoundnesses are caused by injury, while others develop slowly; some are more serious than others or get worse over time. Some might make a horse unfit for strenuous work, such as racing or eventing, but may not bother him in easier work. To avoid buying a pony with a serious unsoundness, always have your veterinarian check the pony before you buy.

Common Blemishes and Unsoundnesses

Front Leg Problems

Splints   These are hard lumps that appear between the splint bones and the cannon bones. The splint bones are attached to the cannon bone by a small ligament. If the splint bone is injured (by being struck) or carries more than its share of weight (often caused by bench knees), this ligament becomes sore. It heals by building up a calcium deposit (new bone growth, or "exostosis") to weld the splint bone to the cannon bone.

SPLINTS

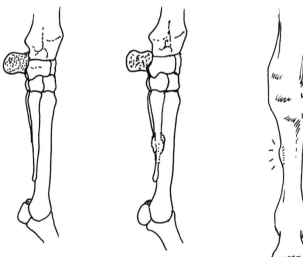

1. Normal splint
   and cannon bone

2. Splint on inside
   splint bone

3. Splint on inside of leg

A splint is usually hot and painful when it first happens. With rest, it becomes "quiet" and usually does not cause any further lameness if it is allowed to heal completely. If it does not cause lameness, an old healed splint is usually considered a blemish, not an unsoundness.

Splints are usually seen in young horses just starting to do hard work. Carrying heavy weight, striking one leg against the other, making tight circles, jumping, and working on hard ground all can lead to splints, especially in horses under five years of age. This is a good reason to wait until young horses are mature before working them hard.

Bowed Tendon   This happens when a tendon is stretched too far, often because of an accident or slip when the horse is overtired. Some tendon fibers are torn, causing pain, heat, and swelling. Later, scar tissue forms, creating a thickening, or "bow," in the tendon. It may be a "high bow" or a "low bow," depending on whether it is up close to the knee or down close to the fetlock joint.

Calf knees (back at the knee), long sloping pasterns, long toes and low heels, and weak "tied-in" tendons put more strain on the tendons and may contribute to bowed tendons. However, any horse can bow a tendon through an accident such as a slip or a fall.

When a bowed tendon first happens, it is extremely painful and the horse will be very lame. After it heals, the horse may not be lame, but the leg may never be quite as strong as before.

BOWED TENDON

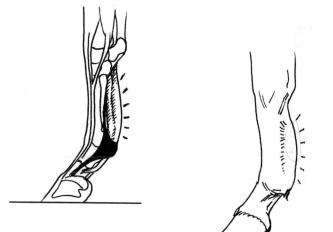

Foot and Pastern Unsoundnesses

Navicular Disease   This is a problem deep within the foot. The deep flexor tendon passes under the navicular bone and fastens to the underside of the coffin bone. The "navicular bursa" is a pad that protects the bone where the tendon crosses over it. The deep flexor tendon presses against the navicular bone and navicular bursa with every step.

Navicular disease occurs when the navicular bursa (pad), the navicular bone, or the end of the tendon becomes inflamed and sore. It usually starts out as a mild lameness that comes and goes, and may disappear when the horse is warmed up. Later, as the bone and tendon become inflamed and roughened, the lameness may become severe and the horse may be lame all the time. Because the heels hurt, the horse tries to walk on his toes, which gives him a short, "tiptoe" gait and may make him stumble.

Navicular disease is more common in middle-aged horses whose conformation promotes concussion. Small feet, narrow heels, upright pasterns, and long toes with low heels all can contribute to navicular disease. The right kind of shoeing and medication may offer some relief.

NAVICULAR DISEASE

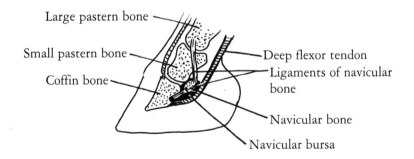

Ringbone   This occurs in the pastern area. It is an exostosis (bony lump) on the pastern bones. If it is not near a joint, the horse may become sound after a period of rest. "High ringbone" is arthritis (irritation and calcification) in the joint between the two pastern bones. Eventually the bones may "fuse," or grow together, and the horse may become sound. "Low ringbone" occurs between the end of the pastern bone and the coffin bone, inside the hoof. This type of ringbone is usually more serious, and the horse usually becomes permanently lame.

Too much concussion contributes to ringbone; it is more common in horses with upright pasterns. It may also occur in horses that carry extra weight on one side of the foot and leg because of crooked legs.

RINGBONE

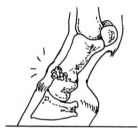
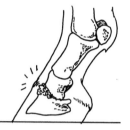

1. High ringbone   2. Low ringbone

Sidebone   This occurs when the collateral cartilages of the coffin bone (which are shaped like wings and form the bulbs of the heel) turn to bone. This process is gradual and usually does not cause lameness unless the sidebones are very large or one gets broken. You can feel the collateral cartilages by pressing just above the bulbs of your horse's heel and the sides of his hoof, just above the coronary band. In a young horse, they feel springy; when they have calcified or turned to "sidebones," they feel hard.

Sidebone problems are more common in large, heavy horses with big feet, especially if they have straight pasterns that cause more concussion. Sidebone is usually not considered an unsoundness unless it causes lameness.

Hind Leg Unsoundnesses   The hind legs do not have to handle as much concussion as the front legs do, so concussion problems such as ringbone, navicular disease, and sidebone are less common in the hind legs than in the front legs. However, the hind legs must push powerfully, especially in collected gaits, jumping, and deep footing, and when going up and down hills. Hind leg problems are more often caused by strain than by concussion.

SIDEBONE

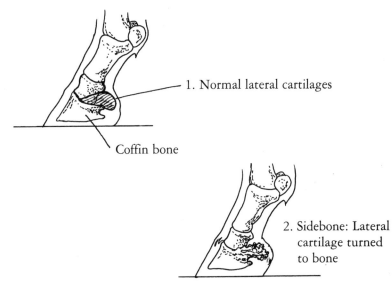

1. Normal lateral cartilages

Coffin bone

2. Sidebone: Lateral cartilage turned to bone

Curb   This is a sprain of the plantar ligament (which runs down the back of the hock), caused by extra strain on the back of the hock, resulting in a thickening at the lower end of the hock joint. It usually causes lameness. Because it is an injury to a ligament, a curb can take a long time to heal.

Curbs are often associated with sickle hocks or horses that "stand under" in the hind legs. This makes the hocks weak and puts more strain on the ligament.

CURB

1. Structures of the hock

2. Curb

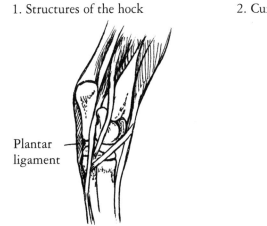

Plantar ligament

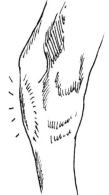

Bone Spavin   This is arthritis in the small bones of the hock. When irritated by stress or concussion, they may form "bone spurs" (calcium deposits, or "exostoses") on the edges of the bone. These are painful and cause lameness. The lower bones of the hock fit closely, like saucers stacked on top of each other; there is not much movement between them. If the calcium deposits eventually cause these bones to grow together, there is no more pain and the horse may become sound again. However, if arthritis or calcium deposits occur in the upper part of the hock joint, the hock cannot move normally and the horse may become permanently lame.

A bone spavin usually produces a hard swelling low down on the inside of the hock joint.

Bone spavin is more common in horses that put extra strain on their hocks. Cow hocks, bowed hocks, and very straight hocks are more prone to develop bone spavins.

BONE SPAVIN

1. Bone spavin:
   Arthritis in bones
   of the hock

2. Appearance of
   bone spavin on
   inside of hock
   (front view)

Bog Spavin   This is a soft swelling on the front of the hock, usually not hot or painful; it seldom causes lameness. A bog spavin usually occurs when a horse's hocks have been under some stress, but not enough to make him lame. The joint produces too much joint fluid (synovial fluid), causing the joint capsule to become enlarged and full of fluid. A bog spavin usually gets smaller when a horse is rested, and may be larger after hard work.

Bog spavins are often seen in horses with straight hocks, or when horses with weak hock conformation do work that is hard on their hocks. A bog spavin is usually considered a blemish, not an unsoundness, but it is a sign that the horse's hocks have been under stress.

1. The hock joint   2. Bog spavin

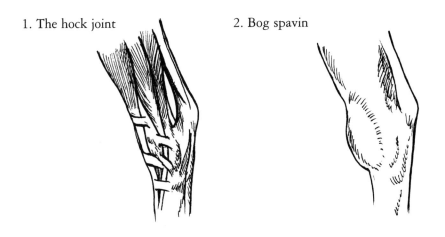

Thoroughpin This usually is caused by stress or strain on a weak hock, especially sickle hocks. The tendon sheath produces extra fluid and stretches, causing a soft, cool swelling in the upper part of the hock. Like a bog spavin, it is a sign of stress but doesn't usually cause lameness.

Thoroughpin

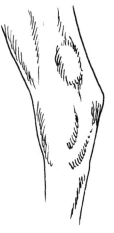

Movement Problems

Specific conformation faults cause problems in the way a horse moves. Any movement problem can range from mild to severe, but all make a horse move less efficiently and may cause injuries. Special shoeing may help, so it is important to let your horseshoer know if your pony shows signs of any of the following movement problems:

Lameness   This is a sign of pain or a serious problem in a leg. When a horse goes lame, it is important to determine which leg is lame and what is causing the problem. (See *USPC D Manual*, page 213, for how to determine which leg is lame.) This usually requires help from your veterinarian.

Stumbling   This can be a momentary accident caused by poor footing or getting off balance, but a horse that stumbles often has a serious and dangerous movement problem. This can be caused by sore feet (especially navicular disease), arthritis, or poor balance, or by neglecting shoeing or trimming and leaving the toes too long.

A horse that has a stumbling problem should be checked by a veterinarian and a farrier, and should not be ridden until the problem has been evaluated and treated.

Interfering   Occurs when a horse strikes one leg against the other. It can cause cuts or bruises, especially if the interfering foot is shod, and can also lead to splints, especially in young horses.

Interfering is commonly caused by toe-out conformation, which causes the legs to wing in (swing inward) during movement. A horse may interfere because his legs are too close together or base narrow. Even a horse with straight legs may interfere when doing lateral work or being longed, which is why protective boots or bandages are recommended for this kind of work. A horse is more likely to interfere when he is tired.

Horses that interfere may be helped by special shoeing, or they may need to wear protective boots.

Plaiting   Occurs when a horse places one leg in front of the other, as if he were walking on a tightrope. It is caused by base-narrow conformation and may lead to interfering or stumbling. Corrective shoeing may help, but the horse may need to wear boots to protect his legs.

FAULTY MOVEMENT

1. Interfering (associated with toe-out conformation)

2. Plaiting (associated with base-narrow conformation)

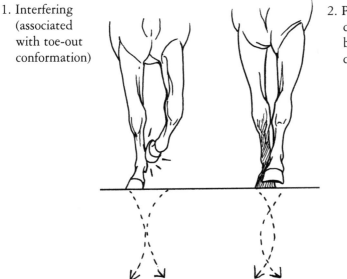

Forging Occurs when a horse hits a front foot with the toe of the hind foot, usually at the trot. Forging is more common when a horse is tired or moving too much on his forehand, and when his toes are too long. It also can happen in a horse that has a very short back and long legs.

FAULTY MOVEMENT

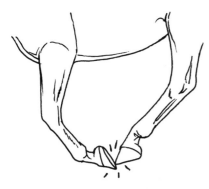

1. Forging: Hind toe strikes front foot.

2. Over-reaching: Hind toe "grabs" heel of front foot.

A good farrier can help with special trimming or shoeing. Riding in good balance is also important.

Over-reaching   Occurs when the toe of the hind foot "grabs" the heel of the front foot, causing an injury. A horse can pull a shoe off when over-reaching; a "high over-reach" occurs when the hind foot hits higher up, on the pastern or the tendon. Over-reaching most often happens when a horse is galloping or jumping in deep or muddy footing. The same things that cause forging (short back and long legs, long toes, moving on the forehand, fatigue) can also contribute to over-reaching.

Bell boots may be used to protect a horse's heels from over-reaches, especially in deep or muddy footing. Protective boots (galloping boots) or exercise bandages protect against high over-reaches. Good shoeing can also help.

Appendix A
CURRENT USPC TEST REQUIREMENTS
FOR C LEVEL RATINGS
(Revised 1995)

The C Rating

The "C" is a Pony Clubber learning to become an active horseman, to care independently for pony and tack, and to understand the reasons for what he or she is doing. The "C" shows development toward a secure, independent seat and increasing control and confidence in all phases of riding. C-1 and C-2 ratings are awarded at the club level. The C-3 is a Regional rating, and reflects a basis of competence in riding and horse care that will make possible a lifetime of pleasure with horses.

C-1 Level

Riding Test Expectations   Candidate should ride with confidence and control on the flat and over fences, demonstrating a basic balanced position and use of natural aids. Candidate should begin to initiate free forward movement and begin to establish a light feel of the horse's mouth.

Riding on the Flat:
- Demonstrate emergency dismount at the trot.
- Demonstrate pony's warm-up routine for everyday work. Discuss value of warm-up exercises.
- Perform rider suppling exercises without stirrups at walk and sitting trot.

- Demonstrate aids for moving pony away from the leg, at halt (sideways).
- Demonstrate riding on long rein, loose rein and light contact at walk.
- Ride at walk, trot, and canter, with smooth transitions. Perform circles and figure 8s at each gait.
- Discuss performance with examiner, including whether or not pony was moving freely forward.
- Describe three artificial aids and their uses.

Riding over Fences:

- Perform simple gymnastic exercises (for rider) over trotting poles, followed by a small jump (2'3").
- Ride over small grid (3 fences, not to exceed 2'3").
- Ride over jumping course of 6 to 8 obstacles (not to exceed 2'9"), including a two-stride in-and-out.
- Discuss performance with Examiner, including steadiness of pace and ways ride could be improved.

Riding in the Open:

- Ride safely with control in a group, on a suitable horse, at walk, trot, and canter.
- Discuss and/or demonstrate riding safely over varied terrain, including hills, ditches, low banks, flat open area, and streams.
- Ride over several cross-country obstacles (not to exceed 2'9").
- Discuss performance with Examiner, giving reasons for any disobediences.

C-1 Horse Management Expectations

Candidate should show a developing awareness of cause and effect in the care of his/her pony, and should be familiar with common horse terms.

Tack and Turnout

- Attire to be correctly formal or informal, or as designated by the DC.
- Pony to be well-groomed, reflecting regular care.

• Tack to be safe, clean, and well-adjusted, reflecting regular care.

Conditioning

• Discuss what is meant by conditioning, and how to condition for a particular Pony Club event.

Nutrition

• Describe how feeds are measured and weighed.
• Know amount and type of feed for own horse or pony.
• Describe characteristics of good and bad feed, watering, and pasture.

Stable Management

• Discuss types of bedding appropriate for your area.
• Put a blanket on a pony safely.
• Discuss types and causes of stable vices.
• Describe and give reasons for three types of clipping.
• Describe conditions which foster internal and external parasites, procedures for parasite control in pasture and stall management, ways to control flies, bot eggs.

Pony Parts, Conformation & Lameness

• Identify good and bad points of basic conformation.
• Describe 5 common unsoundnesses as to location and outward appearance.

Travel Safety

• Discuss basic equipment needed for pony's safety and comfort during trailer travel.
• Know trailer safety check list.

Record Book

• The C-1 is expected to keep a careful Record Book of immunizations, veterinary visits, farrier visits, etc. This book must be brought to the test for review and critique.

Health Care and Veterinary Knowledge

- Describe how to treat minor wounds.
- Discuss: Regular worming control for own pony; how and why to deworm new horses in the barn.
- Know health care schedule for own pony, including: dates of inoculations (tetanus, encephalomyelitis, etc.), deworming, floating teeth, shoeing.

Teaching

- Perform and explain reasons for a safety and tack inspection for a D Pony Clubber (under direct supervision of Examiner).

Longeing

- Discuss reasons for longeing.
- Discuss equipment necessary and safety procedures for longeing.

Foot and Shoeing

- Discuss the 5 steps in shoeing.
- Recognize farrier tools and know their uses.

Bandaging

- Be able to apply a shipping bandage (with assistance).

C-2 Level

Riding Test Expectations   Candidate should ride with confidence and control on the flat and over fences, demonstrating a secure basic balanced position and progress toward an independent seat and coordinated use of the aids. Candidate should initiate free forward movement while developing a steady light feel of the pony's mouth.

Riding on the Flat:

- Demonstrate emergency dismount at trot or canter.
- Demonstrate warm-up for flat work. Discuss warm-up schedule for 3 different activities (of the candidate's choice).

- Perform suppling exercises for the pony at walk and trot, to include large circles, small circles, and serpentines.
- Ride at walk, trot, and canter, changing directions twice in each gait, using coordinated aids and maintaining an even rhythm and smooth transitions.
- Discuss performance with Examiner, including evenness of rhythm and smoothness of transitions.
- Halt squarely and stand quietly for 5 seconds.
- Ride without stirrups at all gaits.
- Develop a hand gallop from a canter, and return smoothly to canter (performed individually).
- Demonstrate aids for moving pony away from leg (sideways) at walk.

Riding over Fences:

- Discuss reasons for adjusting stirrups for different types of work.
- Perform simple gymnastic exercises for rider over grid at trot or canter.
- Develop a plan of how to ride a stadium course (height suitable to pony, not to exceed 3'), and ride course according to plan.
- Discuss performance with Examiner, including impulsion maintained throughout the course.

Riding in the Open:

- Ride in a group at walk, trot, and canter (on a suitable horse).
- Discuss and/or demonstrate safety measures when riding over varied footing, i.e., water, mud, rocks, bog, ice, hard ground, sand, pavement.
- Ride over several cross-country obstacles (not to exceed 3') at appropriate speed (350-375 meters per minute).
- Discuss performance with Examiner, including reasons for any disobediences.

Horse Management Expectations

The candidate should show a solid awareness of cause and effect in horse management skills. Assistance and/or supervision is allowed in demonstrations of bandaging, longeing, and loading a pony.

Tack and Turnout

- Attire to be correctly formal or informal, as designated by the DC.
- Pony to show thorough grooming, with attention to mane and tail, reflecting regular care.
- Tack to be safe, clean, with metal polished, and well-adjusted, reflecting regular care.
- Explain reasons for equipment used on own pony for flat work and over fences.

Conditioning

- Present a written outline of a 6- to 8-week conditioning and feeding program in preparation for a specific event of candidate's choice.
- Measure and record pulse rate, temperature, and respiration rate of own pony (at rest), in front of Examiner.

Nutrition

- Describe own pony's ration when developing fitness, maintaining fitness, taking a day off, sick, roughed off.

Stable Management

- Describe how to care for a pony economically and efficiently when:

   Stabled: feed and water schedule, minerals needed, grooming, clothing, exercise.

   At grass: safety check of pasture, fencing, water, mineral supply, shelter, feed, grooming.
- Discuss knowledge of safety measures, preparation and care of pony and equipment on a day of strenuous work, including: feeding schedule, consideration of pony's condition, consideration of climate and terrain, cooling out, treatment of any injuries, and making pony comfortable after work.
- Discuss pasture safety and fencing.
- Name 3 toxic plants in your area and describe appearance.

Pony Parts, Conformation and Lameness

- Name 5 basic conformation qualities desirable in a pony for your own use.

- Name and locate on a pony the following unsoundnesses: ringbone, curb, bowed tendon, sidebone, spavins, navicular, splint, thoroughpin, sprains.

Travel Safety

- Be able to load and unload (with assistance) an experienced, cooperative pony.
- Discuss preparation of pony for safe and comfortable travel.

Record Book

- Record book (health, maintenance, immunizations, etc.) MUST BE UP TO DATE AND MUST BE BROUGHT TO TEST.

Health Care and Veterinary Knowledge

- List annual immunizations and health requirements appropriate for your area.
- List internal parasites prevalent in your area.
- Describe routine parasite prevention for your pony.
- Describe how tetanus and strangles are transmitted.
- Explain the need for regular care of pony's teeth.

Teaching

- Assist a D-1 or D-2 to prepare for a turnout inspection.
- Candidate must bring a letter from DC stating that he/she is assisting in simple dismounted instructional programs for D Level Pony Clubbers (WITH SUPERVISION).

Longeing

- Longe a pony for exercise in an enclosed area (with assistance).
- Discuss methods, equipment, and safety precautions for longeing.

Foot and Shoeing

- Recognize and describe good and bad shoeing.

Bandaging

- Apply a shipping bandage (under supervision).
- Apply a stable bandage (with assistance) and give reasons for use.

C-3 Level

Riding Test Expectations   Candidate should ride with a basic balanced position, demonstrating coordinated use of aids, developed through an independent seat, and initiate and maintain free forward movement with smooth transitions and a steady, light feel of pony's mouth. Candidate should show confidence and control at all gaits on the flat and over fences.

Riding on the Flat

- Mount and dismount from either side.
- Demonstrate warm-up for flat work.
- Ride schooling figures, to include circles, half-circles, and straight lines at each gait.
- Discuss performance with Examiner, including whether or not pony maintained forward movement, bent correctly on circles, and accuracy of transitions.
- Discuss difference between increase of speed and lengthening of stride.
- Demonstrate ability to ride a different horse or pony, initiating free forward movement at each gait, showing confidence and control. Discuss performance with Examiner, including ways in which the pony was different from candidate's own pony.
- Demonstrate: Moving pony away from the leg at walk or trot in a sideways movement; knowledge of aids for the rein-back; increase and decrease of speed at each gait.

Riding over Fences

- Discuss reasons for different lengths of stirrups and various positions for different work.
- Demonstrate warm-up for jumping, using exercises appropriate for level of horse, including simple gymnastic grid on own horse.
- Ride over stadium course at height appropriate for level of horse (not to exceed 3'3").

- Discuss performance and ways ride could be improved.
- Ride without stirrups over 1 or 2 low fences or simple gymnastic grid on own horse (not to exceed 2'6").
- Demonstrate ability to ride a different pony over stadium fences at height suitable for pony (not to exceed 2'9"), showing confidence and control.
- Evaluate performance and how pony differs from own pony.

Riding in the Open

- Demonstrate a knowledge of pace at 240 mpm, developing an estimated pace of 350 to 400 mpm, using a large circle in an open field.
- Ride at a gallop in the open, alone and in a group.
- Ride over several cross-country obstacles (height suitable for pony, not to exceed 3'3"), at appropriate pace (350 to 400 mpm).
- Discuss performance, pace, and reasons for any disobediences.

Horse Management Expectations

The candidate should achieve a level of competence to care for his/her own horse in a manner that will ensure comfort and health, while knowing when and where to turn for help if needed. Candidate should also be able to explain stable and veterinary routine to D Level Pony Clubbers.

Tack and Turnout

- Correct formal or informal attire, as designated.
- Pony should show evidence of regular grooming and must be clean, with attention to ears, dock, mane, tail, and feet.
- Tack to be safe, clean, with metal polished, and well-adjusted, reflecting regular care.
- Explain the use and function of equipment used on own pony for flat work and over fences.
- Describe basic actions of snaffle, curb, pelham.

Conditioning

- Discuss condition of own pony.
- Know normal vital signs of own pony at rest and after work.
- Discuss different methods of conditioning for various activities.

Nutrition

- List 6 classes of nutrients needed by ponies, and primary feeds that provide them.
- For your area, know availability, cost, and origin of hay and grain needed to meet your own pony's nutritional requirements.

Stable Management

- Discuss safety practices, both human and equine, around barn, including fire prevention.
- Describe 3 toxic plants in your area, including when most toxic, which parts are toxic, symptoms of poisoning.

Pony Parts, Conformation and Lameness

- Describe good and bad conformation points of own pony.
- Know which conformation points might contribute to the following blemishes, unsoundnesses, or way-of-going defects: bowed tendon, curb, ringbone, side-bone, splint, navicular disease, interfering, over-reaching, forging.

Travel Safety

- Discuss preparation of trailer and vehicle for safe and comfortable travel.

Record Book

- Record Book MUST BE KEPT UP TO DATE AND BROUGHT TO TEST.

Health Care and Veterinary Knowledge

- Discuss causes and signs of the following: colic, azoturia, laminitis, heaves, choking, tooth problems, skin diseases.
- Discuss symptoms and preventive measures for the following diseases: influenza, equine encephalomyelitis, tetanus, strangles, rhinopneumonitis.
- Discuss internal parasites and the damage they can cause to a pony.

- Discuss teeth, to include: concept that teeth grow continually, with baby teeth replaced by permanent teeth; location of incisors and molars; number of teeth (in male and female).

Teaching

- Candidate must bring a letter from DC stating that he/she is assisting his/her club in simple mounted instructional programs for D Level Pony Clubbers WITH SUPERVISION.
- Prepare a lesson plan and present a dismounted lesson of choice from D-2 or D-3 Standard to D-1 or D-2 Level Pony Clubbers (time limit: 10 minutes).

Longeing

- Longe own pony (under direct supervision) to pony's level of ability, using properly fitted equipment suitable to own pony, including: longe cavesson or bridle, saddle or surcingle (side reins are not required, but are allowed if appropriate).
- Demonstrate safe longeing technique.
- Demonstrate proper use of equipment and voice.

Foot and Shoeing

- Discuss type of shoes on own pony and why they are used.

Bandaging

- Apply a shipping bandage and a stable bandage, and explain the purpose of each and the dangers involved.

Appendix B
SOURCES FOR FURTHER STUDY

USPC Publications

The following materials, and further information about the United States Pony Clubs, Inc., can be obtained from:

United States Pony Clubs, Inc.
4071 Iron Works Pike
Lexington, KY 40511
606-254-PONY (7669)

1. Harris, Susan E. *The USPC Manual of Horsemanship, Basics for Beginners, D Level.* New York: Howell Book House, 1994. (Book One of this series; essential basics of riding and horse care to USPC D Standard; foundation for skills and knowledge in this book. Required for all Pony Club members.)
2. *USPC Safety Information Packet.* (Important information on safety in riding activities, trailering, attire and headgear, much more! For parents, instructors, and all USPC members.)
3. *USPC Horse Management Handbook.* (Rules, information, and tips on preparation for horse management at Pony Club rallies, competitive rallies and activities. For parents, instructors, and all USPC members.)
4. (Video) *USPC Guide to Successful Longeing.* (Shows equipment, safe procedures, and correct longeing techniques; for C-3 and up.)

Recommended Reading

The following books are recommended by the USPC for further reading and study (as of 1994):

1. British Horse Society, *The Manual of Horsemanship, 10th Edition*; Kenilworth, Warwickshire, England: British Horse Society/The Pony Club, 1993. (Official British Horse Society handbook; worldwide standard for riding and horse care and management; for C-1 through C-3.)

2. Knox-Thompson, Elaine and Dickens, Suzanne, *New Zealand Pony Club Manuals No. 1 and No. 2*; Auckland, New Zealand: Ray Richards Publisher, 1988. (Good information on riding and horsemanship in clear, easy-to-read style; for C-1 and C-2.)

3. Harris, Susan E., *Grooming to Win, 2d ed.*; New York: Howell Book House, 1991. (Covers conditioning, grooming, clipping, special care, and show preparation; C-1 through C-3.)

4. Harris, Susan E., *Horse Gaits, Balance and Movement*; New York: Howell Book House, 1993. (How horses move in all gaits; how anatomy, conformation, shoeing, riding, and training relate to horse movement; C-3 Level.)

5. Kidd, Jane, *A First Guide to Riding and Pony Care*; New York: Howell Book House, 1991. (Good basic information on pony care, management, and common ailments; easy to read and understand; C-1 and C-2.)

6. Ljundqvist, Bengt, *Practical Dressage Manual*; Richmond, Virginia: Press of Whittet & Shepperson, 1976. (Training the horse and rider in dressage, from basics to advanced movements; C-3 Level.)

7. Loch, Sylvia, *The Classical Seat*; Surbiton, Sussex, England: Unwin Hyman Limited and Horse and Rider Magazine, 1988. (Excellent guide to the hows and whys of correct position and use of aids; C-1 through C-3.)

8. Sivewright, Molly, *Thinking Riding*; London, England: J. A. Allen, 1979. (A detailed, progressive training course for instructors and those who would like to become instructors; C-3 Level.)

9. Sivewright, Molly, *Thinking Riding, Book Two: In Good Form*; ibid, 1984. (Companion volume to *Thinking Riding*; more information on anatomy of horse and rider, and what constitutes a good performance; C-3 Level.)

10. Swift, Sally, *Centered Riding*; North Pomfret, Vermont: David & Charles, Inc., 1985. (Helps riders of all levels use mind and body for better balance, performance, and harmony between horse and rider; C-1 through C-3.)

11. Wadsworth, William P., *Riding to Hounds in America*; Middleburg, Virginia: The Chronicle of the Horse, 1987. (Clear and practical introduction to foxhunting, what to expect, and how to prepare rider and horse; C-3 Level.)

12. Threshold Picture Guides; Addington, Buckingham, England: Kenilworth Press Limited, 1986-1994. (Excellent series of full-color, illustrated booklets; clear, concise, and easy to read; C-1 through C-3.) Current list includes these titles:

> *Basic Coursebuilding* by Maureen Summers
> *Beds and Bedding* by Mary Gordon Watson
> *Boots and Bandages* by Jane Holderness-Roddam
> *Colours and Markings* by Jane Holderness-Roddam
> *Conformation* by Peggotty Henriques
> *Feeds and Feeding* by Mary Gordon Watson
> *Feet and Shoes* by Toni Webber
> *Fields and Fencing* by Mary Gordon Watson
> *First Aid* by Jane Holderness-Roddam
> *Fitting Tack* by Jane Holderness-Roddam
> *Flatwork Exercises* by Jane Wallace
> *Grooming* by Susan McBane
> *Jumping Cross-Country Fences* by Jane Thelwall
> *Making Your Own Jumps* by Mary Gordon Watson
> *Manes and Tails* by Valerie Watson
> *Mouths and Bits* by Toni Webber
> *The Outdoor Pony* by Susan McBane
> *Poles and Gridwork* by Jane Wallace
> *Preparing for a Show* by Jane Holderness-Roddam
> *The Rider's Aids* by Peggotty Henriques
> *Rugs and Rollers* by Jane Holderness-Roddam
> *Safety* by Toni Webber
> *Sheds and Shelters* by Toni Webber
> *Show Jumping* by Jane Wallace
> *Solving Flatwork Problems* by Jane Wallace
> *Trimming and Clipping* by Valerie Watson

Index

Felt **colors** (worn behind PC pin)

D1-D3 • Yellow
C1-C2 • Green
C3 • White
H • Purple
B • Red
H-A • Orange
A • Blue